Please Don't Fee

Written, edited, designed, and

ISBN 978-0-9770557-1-5
This is Microcosm #76032

We are proudly distributed by AK Press
510-208-1700 or sales@akpress.org

First Edition - 3,000 copies - August 25, 2006
Second Edition - 3,000 copies - January 10, 2009

Author Proceeds to benefit people living with AIDS

Microcosm Publishing
222 S Rogers St.
Bloomington, IN 47404
812-323-7395
www.microcosmpublishing.com

Printed in Canada

We have a mailorder catalog with other zines, books, stickers, t-shirts, patches, buttons, posters, and more on our website or send $1 for paper catalog.

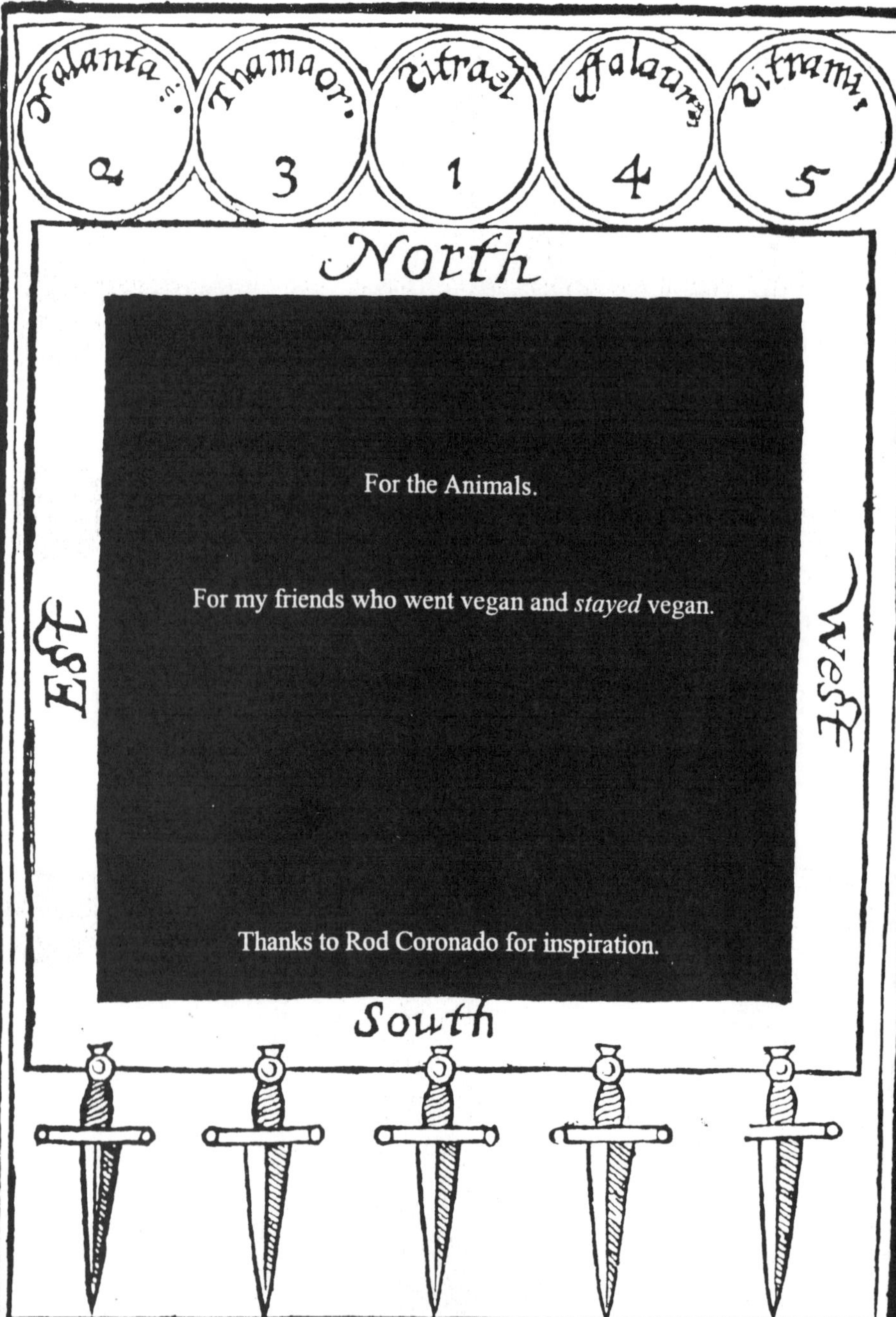
North
East
West
For the Animals.
For my friends who went vegan and *stayed* vegan.
Thanks to Rod Coronado for inspiration.
South

Table of Malcontents

PLEASE DON'T

FEED THE BEARS!

PARK USERS AND CAMPERS . . .

Lock up ALL food and food containers in your vehicle.

Don't invite trouble.

BEARS ARE NOT PETS!

This is a compilation of my favorite recipes...typically the ones I use most often. This project started out as an attempt to organize my recipes for myself and to pay tribute to the greatest cookzine of all time, Soy Not Oi! It soon became an opportunity to share with others...particularly those who are as unskilled in the kitchen as myself. Only a few of the recipes are originals of mine. The rest are from friends, magazines, Internet sources, and so on. I modified them all to my liking, and I certainly hope you will do the same. I had a lot of fun making this cookbook. It is part of a recent attempt to re-reclaim and re-redefine my life through challenge, enjoyment, enlightenment, and good health. I hope that this shows through its darker elements. Enjoy, improvise, and have a good time.

The music in this book is of the obscure, abrasive variety. Perhaps the audial equivalent of berbere or Tellicherry India black pepper. I revel in rarity and obscurity. I have a near-desperate need to seek out the hidden and the partially-revealed. I spend a large portion of my time seeking out rare and forgotten records, films, books, and texts. Part of the modern consumerist world is being able to find and obtain anything you want whenever you want. This has generated an unhealthy and unreasonable mentality in which people believe not only that they *should* be able to obtain whatever item they wish, but that they are *entitled* to obtain whatever item they wish. I like to know that there are things that I cannot have or experience. Things that, if I am lucky, I may one day catch glimpse of...or overhear someone speak of…or see a photocopy of...or hear or see a dubbed tape of. But only if I search hard enough and forge the necessary connections.

Everything in this cookbook is anti-copyrighted. You can repress it and give your friends copies, take out things you don't like, smear tahini all over it, wear its designs in corporate magazines, claim recipes you like as your own, replace my musical suggestions with contemporary Christian rock, lick the pictures, or even take an image out of it, screen it on t-shirts, and sell the shirts on E-Bay for $21 (not that *that* has ever happened or anything).

Seriously, fuck copyrights. This book is now yours. Do with it as thou wilt.

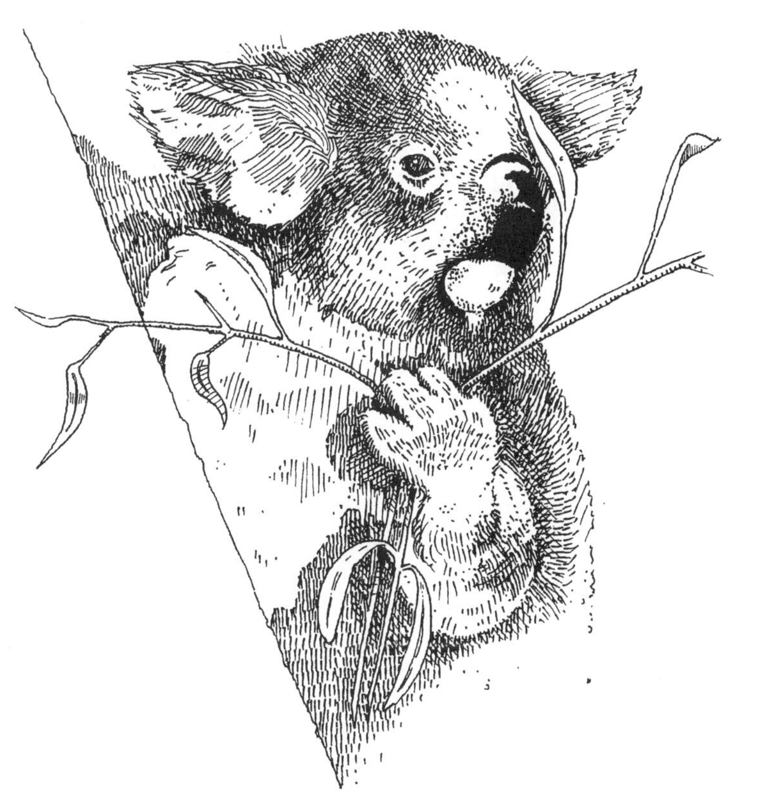

As much as it irritates me to admit, my first serious consideration of a vegetarian/vegan diet was the result of an argument I had with a proponent of the Krishna faith about 12 years ago. The details are irrelevant, but I simply could not argue intelligently in support of a meat-based diet. I tried angle after angle, point after point...only to find myself reduced to hypocritical statements and prey to reductio ad absurdum examples. I began to question myself and my motivations. Why *did* I need animal flesh? Could my body survive without it? What was the impact of my carnivorous diet on the world and its inhabitants? I sought answers to these questions, and, upon finding them, quickly shifted to a vegetarian diet. Veganism did not seem as radical as it once did, yet it was still beyond what I believed I was capable of. I was born in Minnesota and raised in Wisconsin, both states in which the rejection of dairy is considered ridiculous, if not blasphemous. It did not take me long (a couple months) to realize that my health/environmental beliefs were inexorably connected to ethical concerns. Consistency in my own mind was the initial impetus for me to shift from a vegetarian to a vegan diet. I now realize that it is much more than that. For example, I used to visit a bunch of dairy cows (Holsteins, my favorite) on a regular basis. How do you explain to a person who just had cow tongue for dinner last night how wonderful it is to be licked by a cow? It's like being licked by a cat (in that their tongue is like sandpaper)...only hundreds of times more powerful. How do you explain the elegant and ironic juxtaposition of massive size and childish timidity in the cows' collective character? Awkward beauty...so much revolves around that. To me, veganism has become more than just a means to reduce suffering in the world...it has become an acknowledgement of the intricacies and idiosyncrasies of life from an objective, non-human, non-speciesist perspective.

I didn't put notes in the first issue of Please Don't Feed the Bears and everyone kept asking me stuff like "what is sea salt?," "where can I get arrowroot?," "why do I keep ruining my recipes with brewer's yeast?," and so on. Read through these before going into the recipes and refer back to them wherever you get confused. I hope they help.

Agar agar is a flavorless sea vegetable which becomes gelatenous upon being dissolved into boiling water. It's sold powdered, flaked, or whole. Can be used in desserts, jellies, or other sorts of molded dishes. I buy it at the Asian market for cheap, though the natural foods store has it for expensive.

Berbere is an exceptionally delicious Ethiopian spice. Like a more red peppery paprika, perhaps. Excellent in lentil dishes and such. I buy it at the Indian market.

Bragg's Liquid Aminos is a name-brand liquid protein concentrate, derived from soybeans. It is very good for you and is very salty and can often be used as a better-for-you-yet-way-more-expensive soy sauce replacement.

Chipotle peppers are smoked and dried (or oil-cured) jalepeno chili peppers. They have a deep, rich, smoky flavor which adds depth to chili and other similar dishes. Can you think of anything better? No, you cannot.

For the most part, I think that **cornstarch** and **arrowroot powder** are interchangeable though I would definitely recommend the latter over the former. Both are added to soups and sauces to act as a thickener. Do not sprinkle either directly into a hot soup or sauce as it will quickly form clumps. Rather, mix it into a few tablespoons of water first, then add it. Cornstarch is ultra-refined and is not particularly good for you as it can accumulate in your intestines. Arrowroot, on the other hand, is natural and does not have this negative attribute. Look for arrowroot in the baking/spices section of the grocery store. If not there, most spice shops and natural foods stores would have it.

Couscous is a form of pasta which is tiny and somewhat rice-like in appearance. It is light and fluffy (when prepared correctly) and takes about 5 minutes to cook. It is a traditional part of Mediterranean and Middle-Eastern cooking.

Edamame is another word for raw soybeans. They are usually bought fresh, salted, or frozen.

Egg replacer is a powder (mostly potato starch, I believe) which, when reconstituted in a bit of water, serves the binding purpose of eggs. You're not going to be making omelets with it, but it's great for cookies and such. Most natural food stores have it.

Firm tofu, when frozen for 24 hours and thawed, changes consistency. It becomes much firmer and much spongier. This makes it highly amicable to marinades and is highly recommended.

Garam masala is a blended South Asian spice which is common in Indian cooking. It is recommended that you only use a little bit at a time, as the flavor may quickly overpower whatever dish it is included in.

Gumbo file is another soup thickener which is made from ground sassafras leaves. It can be found in the spice section of any supermarket.

Habanero peppers are hot peppers which are typically 50-200 times hotter than the average jalapeno. They are small and have a mildly fruity taste before the heat sets in. They may cause food poisoning if eaten plain and can cause burns to the skin and eyes through contact. Typically, they are available fresh or dried at grocery stores.

Hominy is a form of corn which can be found dried or canned. Often used in Southwestern and Mexican cooking.

Two words for you: **liquid smoke**. This is probably the most glorious thing ever invented and can be put on **damn-near-anything** to add depth and subtle flavor. Find it near the barbecue sauces at the grocery store.

Miso is a paste made from fermented soy beans. It has a potent, salty flavor and is delicious in soups and other Asian dishes. It is rich in B vitamins and protein. **Red miso**, I believe, has a stronger flavor than **white miso**. Both are rather expensive, but a little package lasts a long, long time.

MSG (monosodium glutimate) is a "flavor enhancer" which helps to make tasty food tastier. I love the stuff. However, it is sourced from wheat, and those with wheat allergies can have mild to severe reactions to it (typically headaches). Perhaps you'll want to research this a bit before purchasing a 20 lb bag of it.

Nutritional yeast is a yellowish, flaky substance which can be used to add a cheesy, nutty flavor to food. It can be found at any natural foods store and is an excellent source of iron and the elusive B-12. It is typically not cheap, but a package of it lasts a while. Cats tend to love it, so don't leave it out in the open unless you want a big mess. It is NOT the same thing as brewer's yeast or baking yeast.

Polenta is a soft, yellow substance made from corn meal. It can be used with tomato-based sauces like a form of pasta or it can be used as a base in more traditional Mexican dishes.

Sea salt and regular salt are interchangeable. Sea salt does not have iodide and allegedly retains many of the minerals of the sea.

Seitan is a meat substitute which is derived from wheat gluten. It is seasoned with ginger, **kombu** (a sea vegetable), peppercorns, and soy. It can be found at natural food stores and is one of my favorite things to put in chili.

Silken tofu is not the same as **firm or extra-firm tofu**. I don't know why, it just isn't. The former is of Japanese origin and tends to have a soft, smooth texture that is ideal for whipping into cakes and sauces. The latter is of Chinese origin and tends to be firmer and meatier. It is ideal as a meat substitute.

Tahini is a smooth paste made from sesame seeds, perhaps akin to natural peanut butter in the way that it is processed. It has a very rich flavor and is best when mixed with other ingredients (though I do know some folks who spread it on toast like peanut butter). It is a staple of Middle-Eastern cooking and can be found at any Indian, Asian, or natural foods market.

Tamari is a naturally brewed soy sauce that contains no sugar. It is available wheat-free and is interchangeable with regular soy sauce.

Teff Flour is a highly nutritional flour made from the teff grain. It is common throughout Ethiopia and India. I find it at the Indian market.

Tempeh is a pressed form of whole, cultured soybeans. It's flavor is mildly nutty and it is available at any natural foods store. It can be shredded or cooked whole and is typically easiest to work with if steamed first.

Turbinado sugar is a raw sugar that is obtained or crystallized from the initial pressing of sugar cane. Its flavor is much stronger, its color is much darker, and its crystals are significantly larger than that of white sugar. It works well for some desserts, not for others.

TVP (textured vegetable protein) is a dried meat substitute which is rich in vegetable protein. I like to rehydrate it with a mix of water, soy sauce, ketchup, dried ginger, and liquid smoke to give it a meaty flavor. It is cheap and is available at any natural foods store.

Umeboshi vinegar is a salty, Japanese vinegar made from pickled plums. Try your local Asian market or natural foods store.

I want [his] heart. I want to eat his children. Praise be to Allah.-Mike Tyson

He's gotta eat my left and right hands first.-Lennox Lewis

That said, let's begin.

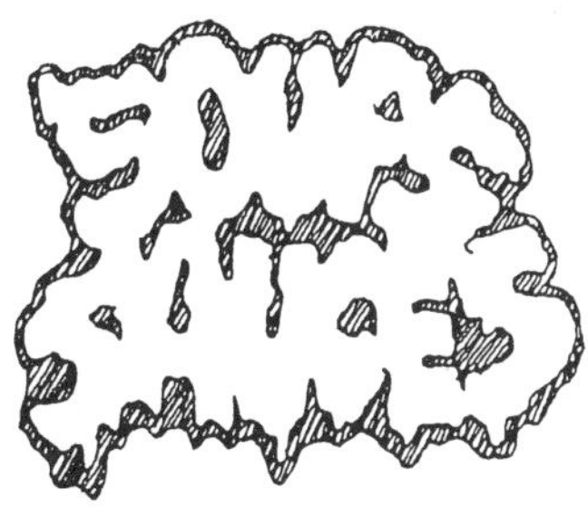

The Best Damn Cheese Dip I Ever Ate

Music: Cianide-The Dying Truth lp (1992)

The best. Dip your chips in it. Pour it on potatoes or broccoli. Serve it over shell-shaped pasta and pretend you're eating those bourgeois shells and cheese you could never afford if you wanted to.

2 cups water
1/3 cup nutritional yeast
¼ cup tahini
¼ cup arrowroot
2 Tbsp lemon juice
1 Tbsp onion powder
1 tsp sea salt
Dash or two of turmeric for color
2 dashes of liquid smoke
3 Tbsp red bell pepper, minced
2 jalapeno peppers (the kind you get in a bottle), minced

Blend everything in a blender except the jalapenos and red pepper. Pour the mixture into a saucepan and add in the hot and red peppers. Whisk rapidly over high heat until the mixture thickens. This should only take a few minutes. Eat hot. For a heartier cheese dip, add in a can of vegan chili or a couple cups of tasty salsa.

Trident of Neptune Seaweed Sauce

Music: Temple of Baal-Faces of the Void mlp (2001)

½ oz dulse flakes
½ oz kelp granules
2 sheets toasted nori seaweed, crumbled
¼ cup shoyu
1 cup cider vinegar
½ cup olive oil
3 Tbsp toasted sesame oil

Mix all ingredients and blend. Refrigerate two days before using.

Gloria Cubana's Fresh Pasta Sauce

Music: Amebix-Monolith lp…keep in mind, however, just as there is no universal morality, there is also no universal lp to go with this recipe and the various situations and circumstances at which it might be evoked. Choose wisely.

I'm taking this recipe pretty much word-for-word from Gloria...she's definitely a lot more eloquent than me:

Mmmm…fresh pasta sauce. Nothing can compare with a rich, homemade tomato sauce. Traditionally, Roma tomatoes are used, since they are fleshier, with fewer seeds. But when Food Not Bombs is providing the produce, who needs to be picky?

Lots and lots of tomatoes (10-20 small ones)
½ onion
2 or 3 cloves garlic
Any vegetables you might have
Spices and herbs as desired*

Boil a pot of water and plunge the tomatoes into the water for 10 to 15 seconds each. This will make them easier to skin. Remove the skins and seeds. I don't really have a system for this. It usually involves ripping open the tomatoes and scraping the insides out into a bowl. It's a messy (and time-consuming) job, but somebody's got to do it.

While you're gutting the bellies of the tomatoes, you should saute whatever vegetables you wish to add to the sauce in some olive oil (see Evan's faux meat recipe for one idea). Even if you turn the heat way up in order to get the oil hot faster, please turn it back down at least to medium heat upon adding your ingredients. Minced garlic, especially, can burn almost instantly if you aren't careful. Tofu is better if sauteed first, but I'd leave things like spinach, rughetta, olives, etc. out until there are a few minutes of cooking left. So chop your onion, cut up your broccoli, cube your tofu, and throw it all in a skillet.

When you've finished amassing a mound of tomato, add that to the skillet as well. You did set aside all afternoon for this, didn't you? Because it's going to take a couple of hours for this to all cook down. But it's so relaxing, and it smells so good!

So let's discuss tomatoes. I like my pasta sauces chunky, so I chop the tomato pretty loosely. But depending on your preference, you can chop more finely, or even put it in a blender. Of course, if you didn't read the whole recipe first and already put your tomatoes in the skillet, you're stuck. Let that be a lesson to you.

As the sauce simmers on the stove, you will discover something shocking: you haven't made nearly as much sauce as you thought you had. All those tomatoes, so little product? If only our values weren't so centered around quantity and efficiency. If only we could appreciate putting so much effort out for results that couldn't be measured in those ways, we might be more generous, passionate people. But the fact remains: this is not enough pasta sauce for a large dinner party, it's probably only enough for a romantic dinner for two. But that might be much more enjoyable anyway…

**A note on spices and herbs: You have as many options here as you do with vegetable ingredients. Fresh herbs like basil and oregano do amazing things in tomato sauces. Fresh-ground black pepper (usually coarsely ground) is great, too. I also love marjoram, a vastly underrated herb. In Spain, cooks often add cumin to tomato sauce (less and less now, as Italian cooking takes over the world). Please don't think I'm criticizing Italian cooking-it's delicious-and far be it from me, as an American, to point fingers and scream "cultural imperialism!" All I'm saying is, cumin added to tomato sauce gives an incredible flavor. You can add a little sea salt, too, but why don't you try cutting it out of your diet?*

Sweet Onion Bisque

Music: Darvulia-Shabattu, Danse Lunaire demo (2001)

¼ cup margarine
3-4 lbs large, diced vidalia (sweet) onions
2 Tbsp flour
5 cups vegetable stock
1 cup soy milk
Sea salt and pepper to taste

Melt margarine in stock pot; add onions, cooking until soft or about 15-20 minutes. Stir in flour and add remaining ingredients. Bring to a boil, stirring occasionally.

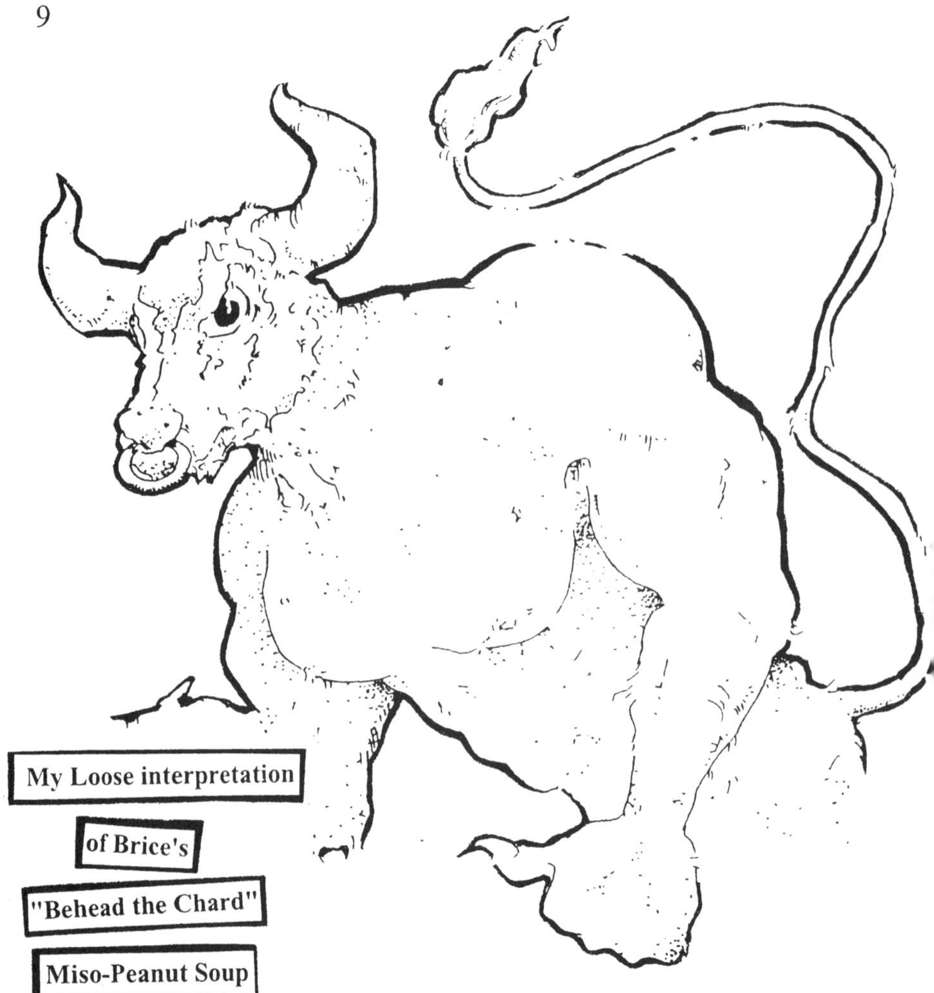

My Loose interpretation of Brice's "Behead the Chard" Miso-Peanut Soup

Music: Behead the Prophet No Lord Shall Live-I Am that Great and Fiery Force lp (1996)

4 cups water
¼ to ½ cup soy sauce (start at ¼ cup and add more if necessary...you don't want it to be too salty)
2 Tbsp natural peanut butter
A bunch of superfine rice noodles (aka rice stick)
½ lb extra firm tofu, cubed
A bunch of chard
2 Tbsp red miso

Bring the water, soy sauce, and peanut butter to a boil. Put in the rice noodles (as many as you want to eat) and the cubed tofu as you turn the stove down to simmer. For as fragile as they look, these rice noodles are pretty damn durable until you cook them. Wait a couple minutes and put in the chard (once again, as much as you feel suitable). Finally, add the miso. Your kitchen should smell wonderful by now. Make sure the miso is fully dissolved into the broth and serve hot.

Priscilla's Gumbo des Herbes

Music: Amon-Zrozeni Smrti lp (2002)

Start with the greens...the story is that this is a veggie gumbo for Lent when Catholics don't eat meat on Fridays. The story also is that for each kind of green put in the gumbo, you would make a new friend during the year, so go for lots of kinds of greens and eat up!

Wash, trim, and dry lots of kinds of greens (collards, kale, spinach, chard, mustard, turnip, etc.; you'll need a big pot if you use pounds and pounds, but greens do cook down). So 4 pounds, or 12 cups, or 2-4 bunches, whatever. Then get a pot going with 8½ cups water, 1 tsp sea salt, ½ tsp cayenne, and 5 bay leaves. Get the water to a good boil and then reduce the heat to medium. Put the greens in the water a handful at a time and blanch until wilted; then fish them out with a slotted spoon and put them in a separate bowl. Repeat until all greens are done. Keep the liquid separate and cover. If you only have one pot, find a place to put the liquid (stock) and dry out your pot. You do need to eventually chop up the greens coarsely, so you can do this now or wait until right before you add them back (I'm getting to that) when they are cooler.

Okay! So now you have 1 bowl of greens, 1 pot or bowl of stock (covered), and one empty pot (that should be pretty big and have a heavy bottom). Quick chop up 2 cups of yellow onions, 1 cup green bell pepper, and maybe 1 cup celery.

Now the roux! Roux is what makes gumbo so fucking good. Traditional roux is made from 1 cup flour and 1 cup canola oil. This makes rich gumbo…you can use less of each in a 1:1 ratio (down to ½ cup and ½ cup). Or, if you want less fat, do less oil to flour-like ½ cup oil to ¾ cup flour.

So put the oil in the pot over high heat and immediately add the flour. Stir constantly and slowly for about 20-25 minutes, until the roux is very dark brown, like chocolate. Don't be afraid to burn it, as dark brown roux is the key to good gumbo. Once it gets brown, add the onions, green pepper, and maybe celery. Stir often for about 10 minutes.

When veggies are wilted and kind of golden, add the chopped greens, stock, ½ tsp dried thyme (or several sprig fresh), ½ tsp dried oregano, and ¼ cup fresh parsley. Bring to a gentle boil and simmer an hour and a half. Enjoy a couple Abita Turbodogs (or Dixies if you're short on cash) while you wait. Remove the bay leaves and sprigs of herbs (if you used fresh ones).

Put some cooked rice in a bowl and serve the gumbo over it. Add a tiny bit of gumbo filé for flavor and to thicken, as well as some Tabasco to taste. You might want to make some garlic bread to serve with it as well. This gumbo tends to be thick, so add more water if you want while cooking or when you reheat.

The Chili of Holy Terror

Music: Deathspell Omega-Si Monvmentvm Reqvires, Circvmspice 2Xlp (2004)

1 can chili beans
1 can black beans
1 small can tomato sauce
1 black bean can's worth of water
1 can tomatoes, cut up into chunks
1 onion, diced
1 green pepper, diced
½ package vegan meat crumbles
6 oz dark beer
2 Tbsp chili powder
1Tbsp cumin
1 Tbsp dried cilantro
1 tsp garlic powder
1 tsp liquid smoke
1 tsp sea salt
1 tsp black pepper
2 bay leaves
2 chipotle pepper, minced
2 habanero peppers, minced
Hot sauce
3 drops of your own blood

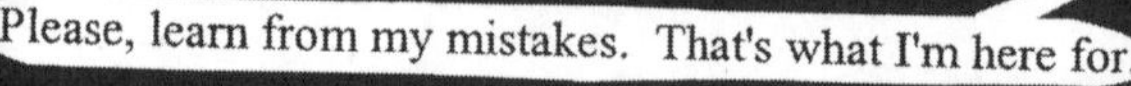

This is pretty simple. Get a large pot and put all of the ingredients in it in any order...even backwards. Add more or less of the spices, according to your taste. Feel free to add other vegetables or tofu as you see fit. However, you put carrots, celery, or beets in my chili, I punch you in the fucking face. Got it? Okay, bring it all to a boil and then reduce heat to low. Let it simmer for a good two hours or so. Remove the bay leaves. Consume with inhuman voracity. It's actually best after being refrigerated overnight and then reheated the next day as this gives the spices and flavors time to meld, but not all of us have that kind of time to spare you know.

Warning: A word from the not-so-wise...

Common sense should preclude the need for this warning, but I figured it's entertaining if nothing else. Here are two examples of how *not* to handle habanero peppers:

1. So I'm making the hellfire chili and it's time to put in the habanero peppers. I got some dried ones from a co-worker at the factory and she told me to be careful handling them as they tend to burn your skin (they are 50-200 times hotter than the average jalapeno). Whatever, I thought, and didn't take any precautions when picking them up. I must have inadvertently picked my nose, as I soon had the sensation of having a nosebleed. I scratched my nose (thereby rubbing more pepper on it) and the feeling intensified. It soon felt as if I had been suckerpunched in the nose. The real pain only lasted a half hour or so, but the burning sensation lasted quite a while after...as if to remind me of what a dumbass I can be.

2. Okay, try two. I decided to saute some minced, fresh habanero peppers to put in my supaburritos. I was *very* careful this time not to touch them directly. I started frying them in the oil, feeling quite cocky after not hurting myself again. Little did I know, frying peppers causes them to release their capsicum (the active ingredient in self-defense pepper sprays). My throat started burning and I started coughing. My nose and eyes started burning and watering and I could not for the life of me figure out what was going on. I had to bail out the side door to get away from the kitchen. I couldn't go back into the kitchen for about 20 minutes until it aired out. It's all fun and games until the chef maces himself.

Born/Cook/Consume Chili/Die

Music: Sadistic Intent-Impending Doom mlp (1990)

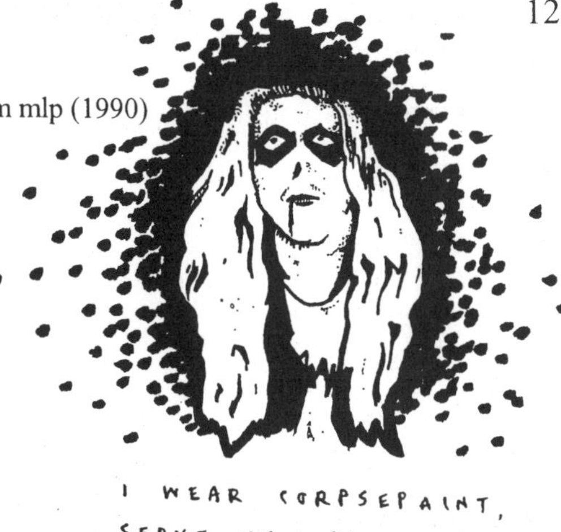

2 tsp olive oil
2 medium onions, chopped finely
4 cloves garlic, minced
3 cups vegetable stock
2 Tbsp apple cider vinegar
1 large bay leaf
5 allspice berries, ground
2 tsp sea salt
3 Tbsp chili powder
1 tsp cocoa powder (or carob)
2 cups tomato sauce
1/2 tsp cayenne pepper, or to taste
1 tsp cumin
1 tsp cinnamon
2 cups cooked pinto beans
2 cups tofu, frozen, thawed, and crumbled

In large heavy pot, over medium-high heat, heat oil and saute onions for 8 to 10 minutes. Add remaining ingredients. Bring to a boil, then lower heat and simmer for 1 1/2 hours. Take out the bay leaf before eating, eh?

As Tzu-gung was traveling through the regions north of river Han, he saw an old man working in his vegetable garden. He had dug an irrigation ditch. The man would descend into the well, fetch up a vessel of water in his arms, and pour it out into the ditch. While his efforts were tremendous, the results appeared to be very meager.

Tzu-gang said, "There is a way whereby you can irrigate a hundred ditches in one day, and whereby you can do much with little effort. Would you not like to hear of it?" The gardener stood up, looked at him, and said, "And what would that be?"

Tzu-gang replied, "You take a wooden lever, weighted at the back and light at the front. In this way you can bring up water so quickly that it gushes out. This is called a draw-well."

Then anger rose up in the old man's face, and he said, "I have heard my teacher say that whoever uses machines does all his work like a machine. He who does his work like a machine grows a heart like a machine, and he who carries the heart of a machine in his breast loses his simplicity. He who has lost his simplicity becomes unsure in the strivings of his soul. Uncertainty in the strivings of the soul is something which does not agree with honest sense. It is not that I do not know of such things; I am ashamed to use them."

Chang-tzu; Fourth century B.C.

Ital Stew

Music: Procreation-Rebirth into Evil demo (1990)

2 cups kidney beans, soaked overnight and drained
6 cups vegetable stock
8 to 10 whole allspice
3 scallions, chopped
3 cloves garlic, minced
3 sprigs fresh thyme
3 medium carrots, peeled and diced
1½ cups sliced okra
2 cups corn
2 medium sweet potatoes, peeled and diced
1 large russet potato, diced
1 whole habanero pepper
3 cups canned, unsweetened coconut milk (or fresh)

Combine the beans, vegetable stock, and allspice in a large pot. Cook at a low boil for 1½ to 2 hours, stirring regularly, until the beans are almost tender. Add the scallions, garlic, thyme, carrots, okra, corn, potatoes, and habanero. Stir in the coconut milk. Bring to a boil, then reduce heat and simmer, covered, for 30 minutes while stirring regularly. Remove the habanero, allspice, and thyme before eating.

So I was passing through D.C. a few years ago now. I had just been dissed from the Lumberjack store over in Arlington, VA. Unbeknownst to me, their store is only open to the public on Saturdays. Anyway, I decided to go over to the Dischord house and say "hi" or whatever. I knew it was just going to be a house, but I wasn't looking to buy anything...just a friendly hello. I finally found it (after fighting through the masses of tourists over by the monuments). I knew something was wrong as I climbed the steps...no sign, no nothing. I rang the bell and an older woman opened the door. "okay," I thought, "think quick. They either moved or you got the wrong address. You're such a fucking idiot." Before I had the chance to blabber out some nonsense, the woman smiled and said, "You're looking for Dischord, aren't you?" "Uh, yeah," I think I said. "They moved out over ten years ago, you know." "I'm really sorry to bother you," I stammered as I looked down at my old Minor Threat tape to check the address one more time against the one that stood in front of me. "That's okay," she replied. "We still get people every now and then. I'm Ian's Mom. They moved to the other side of the river but kept the address here...as much as they appreciate the support, they really aren't equipped for people to drop by and such. Let me get a sheet that explains it all." She left the doorway and I could hear her shuffle some papers around in another room. I saw a shadow move down the hall. Could that have been Ian?...No, I didn't need to know. I felt in a daze with the inconvenience I'd created. Mrs. MacKaye returned with a dusty, faded flyer which politely explained my faux pas. "Not many of these left," she mused. My head hot, I thanked her for her time and stumbled back down the stairs. The cherry blossoms that the tourists flocked from all over the country to see didn't seem quite as glorious as they did on the way over.

Eric the Bearded Quoits Warrior's Vegan Power Seitan Stew

Music: Arkangel-Dead Man Walking lp (1999)

3 cups vegetable broth
16 oz seitan
3-4 medium carrots cut into rounds
2 smallish potatoes cut into small chunks
2 small to medium onions cut into chunks
1/4 cup ketchup
1/4 cup soy sauce
1 to 2 glugs of olive oil (for richness!)
1½ -2 tsp garlic powder
Fresh cracked black pepper to taste
¼ cup flour
1/3 cup cold water

Put everything EXCEPT the flour and 1/3 cup water in a large pot. Bring this to a boil. Lower the heat and simmer for about 25 minutes stirring every now and again.

Put the flour in a bowl, add water and stir with a fork to make a slurry. Try to get this smooth but don't worry too much about it. Stir the slurry into the stew and cook for another 5 minutes. It will get thick and wonderful. Vegan Power!

Zak Holochwost's Suicidal Peanut Stew

Music: Suicidal Tendencies-Lights...Camera...Revolution.lp (You Can't Bring Me Down in particular; 1990)

Serves 5-7 suicidal thrashers and skaters

2 or 3 Tbsp olive oil
1 or 2 large onions, diced
4 cloves garlic, minced
1 green pepper, diced
1 red pepper, diced
2 or 3 large carrots, sliced

You can add just about any other veggies you like zucchini, squash, mushrooms, etc. The ones mentioned above are a must though.

1 28 oz can of diced or stewed tomatoes (or equivalent of that in fresh tomatoes)
4-5 cups vegetable stock
Jar of peanut butter
1 block of extra-firm tofu, cubed
Tabasco, cayenne, sea salt, pepper, nutritional yeast, and any other seasonings you like. I've thrown basil, thyme, dill, and a million other things into this and they all taste good.

Cut up all the vegetables as big or as little as you like. Sauté them all in oil until they are tender. Add the tomatoes and let simmer for a few minutes. Add the stock and let that come to a boil. Once boiling, start adding the peanut butter. Depending on how thick you want the stew add enough peanut butter and stir until it is all dissolved. I usually add one full normal-sized (12 or 13 oz?) jar per 4 cups of stock. If the stew is not thick enough add more peanut butter, if its too thick add more stock. It is purely guess work. Bring the stew down to a simmer and add the tofu and all the spices you want, to taste. I like it hot and add a lot of Tabasco and salt and nutritional yeast. Serve it over rice.

Corn and Potato Chowdah

Music: Witchfinder General-Death Penalty lp (1982)

3 medium potatoes, peeled and diced
1½ cups water
1 tsp canola oil
1 small onion, chopped
1 stalk celery, chopped
1 medium carrot, pared and chopped
1 small red pepper, finely chopped
½ tsp dried thyme and/or oregano
2/3 cup unsweetened soymilk
1 cup fresh or frozen corn kernels

Place the potatoes and water in a large pot and bring to a boil. Reduce the heat to low, cover, and let simmer for 20 minutes. In the meantime, place the oil in a skillet and heat to medium-high. Add the onion, celery, bell pepper, and thyme and/or oregano. Cook, stirring constantly, until the vegetables are just tender...about 5-8 minutes. Take them off the heat and set aside. When the potatoes are tender, remove them from the heat as well. Remove about 1½ cups of the potatoes and put them in a blender. Add the soymilk to the blender and puree until smooth. Pour the puree back into the pot with the remaining potatoes and their cooking liquid. Stir in the corn and the other vegetables. Warm the mixture for about 10 minutes and serve hot.

> Art is always subversive. Art and Liberty, like the fire of Prometheus, are things that one must steal to be used against the established order.
>
> Pablo Picasso

Potato-Chile Soup

Music: Minotaur-The Oath of Blood demo (1986)

10 cups water
1 bell pepper, chopped
1 celery rib, chopped
2-3 cloves garlic, minced
1 Serrano chile, minced
1 small cauliflower head, cut into flowerettes
2 cups Yukon potatoes, cut into ½" cubes
1½ tsp dill weed
2 Tbsp liquid aminos (or soy sauce)
1 cup fire-roasted green chile, diced
1 Tbsp arrowroot powder, mixed with ¼ cup water
1 cup soymilk

Bring water to boil. Add the next 8 items, cover, and simmer for 20 minutes. Stir in the remaining ingredients. Ladle half of the vegetables into a blender and puree. Return to soup pot. Repeat. Serve hot.

Powerkraut Soup

Music: Protector-Golem lp (1988)

This goes out to Dave and Demian, my brothers in kraut and metal.

2 16 oz cans sauerkraut
1 10 oz can sauerkraut juice
¼ cup dried mushrooms, chopped
1 ½ quarts water
1 large onion, diced
5 Tbsp margarine
½ cup uncooked barley
5 Tbsp flour
Sea salt and black pepper

Put the sauerkraut, juice, water, and mushrooms into a pot. Bring to a boil, turn down the heat, and let simmer one hour. Add the barley, and cook until barley is done.
In the meantime, saute the onions in the margarine until they are soft. Add the flour into the margarine/onion mixture to thicken. Add a bit of the soup stock in and stir until smooth. Add this mixture to the rest of the soup.

Add sea salt and pepper to taste. Enjoy with sourdough bread.

Evan's Faux Meat Sauce

Music: Malignancy-Cross Species Transmutation mlp (2003)

This should be nothing less than exceptional if you prepare it using Gloria Cubana's pasta sauce

4 cups mushrooms (domestic, portabellos, a mix, whatever)
1 vidalia onion, minced
5 cloves garlic, minced
Olive oil
Pasta sauce

Chop the mushrooms up into tiny pieces using a sharp knife…you want the pieces to be small enough that they resemble hamburger. Sweat the onion and garlic at low heat in a bit of oil with a bit of sea salt and pepper. Cook until they have no crunch, nice and soft. Add the shrooms. Stir them frequently, as they tend to stick at first. Add more sea salt and pepper to taste, if necessary. Once the shrooms start to soften they will release their water. Cook them over low heat until they are dry and have the consistency of hamburger. Add the pasta sauce, heat, and enjoy over pasta or rice.

Typhoid Ellie's Tortilla Lime Soup

Music: Sacred Reich-Surf Nicaragua ep (1988; Viva Arizona!)

Preheat oven to 375° F

Sáute until onion is translucent:
1 Tbsp olive or vegetable oil
1 cup chopped onion (yellow or white)
2 Tbsp minced garlic

Add:
8 cups vegetarian "chix" broth (made with that powder shit)
1 medium (28-30 oz) can diced tomatoes, with juice
1 medium can hominy, with liquid
1 small can diced green chiles
3/4 cup lime juice
1/4 cup jalapeno juice (add more later if needed)
1 Tbsp salt
2 Tbsp cumin
2 Tbsp chili powder (more as needed)
1/2 bunch cilantro, chopped

Simmer over low to medium heat for a half hour, or until hot. After soup has simmered for a while, add more jalapeno juice, chili powder, and/or cayenne pepper as desired.

While you're waiting:
1 package medium-sized flour tortillas
1/4-1/2 cup oil
1 Tbsp salt (preferably kosher or coarse)

Cut tortillas into 1/2" strips, brush with oil/salt mixture, and place on a cookie sheet. Bake in preheated oven 10 minutes or until golden and somewhat crisp, flipping halfway through bake time. Tortillas will crisp up more upon cooling. Serve these bad bitches on the soup...YUM!

Eric the Red's Militant Vegan Tofu Marinade

Music: Purified in Blood-Last Leaves of a Poisoned Tree ep (2003)

I suggest pan frying the marinated tofu and serving with Kale and rice. This will make enough for 1 pound of tofu.

2 Tbsp soy sauce
1½ Tbsp Grade B maple syrup
1 Tbsp organic brown rice vinegar
1Tbsp extra virgin olive oil
½ tsp ground ginger
½ tsp garlic powder

Place all ingredients in a small mixing bowl and mix well with a wire whisk. I'm serious here...mix this together for some time. Ponder the following thought as you whisk: "Perpetrators of this madness, your right to live is gone. Your burning bodies shall light the path to a glorious new dawn." Now get the ginger and garlic incorporated. Pour over sliced tofu and marinate in the refrigerator (covered) for anywhere from 30 minutes to over night. Usually, the longer the better!

Plain Ramen Just Isn't Going to Cut it Today Soup

Music: diSEMBOWELMENT-Transcending into the Peripheral lp (1993)

1 package ramen noodles and included spices
1 Tbsp red miso
1 or 2 cloves garlic, minced
1 Tbsp peanut butter
¼ cabbage, chopped
2 tsp red pepper
A bit of cayenne
¼ tsp black pepper

Cook the ramen as instructed.

Add the rest.

Cook a few minutes. Subsist.

Creole Sauce

Music: Brenoritvrezorkre-Vasagraèbe éakr vatrè Brenoritvrezorkre demo (1996)

Try it over rice, blackened tofu, vegan sausages, or whatever.

1 green pepper, coarsely chopped
1 yellow onion, peeled and chopped
1 large clove garlic, minced
½ oz margarine
½ Tbsp corn oil
1 14 oz can Italian tomatoes
1 Tbsp tomato paste
1 bay leaf
½ tsp chopped oregano
¼ tsp chopped thyme
½ tsp sea salt
Black pepper to taste
1½ tsp sugar

In a large, thick-bottomed saucepan fry the onions in the margarine and oil until amber colored, then add the green pepper and garlic and continue frying for another 4-5 minutes. Stir in the rest of the ingredients, bring to a boil, and simmer, covered, for 1¼ to 1½ hours, stirring occasionally. Freezes well.

It seems hard for people to understand that not everyone caught in a thunderstorm will b frightened, and some will go there on purpose.

Skepticism

Virgil Tate's Mean Green Bean Soup

Music: Because this is an Austrian recipe, I would suggest any Pungent Stench album as the accompanying soundtrack (let's go with the Been Caught Buttering lp; 1991).

Fresh Beans are always best, but frozen ones can work if the money's tight or you live somewhere that fresh ones are harder to come by. Serves 4-6.

¾ lb of young green beans or a 10 oz. package frozen cut beans, thawed
8 Tbsp margarine
1 medium onion
1 garlic clove minced
½ cup finely chopped celery
8 cups vegetarian vegetable stock (Swanson makes a great organic veggie stock if you don't have the time or patience to make your own)
1/3 cup pearl barley
½ cup dried tarragon or 1 Tbsp of fresh
6 to 8 sliced fresh mushrooms or 1 4oz. can, drained
2 Tbsp flour
½ cup vegan sour cream
¼ cup chopped parsley to garnish

Basically all you need to do to prep is make sure all your veggies are chopped and ready to go. Keep 'em separated as it makes things a bit more orderly and easier to add when the time calls for it. I like to chop the beans so they are the size of the distance between knuckles on my thumbs.

In a medium sauce pan (4-quart) heat 6 Tbsp margarine until it foams and then add the garlic, onion, and celery. Cover and cook for 8 minutes. Then add the chopped beans and continue to cook, covered, for an additional 10 minutes over medium-low heat.

Pour the stock into the saucepan with the veggies. Add the barley and tarragon. Bring to a gentle boil, reduce heat to simmer, and cook for 30 minutes.

Meanwhile, you sauté the mushrooms in 2 Tbsp of margarine in a medium skillet over medium heat for about 10 minutes. Set 'em aside after that. When the soup has cooked for 30 minutes, pour the mushrooms and the liquid into the sauce pan. Simmer for 15 more minutes and then remove from the heat.

Whisk together the flour and vegan sour cream. Beat 1 cup of the hot soup into this mixture. While stirring, slowly pour this back into the saucepan with the soup. Serve this HOT with the parsley sprinkled on top.

Super Savory Shub Niggurath Sauce

Music: Thergothon-Fhtagn Nagh Yog-Sothoth demo (1991)

Simply excellent...definitely one of my favorite sauces.
It's creamy and alfredo sauce-like.
Goes well over angel hair.

½ lb firm tofu
¾ cup vegetable stock
¼ cup olive oil
2 Tbsp soy sauce
2 Tbsp nutritional yeast
2 Tbsp chopped fresh basil (1 tsp dried)
2 Tbsp lemon juice
1 tsp yellow mustard
1 garlic clove, peeled

Put all of the ingredients into a blender. Puree until smooth. Reheat on the stove if necessary and serve hot over your favorite pasta.

> Extreme Noise Terror were amazing. So were their fans. Any track more than 20 seconds long was greeted with derisive cries of "too long, too slow" or "fucking prog-rockers" from the faithful, most of whom looked as though they had but recently risen from shallow graves alongside the A12, the arterial road that runs from London to Ipswich. The only disappointment for Sheila, William and me was that the band weren't loud enough. We wanted to leave the show with blood trickling from our ears.
>
> John Peel (R.I.P)

Cold Defense Soup

Music: Morbid-December Moon demo (1987)

2 14 oz cans vegetable broth
1 head garlic
1 medium onion, quartered
1½ Tbsp minced fresh parsley
1½ Tbsp minced fresh cilantro
1 tsp minced fresh mint
1 tsp minced fresh basil
1 tsp curry powder
¼ tsp red pepper flakes
Sea salt to taste
1 Tbsp fresh lemon juice

Combine all ingredients except the lemon juice and bring to a boil over high heat. Reduce heat and simmer, covered, for 30 minutes. Remove from heat and cool a bit. In a blender, puree the soup in batches. Return each batch to the saucepan, add the lemon juice, and reheat.

Roald Dahl Soup

Music: Master's Hammer-Finished demo (1988)

This soup is spectacular. Thick, rich, and creamy.

3 Tbsp yellow split peas
3 Tbsp mung beans
3 Tbsp Basmati rice
2 Tbsp margarine
1/2 tsp turmeric
1/8 tsp asafetida
1/2 small seeded green chili
A 1/2" piece of ginger root
2 medium sized carrots, sliced
1/2 small cauliflower, in florets
6 red radishes
5 1/4 cups vegetable stock
1 Tbsp cumin
1 Tbsp coriander
1 tsp garam masala
1/2 tsp black pepper
1 tsp sea salt
2 Tbsp minced coriander

Soak the split peas in hot water for 1 hour and drain. Wash the Mung beans well and pick out any loose stones and sticks, etc. Combine rice, legumes, margarine, turmeric, asafetida, chili, ginger root, vegetables, and stock in large pot. Cook for about one hour. Blend the vegetables at high speed to make a very creamy and smooth soup and return to the pot.

Sprinkle in the ground coriander, cumin, and garam masala. Heat until almost boiling and simmer gently for 2 to 3 minutes, stirring to prevent burning. Add the black pepper, salt, and minced coriander and serve.

The importance of nonsense hardly can be overstated. The more clearly we experience something as "nonsense," the more clearly we are experiencing the boundaries of our own self-imposed cognitive structures. "Nonsense" is that which does not fit into the prearranged patterns which we have super-imposed on reality. There is no such thing as "nonsense" apart from a judgmental intellect which calls it that.

Gary Zukav

Eight Ball in the Corner Pocket Chili

Music: Casbah-Infinite Pain demo (1987)

I always like to have new chili recipes. This one is from someone called the "masked idiot."

-10 cloves garlic, minced
yellow onion, chopped
green bell pepper, chopped
cup tofu, crumbled
-10 large button mushrooms, chopped
cans black beans
cans Great Northern (white) beans
cans whole tomatoes, chopped
small can tomato sauce
jalepeno peppers, minced
Turbinado sugar
Sea salt and pepper
Red pepper flakes
Cayenne pepper
Cumin
Basil
Olive oil
Hot sauce
Green onions, minced

In a large pot, saute the garlic, onion, and bell peppers in the olive oil and a bit of salt, until soft. Add the mushrooms and tofu. Add a pinch of each of the spices and simmer for a bit.

Add the beans, tomatoes, and tomato sauce. Add some sugar. Add more spices to taste. Bring to boil for a few minutes, adding water if necessary. Lower the heat and let it simmer a while. The longer it simmers, the more time the spices have to meld. Serve with green onions on top.

Creamy Spinach Artichokehold Dip

Music: Foetopsy-Dyspartum lp (2002)

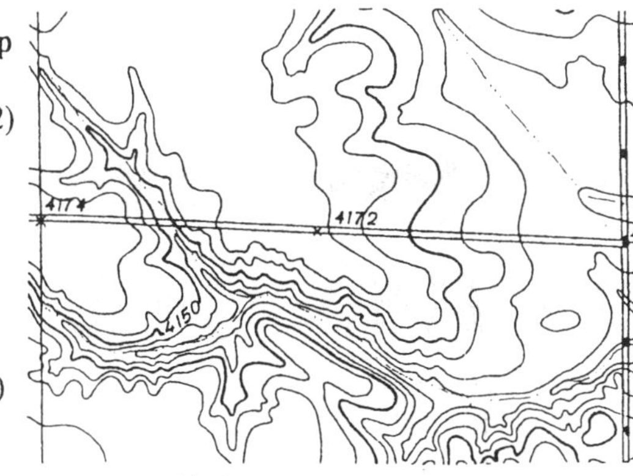

cup silken tofu
Tbsp nutritional yeast
tsp garlic powder
½ tsp balsamic vinegar
½ tsp black pepper
8 oz can artichokes (non-marinated)
/3 cup cooked spinach

Blend tofu, nutritional yeast, garlic powder, balsamic vinegar, and black pepper. Stir in cut up artichokes and spinach. Bake in a casserole dish uncovered for 15 minutes at 275° F or until cooked through.

French Onion Soup with Vegan Mozzarella Cheese

Music: Blut aus Nord-The Work which Transforms God lp (2003)

3 large Vidalia onions, sliced
½ cup water
3 cloves garlic, minced
7½ cups water
1/3 cup soy sauce
2½ Tbsp nutritional yeast
2 Tbsp dry white wine or dry sherry
1 tsp dry mustard
¼ tsp onion powder
¼ tsp paprika
¼ tsp black pepper
Pinch of turmeric, thyme, marjoram, and dill
Vegan mozzarella cheese (see recipe this book)
6 pieces French bread, sliced ½" thick and toasted
Nutritional yeast
1½ tsp sea salt and pepper (or to taste)

Cook the first three ingredients in a large pot over medium-low heat until the onions are tender. Add more water if the onions begin to stick to the pot. Stir in the next 9 ingredients to complete the broth. Bring it up to a boil, then reduce the heat and simmer for 15 minutes.

Get out six soup bowls and place a piece of toasted French bread in the bottom of each. Ladle the soup in over the bread. Top each bowl with several spoonfuls of mozzarella cheese mixture and sprinkle with a little nutritional yeast. Alternately, you can spread each of the toast slices with a thick layer of cheese sauce, sprinkle them with a little nutritional yeast, and then float them atop the soup in each bowl.

Black Death Chili

Music: Black Death-self titled lp (1984)

1 can (14.5 oz) diced tomatoes
1 can (15.25 oz) black beans
1 can (15.25 oz) whole kernel corn
1.2 lb extra firm tofu, cubed
1 Tbsp chili powder
1 Tbsp cayenne powder (less if you can't deal)
¼ cup chopped cilantro (crucial)
A couple finely sliced green onions

Fry the tofu in a bit of olive oil in the pot you intend to use. When finished, dump everything else in. This will be very thick so you may want to add a can's worth of water and let it simmer down.

Bernadette's Vegetable Soup from the Great White North

Music: Infernäl Mäjesty-None Shall Defy lp (1987)

Straight from Bern's mom's kitchen in Canaduh to yours.

2-3 stalks celery
2 cooking onions
2-4 cloves chopped garlic
2 Tbsp oil
1 large carrot (cubed)
1 medium potato (cubed)
1 1/2 cup shredded cabbage
1 Tbsp basil
1 tsp parsley
1 small can red kidney beans
1 5 oz can tomato paste
Sea salt & pepper & hot sauce to taste

> We now know that
>
> the moon is
>
> demonstrably not there
>
> when nobody looks.
>
> N. David Mermin

Saute celery, onion, & garlic in oil. Add very hot water with tomato paste. Add remaining ingredients-bring to a boil, then turn to a simmer for 2 hours. Ten minutes before serving, add 1/2 cup alphabets or other soup pasta.

Drunk-Punk Winter Stew

Music: Winter-The Hour of Doom demo (1990)

3 potatoes, peeled and cubed
¼ cup chopped onion
½ head cabbage, sliced
can kidney beans
3 cups water
2 oz beer (porter, if possible)
Tbsp spicy mustard
tsp garlic powder
½ tsp black pepper
tsp sea salt

Bring potatoes, onions, and water to boil. Lower heat to simmer. Add cabbage and mustard. Slowly add about ½ the beer (it will foam up a bit). Cover loosely. Let immer 15 minutes, stirring occasionally. Add the beans, spices, and the rest of the beer take a swig first, of course). Remove lid and let simmer until the potatoes are tender, dding water if necessary. Re-spice if necessary before serving.

Terror of the Thai Soup

Music: Nuctemeron-The Unexpected demo (1988)

1 shallot, chopped
2 Tbsp fresh ginger, chopped
1 can vegetable broth
1 can coconut milk (unsweetened)
¼ cup cilantro, chopped
Juice of 1 lemon
A few drops of chili sauce to taste
2 Tbsp soy sauce
1 cup fresh spinach leaves

Saute the shallot, garlic, and ginger in a small amount of vegetable oil. Add the coconut milk and vegetable broth. Bring to a boil. Turn down to a simmer and add the cilantro, lemon juice, chili sauce, soy sauce, and vegetables. Simmer about 5 minutes or until the spinach is wilted and serve with rice.

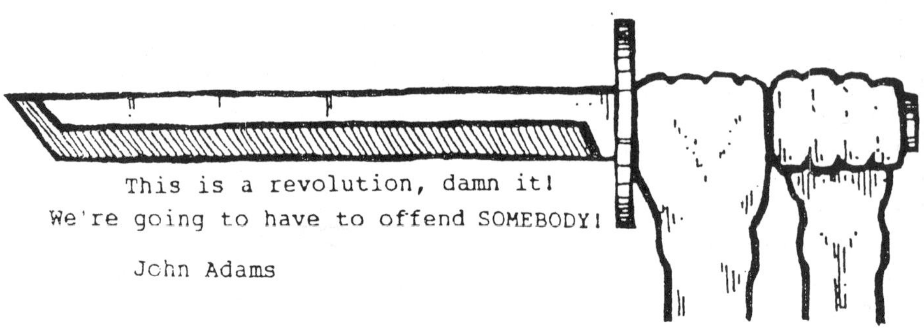

Life's Blood Soup

Music: Slaughter Lord-Taste of Blood demo (1986)

1 small head cauliflower, chopped
2 carrots, chopped
2 roasted Anaheim green chiles (6" long), skinned, stemmed, seeded, and chopped
1 dried red chile (6" long), softened in hot water, skinned, stemmed, seeded, and chopped
2 garlic cloves
1 tsp chile powder
1 tsp oregano
2 tsp ground cumin
1 tsp liquid aminos (or 1 Tbsp soy sauce)
A dash of clove powder

Steam the cauliflower and carrots in a medium pot with one cup of water until tender. Put everything in a blender and puree (in batches, if necessary), then return it all to the pot. Stir in water, if needed, and simmer before serving.

Iuman Marinade/Baste Dip

Ausic: Necrofago-Desire for Blood demo (1987)

'rom your "friends" at the Church of Euthanasia.

8 oz can tomato sauce
6 oz can tomato paste
cup black coffee
/4 cup beer (Genessee Red preferred)
/4 cup pineapple juice
Tbsp whiskey
Tbsp lemon juice
Tbsp vegan Worcestershire sauce
Tbsp vinegar (red wine garlic preferred)
cloves garlic, minced
jalepeno peppers, minced
/4 large onion, minced
½ tsp liquid smoke
Tbsp brown sugar
Tbsp molasses
½ Tbsp crushed red pepper
cube vegetable bouillon
½ tsp sea salt
½ tsp ground black pepper
½ tsp paprika
½ tsp cayenne pepper
dashes basil
dashes oregano
dashes savory
.shes of one fine thin joint (optional)

Aix all the ingredients well. Marinate the insalubrious.

:abin Fever Chowder

Ausic: Ildjarn-Forest Poetry lp (1996)

cup white beans, rinsed and drained
cup canned potatoes, rinsed and drained
can (14.5 oz) vegetable broth
Tbsp finely chopped onion
Tbsp finely chopped fresh dill
Tbsp white wine
ea salt and pepper to taste

uree the beans and potatoes in a blender. Add the remaining ingredients and give it nother whirl. Pour into a pot and heat on the stove, simmering for 10 minutes. Make ure to stir occasionally. Serve in heavy bowls. Avert hypothermia.

Creamy Herbgrinder Dressing

Music: Warloghe-Desecration rehearsal (1997)

3 Tbsp lemon juice
2 tsp vegetable oil
1 Tbsp miso
3 cloves garlic
1/4 cup chopped fresh parsley
2 tsp dried dill
1/8 tsp celery seed
1/4 tsp marjoram
2/3 cup soft tofu

Turn tofu into a strainer to drain for few minutes. Place the other ingredients in a blender and puree. Add tofu to blender, bit by bit, blending until a creamy consistency is reached. Keep refrigerated. Use as a salad dressing, a topping for baked potatoes, or party dip.

Stupid Jerk Sauce

Music: Carcass-Flesh Ripping Sonic Torment demo (1987)

8 habanero peppers
¼ cup lime juice
¼ cup orange juice
1/3 cup prepared yellow mustard
1/3 cup olive oil
1 coarsely chopped onion
5 large garlic cloves
1 Tbsp ground allspice
2 Tbsp fresh parsley
2 Tbsp vinegar
1 Tbsp cumin
1 tsp ground cinnamon
1 tsp rosemary
1 tsp sea salt
1 tsp black pepper
½ tsp ground cloves
½ tsp thyme

Combine all ingredients in a blender and blend until smooth. Coat tofu (or whatever you deem appropriate) with the mixture and marinate 2 hours or longer before grilling.

Black Legions Bouillabaisse

Music: Moëvöt-Ézléýfbdréhtr Vépréùb Zùérfl Màzàgvàtre Érbbédréà demo (1994)

2 8 oz packages of tempeh, cut into ½" cubes
8 cloves garlic, thinly sliced
1 medium Spanish (or yellow) onion, chopped
2 Tbsp drained capers, coarsely chopped
8 Tbsp chopped kalamata olives
4 cups vegetable broth
1 cup dry white wine
14 oz can diced tomatoes, **un**drained
2 large dried bay leaves
1 tsp dried oregano
½ tsp dried thyme
1 tsp dried tarragon
1 tsp dried basil
1 tsp fennel seed
½ tsp celery seed
1 cup loosely packed flat-leaf parsley, chopped

HEY BOB, COULD YOU TURN DOWN THE BASS A BIT?..

In a large, heavy saucepan, place all ingredients except the parsley. Season with sea salt and freshly ground black pepper to taste.

Bring to a simmer. Cover and cook over medium heat for 45 minutes (Bouillabaisse means "to boil and reduce," you know). Recite the following six times: Insensé que vous êtes pourquoi...Vous promettez vous de vivre...longtemps, vous qui ne pouvez...Compter sur un seul jour. Remove the bay leaves and stir in the parsley just before serving. Serve in bowls with crusty French bread and crusty French (or French-Canadian) friends.

Golden Dawn Gravy

Music: Magus-Ruminations of Debauchery ep (1992)

2 Tbsp safflower oil
1/4 cup flour
2 Tbsp nutritional yeast
2 cups vegetable broth
Black pepper to taste

Add safflower oil to saucepan. Place over medium heat until hot. Add flour and nutritional yeast, stirring constantly until mixture starts to bubble. Whisk in vegetable broth. Stir until mixture thickens and comes to a boil. Reduce heat and simmer 1-2 minutes, stirring occasionally. Add black pepper to taste.

I saw a dead woman today. It's hard to prepare yourself for that kind of thing. I was riding my bike home, and, as I crossed the Schuylkill River and approached 30th Street Station, I noticed a couple cops wildly gesturing to each other at something over the edge about 50 feet down.

The body floated face-down-head-underwater-legs-sunk. Not much dignity in this kind of death. Not much dignity in death in general, I imagine. Dignity is a living characteristic…an expression of the tenacious grasp one maintains on the integrity of the self. Take away the subject and its internal forces and you have nothing but the object, left to be manipulated by the forces at hand. The waves carelessly pulled the dead woman's shirt up and exposed her naked back. A life preserver bounced gently and ironically against her head with each aquatic oscillation.

Another woman had seen the fall…said it looked like a suicide. The deceased had just let herself fall face-forward off the ledge. Her purse and belongings sat below the railing as a temporary memorial at the spot where she fell. No one laughed. Few people spoke. Distress was visible. This wasn't a 20 second video clip on the news…this was real. The body was floating right there. No changing the channel. The body was floating right there. No cut to commercial, no diverting the conversation, no speaking in euphemisms, no denial. The body was floating right there. No one could get to it and it had nowhere to go. The body was floating right there. Perhaps this was the only real, undeniable thing these people had seen all day. All week. I thought of all the abstractions I dealt in. All the symbolism. All the filtered, watered-down, mediated, indirect perceptions. This was fucking real and we knew it. We stared because we had to.

A diver arrived and tugged and twisted her arms to stuff her in a harness. As he cradled her lifeless body, the woman's head fell back and revealed her face for the first time, blue and pained. Her body flopped heavily against the seawall as she was hoisted up, up, and onto the side of the road.

The man next to me shook his head and sighed. "It's never so bad you got to go and do that," he said to no one in particular. I turned to him and our eyes wearily met. I wanted to tell him that yes, sometimes things are that bad. In fact, oftentimes things are that bad. But I wasn't certain he even believed what he had just said. It wasn't my place to challenge him. "I know that's right," I mumbled.

Simple Ginger Dipping Sauce

Music: Blue Holocaust-Twitch of the Death Nerve lp (2004)

¼ cup chopped onion
1 small piece of ginger root or 1/8 tsp ground ginger
½ cup soy sauce
¼ cup rice wine vinegar

Combine all ingredients in blender and process until smooth. Serve with spring rolls.

Basic Guacamole

Music: Rottrevore-Copulation of the Virtuous and Vicious ep (1991)

1 large, ripe avocado
2 green onions, finely chopped
2 Tbsp fresh lemon or lime juice
¼ tsp garlic powder
¼ tsp cayenne
1 pinch sea salt

Mash it all together. Eat.

Creamy Italian Salad Dressing

Music: Necrodeath-Fragments of Insanity lp (1989)

¼ tsp fresh thyme
¼ tsp fresh basil
¼ tsp fresh oregano
5 oz lite, silken tofu
1 clove garlic, minced
1 Tbsp olive oil
2 tsp red wine vinegar
1 tsp minced onion or shallot
Sea salt and pepper to taste

Combine all ingredients into a blender and mix until smooth.

Splattered Spinach Soup

Music: Saprogenic-The Wet Sound of Flesh on Concrete lp (2002)

1 largw onion, coarsely chopped
6 cups water
3 potatoes, peeled and chopped
3 zucchini, thickly sliced
1 Tbsp soy sauce
2 cups fresh spinach leaves, tightly packed
Black pepper to taste

Place the onion in a large pot with ½ cup water. Cook and stir until the onion softens slightly...about 3 minutes. Add the remaining 5 or so cups of water, potatoes, zucchini, and soy sauce. Bring to a boil, reduce heat, cover, and simmer for 35 minutes. Add the spinach and pepper. Cook for another 2 minutes. Remove from heat. Puree the soup in batches in a blender. Return each batch to the pan. Heat gently for 5 minutes and serve hot.

Roasted Garlic Spread

Music: Pustulated-Pathognomonic Purulency mlp (2002)

It's amazing how mild and mellow the garlic flavor becomes with roasting. Use in place of butter on hot, fresh bread.

4 large heads (not cloves) garlic
1 Tbsp olive oil
1 tsp sea salt
½ tsp white pepper
2 Tbsp fresh basil, minced

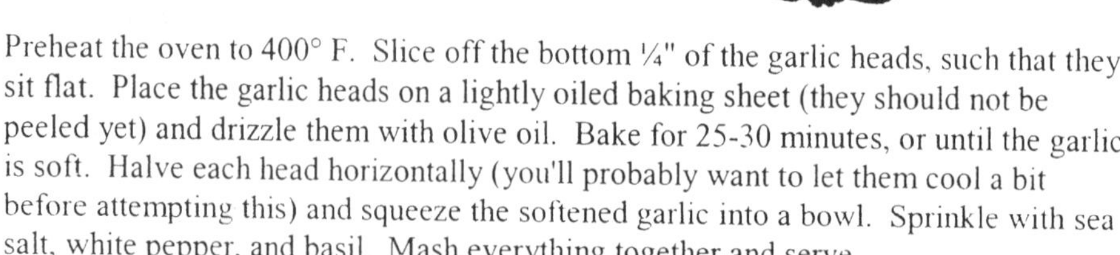

Preheat the oven to 400° F. Slice off the bottom ¼" of the garlic heads, such that they sit flat. Place the garlic heads on a lightly oiled baking sheet (they should not be peeled yet) and drizzle them with olive oil. Bake for 25-30 minutes, or until the garlic is soft. Halve each head horizontally (you'll probably want to let them cool a bit before attempting this) and squeeze the softened garlic into a bowl. Sprinkle with sea salt, white pepper, and basil. Mash everything together and serve.

> Anybody's music is made up of a lot of things that are not musical. Music is an attitude, a group of symbols of a way of life, whether you're conscious of it or not...and of course, it naturally reflects the social and economic and educational attitudes of the players. And that's why the fools don't think I play jazz.
>
> Cecil Taylor

Naomi's Marvelous Mango Salsa

Music: Angel Witch-1979 demo (1979)

1 red or yellow medium-sized pepper, diced
3 medium-sized ripe tomatoes, diced
½ to 1 cup red onion, diced
1 cup red wine vinegar
Jalapeno peppers, chopped
Cilantro, chopped
A bit of sugar

Combine the first five ingredients in a bowl and let it sit a while after mixing thoroughly. Add the cilantro and some sea salt and fresh ground pepper to taste. Next, add as many jalapenos as you can handle and a bit of sugar to cut the acidity. Mix again. If necessary, you may want to drain out a bit of the liquid if the salsa is excessively watery. Garnish with cilantro and mango slices and let it sit in the refrigerator for several hours before serving with tortilla chips.

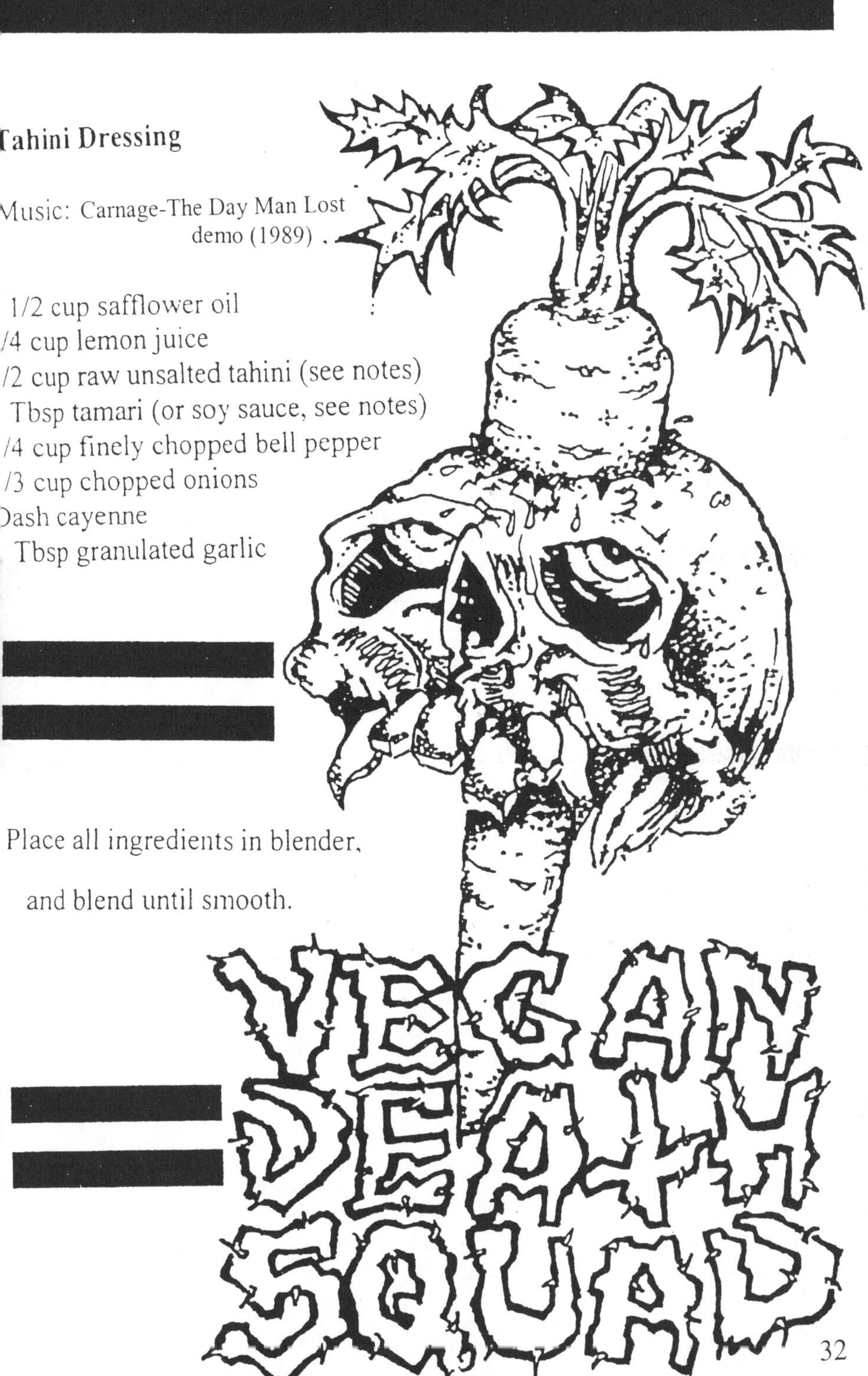

Tahini Dressing

Music: Carnage-The Day Man Lost demo (1989)

1/2 cup safflower oil
/4 cup lemon juice
/2 cup raw unsalted tahini (see notes)
Tbsp tamari (or soy sauce, see notes)
/4 cup finely chopped bell pepper
/3 cup chopped onions
)ash cayenne
Tbsp granulated garlic

Place all ingredients in blender, and blend until smooth.

Luther's Bastardized Barbecue Sauce

Music: Hellish Torment-1986 demo (1986)

3 small cans tomato sauce
¼ onion, finely minced
½ cup sugar
1 tsp black pepper
½ tsp mustard powder
1 tsp sea salt
1 Tbsp molasses
1 Tbsp corn syrup
¼ tsp cayenne pepper
1 tsp garlic powder
2-3 tsp liquid smoke

Mix all ingredients in a medium pot and simmer for 1 hour. Cool and serve.

Green Hell Sauce

Music: Celtic Frost-To Mega Therion lp (1985)

2 cups hot vegetable stock
3 Tbsp margarine
1 medium onion, chopped
2 cups canned, hot green chili peppers, chopped
4 Tbsp flour
1 tsp garlic powder
1 tsp sea salt
¼ tsp pepper
Vegetable oil as needed

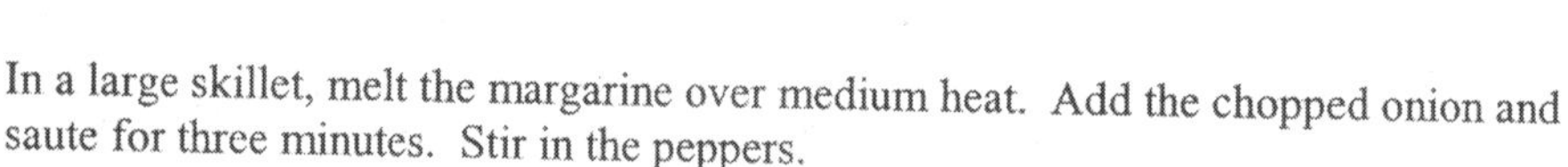

In a large skillet, melt the margarine over medium heat. Add the chopped onion and saute for three minutes. Stir in the peppers.

In a small bowl, mix together the flour, garlic powder, salt, and pepper. Add oil until the mixture is not hard to stir but not overly runny. Add the flour mixture to the skillet and stir for 1 minute. While stirring constantly, slowly add the vegetable stock. Bring the sauce to a boil, then reduce heat and simmer 10 minutes, stirring occasionally. Serve over tacos, burritos, and so on.

Thickeners Demystified (Thanks to the Milwaukee Journal)

Cooks use starches to thicken sauces and gravies, to set pies and custards, to prevent proteins from curdling, and to bake cakes. Starches look like fine powders. They are not composed of cells or crystals, though, but are a semi-crystalline structure scientists call "granules." These granules contain starch molecules packed together, layer on top of layer, like an onion. When we stir starch granules into cold water, a little water begins to seep into the granules. As we heat the starch and water, more and more water seeps in. At 90° F, a starch granule can hold more than a hundred times its weight of liquid. Between 150 and 212° F, depending on the type of starch, the granule may hold more than a thousand times its weight. At this point, the granules pop, and starch rushes out into the solution. This is when the sauce or gravy thickens. When making a sauce, we can't see the starches swelling. So we often add a little more starch than necessary to hasten the job. Then, all at once, the magic temperature is reached and the starch granules pop and the result is food glue. If you've had this happen, you know how bad it sucks. One of the secrets to perfect sauces, then, is to wait until the sauce reaches a gentle boil before adding any more starch.

All starches can absorb a large weight of water, but the granules are different sizes and swell to different sizes. For example, cornstarch swells to about 20 times its original volume before it pops, while potato starch can swell to 100 times its original size. So which starch should be used for a given recipe? Each granule contains two kinds of starch molecules. They are amylose (a long, straight bar-shaped molecule), and amylopectin (a little branched molecule with points sticking out in many directions like a multi-pointed star). When amylose reaches the temperature at which the granule pops and the starch molecules rush out into the sauce, both the long, bulky amylose molecules and the puffed, empty granules contribute to the thickening. When the starch cools, amylose molecules bond to each other to make a firm, slightly opaque gel. Amylopectin molecules and the empty granules contribute thickening, but the little amylopectin molecules do not join together to form a solid gel. So these two starches have very different characteristics. Amylose makes sauces and gravies that are clear when hot but cloudy when cooled and very thick when cold; in fact, they are thick enough to cut with a knife. Amylopectin makes sauces that are crystal clear, hot or cold, but never get firm enough to cut with a knife. How do we know which starches contain a lot of amylose or a lot of amylopectin? Ordinary grain starches, such as wheat and corn, are relatively high in amylose, containing about 26%, while root starches, such as arrowroot and tapioca, contain only about 17 to 21%. Potatoes are a tuber, not a true root, so potato starch falls somewhere in between with about 23% amylose. So sometimes we need one kind of starch and sometimes another. Coconut cream pie, for example, must be firm enough to cut and it doesn't matter if it is opaque. But for cherry pie, we want a clear thickener so as not to have a cloudy covering on bright red cherries.

So, how much starch should one use to thicken a sauce for a given recipe? Depends on the thickener. The following measurements are meant per 1 cup of liquid:

Flour:	1 Tbsp (thin sauce) 2 Tbsp (medium sauce) 3 Tbsp (thick sauce)
Cornstarch:	1 Tbsp + 1 tsp (medium sauce)
Rice Starch:	1 Tbsp + ½ tsp (medium sauce)
Arrowroot:	1 Tbsp + 1 tsp (medium sauce)
Potato Starch:	2¼ tsp (medium sauce)
Tapioca Starch:	1 Tbsp + ¼ tsp (medium sauce)

As always, don't forget to mix the thickener into 2 or so Tbsp of cold water before adding it to a recipe. Otherwise, you'll end up with pretty disgusting clumps. No good at all.

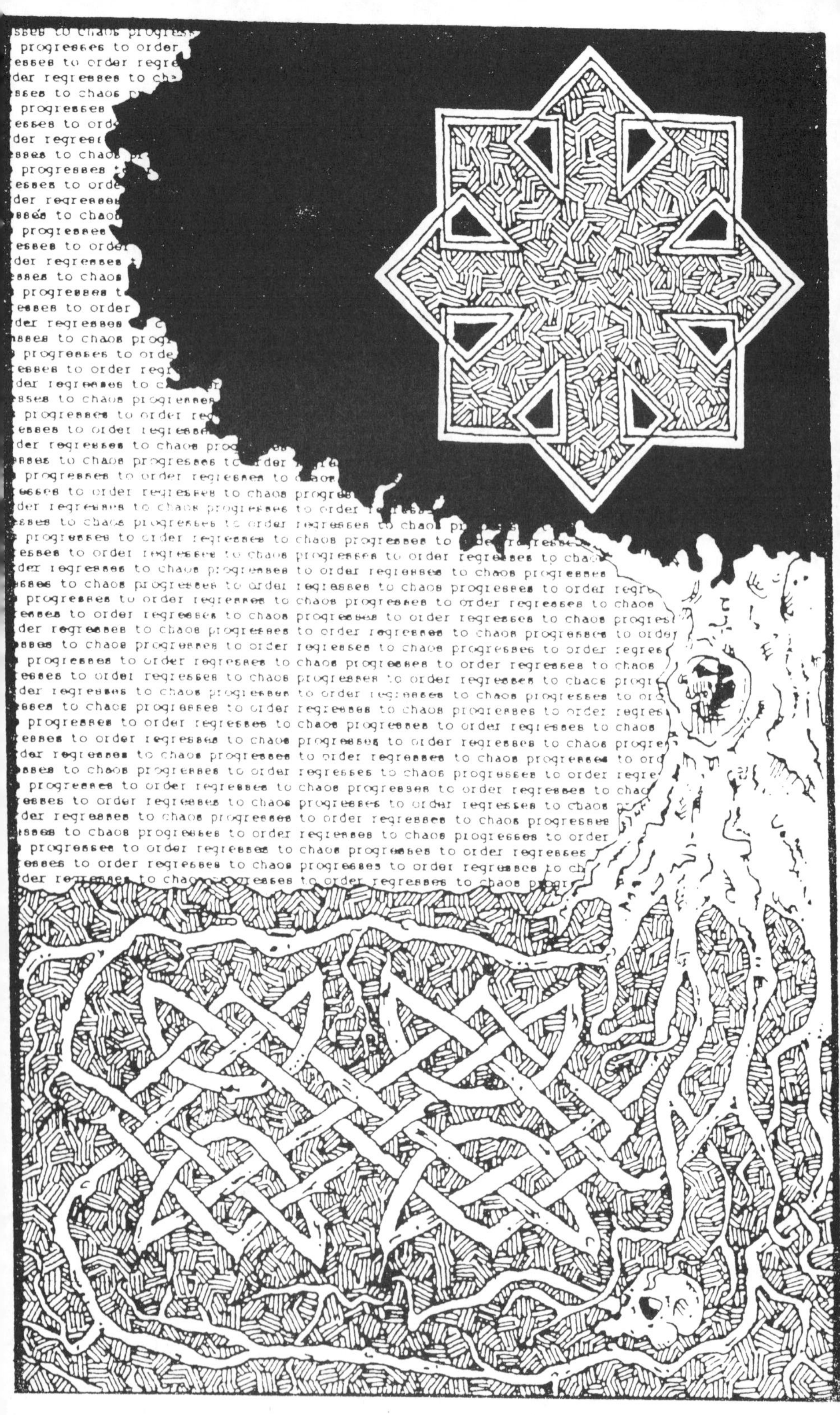

der regresses to chaos progresses to order regresses to chaos progresses
sses to chaos progresses to order regresses to chaos progresses to order regre
progresses to order regresses to chaos progresses to order regresses to chaos
esses to order regresses to chaos progresses to order regresses to chaos progres
der regresses to chaos progresses to order regresses to chaos progresses to order
sses to chaos progresses to order regresses to chaos progresses to order regres
progresses to order regresses to chaos progresses to order regresses to chaos
esses to order regresses to chaos progresses to order regresses to chaos progr
der regresses to chaos progresses to order regresses to chaos progresses to or
sses to chaos progresses to order regresses to chaos progresses to order regres
progresses to order regresses to chaos progresses to order regresses to chaos
esses to order regresses to chaos progresses to order regresses to chaos progre
der regresses to chaos progresses to order regresses to chaos progresses to ord
sses to chaos progresses to order regresses to chaos progresses to order regre
progresses to order regresses to chaos progresses to order regresses to chac
esses to order regresses to chaos progresses to order regresses to chaos
der regresses to chaos progresses to order regresses to chaos progresses
sses to chaos progresses to order regresses to chaos progresses to order
progresses to order regresses to chaos progresses to order regresses
esses to order regresses to chaos progresses to order regresses to ch

Chicago Not Dog

Music: Deathstrike-Fuckin' Death lp (1985)

Here it is: the vegan version of the highly revered Chicago hot dog. Definitely one of my favorite things to eat. I once witnessed my friend Josh eating four of these (the non-vegan version, unfortunately) in one sitting at Chicago's (RIP) in Milwaukee during hot dog happy hour.

1 soy/tofu not dog
1 poppy seed hot dog bun
1 tsp yellow mustard
1 tsp bright green sweet relish
1 tsp freshly chopped onions
1 Kosher dill pickle spear (Claussen, if possible)
2 tomato slices
2 serrano sport peppers
A dash of celery salt

Heat not dogs in boiling water to 170° F. Do not grill them. Place the not dog in a steamed poppy seed bun, then pile on the toppings in this order: mustard, relish, onions, pickle, tomatoes, peppers, and celery salt. Don't even think about putting ketchup on it or you may find yourself banned to the outskirts of the Chicagoland area, aka Iowa.

Blasphemer Burritos

Music: Profanatica-Broken Throne of Christ demo (1990)

3 cups cooked rice, brown or white
1 tsp lime zest
1-2 Tbsp fresh lime juice
2-3 Tbsp finely minced cilantro
Sea salt to taste
Black beans (1 or 2 cans, drained)
Bay leaf
Habanero sauce
The biggest danged burrito shells you can find

Toss the lime zest, lime juice, salt, and cilantro with the cooked rice while heating the beans, the bay leaf, and some salt to taste on the stove. Lay out the burrito shell on the counter. Put on as much rice and beans (remove the bay leaf first) as you think you can and still be able to roll it all up. Slather habanero sauce all over the top. Roll it up. Eat with ice-cold, unsweetened ice tea at hand.

Chef Sluggo's "Cheese Steak"

Music: Funerus-Festering Earth lp (2003)

Three words: FUCK GIANNA'S GRILLE. This Philly-based "vegan-friendly" restaurant stabbed the entire vegan community in the back when it recently (late 2004) admitted that its "vegan" cheese had never been vegan, despite repeated (oftentimes indignant) assurances over the years that the cheese was vegan. This is inexcusable. You do not fuck with people's ethics in order to turn a profit. You do not treat your customers like shit. Seriously, fuck them. Make your own (it's simple enough, as you can see), or try the vegan delicacies at Govinda's (at Broad and South) instead.

1 lb seitan (see recipe this book)
1 small green and red pepper, cut in long thin strips
1 onion, diced
Olive oil
3-4 Tbsp teriyaki and soy sauce
1 tsp liquid smoke
Some pinches of chili powder
Italian seasoning
Garlic powder
Few pinches of black pepper
Vegan soy cheese slices (the tasty kind...like Tofutti makes)
Hoagie rolls

Saute the seitan in the oil on low for a while, when it browns add in the seasonings. Add the peppers and onions with a little more oil, and saute until done. May need more of teriyaki and soy sauce. Put into hoagies and put slices of soy cheese on the pan so they melt a little then drop 'em on top.

Mystics in Balinese Tempeh

Music: As Sahar-Primitively Eastern Winds demo (1993)

1 large onion, chopped
1" piece ginger, grated
Some green chiles, chopped
¼ tsp turmeric
2-3 cloves garlic, minced
½ cup peanuts, chopped
1 package tempeh, crumbled
Red chile flakes
1 Tbsp soy sauce
1 large tomato, chopped
Rice, prepared

Saute the onion together with the ginger, green chiles, and the turmeric. Stir constantly so nothing burns. When the onion starts to brown, add the garlic and saute carefully for a minute. Add the tempeh, red chile flakes to taste, and the soy sauce. Fry for a minute. Add the chopped peanuts. Fry for a couple minutes more. Add the tomato. Fry for a couple minutes more. Serve over rice.

Chinese Take-Out

Music: Mekong Delta-self titled lp (1987)

This reminds me a lot of the vegetables in brown sauce my parents used to get when we would order out. It really doesn't matter which vegetables you use here. The ones listed are the ones I tried and it tasted very good.

1 green pepper, sliced into strips
1 red pepper, sliced into strips
Some broccoli, chopped
Pea pods
1 cup water
1 Tbsp arrowroot
1 Tbsp soy sauce
1 Tbsp miso
1 tsp garlic, minced
1 tsp ginger, minced
1 tsp natural peanut butter
A bit of sesame oil
Black and red pepper
Brown rice

Get the brown rice going…it takes a while to cook. Put the water, arrowroot, soy sauce, miso, garlic, ginger, and peanut butter in a blender an blend. Stir fry the vegetables in a wok or pan in the sesame oil. Add black and red pepper to taste. Pour in the brown sauce and stir over high heat. The sauce will thicken as the vegetables cook. Serve over rice.

Okara (no, not okra) Burgers

Music: Necropolis-Contemplating Slaughter lp (1988)

Okara is a by-product of the soymilk/tofu making process. I don't think you can buy it in the store, but if you make Merrydeath's soymilk recipe you'll have plenty to work with. No sense throwing that stuff out...it makes delicious burgers! To make super-easy burgers, simply add some flour, sea salt, and smoke sauce, make patties and fry them. For a more extravagant burger, try this:

Place the okara in a big bowl. Mince about four cloves garlic and a small onion and fry in a skillet. Add it to the okara. Now add 2 Tbsp natural peanut butter. Now add a half of a small banana. Pour in ¼ cup soy sauce, ¼ cup tomato sauce, and ¼ cup nutritional yeast. Add 1-2 Tbsp basil, ground ginger, and cayenne. Add ½ cup unbleached flour and ½ cup textured vegetable protein to absorb some liquid.

Now...mash it up. Necropolis should provide a pretty good mashing/moshing beat for this. Form patties out of the mixture. I will make lots and lots, so either have a really, really big barbecue with all your friends or put them in the freezer for later enjoyment. Cook them as you would any other burger (fry them, grill them, etc.).

Erik's Touring Band After-Show Drunk Food AKA: Fuck Yea!

Music: This is a coat-your-bones-and-pass-out content. The kinda meal for the touring musician. Because of this, nothing says FUCK YEA! quite like Entombed's Morningstar lp (2001)

Serves about 6-7 folks depending on roadies and such. Adjustments can be made depending on the amount of people you are feeding.

4-6 red potatoes. Any potato will do really, but I like the red ones because they are a bit sweeter

3 large garlic cloves
1 red bell pepper
1-2 decently sized hot peppers
½ medium sized onion
6 good-sized mushrooms
3 Tbsp vegetable or olive oil
1 cup vegan cheese, shredded

Fill a large pot (6 quart) with water and put on high heat. Chop all the vegetables to a manageable size. Mince the garlic. Chop the potatoes into pieces the size of a ½ dollar coin, adding them to the water as you cut them.

Once all the potatoes are in the pot bring that sucker to a boil and let 'em cook until they are tender but not breaking apart on a fork. Meanwhile, as the potatoes are doing their thing in the big pot, sauté the garlic, red bell pepper, onion, and mushrooms in 2 Tbsp of oil in a large pan. Stir this frequently so as not to burn the vegetables or lose too much oil.

Drain the potatoes and add them to the pan of vegetables. Add the hot peppers and 1 Tbsp of oil and cook it all over medium heat for about 15 minutes, stirring semi-frequently so as to brown the potatoes. Once the mixture is good and browned remove it from the heat and add the cheese on top. Cover and let sit for 2 minutes. Finally, serve hot to drunk musicians.

Side notes: Ketchup makes an excellent condiment as does hot sauce for those who need it. Something I like to do to really spice up the natural flavors of the garlic is this: Get a small jar of cocktail olives (make sure they're vegan...the green ones often have lactic acid in them). Eat the olives and save the liquid they come in. Add an entire garlic bulb's worth of cloves to the liquid and let it sit in the refrigerator for a few days before using. The olive oil juices really kick-start the spiciness of the garlic.

Sheepherder's Pie

Music: Rotor-Tepj Szet Minden Lancot! lp (1991)

4 large russet potatoes, diced
1/2-1 cup soymilk
1/2 tsp sea salt
1/2 cup water or vegetable stock
2 onions, chopped
1 large bell pepper, diced
2 carrots, sliced
2 celery stalks, sliced
1/2 pound (about 2 cups) mushrooms, sliced
1 15-ounce can chopped tomatoes
1 15-ounce can kidney beans, drained
1/2 tsp paprika
1/2 tsp black pepper
2 Tbsp soy sauce

Dice the potatoes and steam them until tender. Mash, adding enough soymilk to make them smooth and spreadable. Add sea salt to taste. Set aside.

In a large pot, heat the water or stock and cook the onions for 3 minutes. Add the pepper, carrots, and celery and cook for 5 minutes over medium heat. Add the mushrooms, then cover the pan and cook an additional 7 minutes, stirring occasionally. Add the tomatoes, kidney beans, paprika, pepper, and soy sauce, then cover and cook 10 to 15 minutes.

Preheat the oven to 350° F.

Put the vegetables into a 9" x 13" baking dish and spread the mashed potatoes evenly over the top. Sprinkle with paprika. Bake for 25 minutes, until hot and bubbly.

Breakfast Scramble, Mexican Style

Music: Diamanda Galas-Plague Mass lp (1984)

2 lbs firm tofu
2 Tbsp yellow miso
1 tsp turmeric
1 Tbsp chile powder
2 tsp dried oregano
1 tsp cumin
1 Tbsp olive oil
Sea salt and pepper to taste
¼ cup vegetable broth or water
4 plum tomatoes, seeded and diced
1 cup crushed corn chips
¼ cup corn kernels
2 roasted red bell peppers, chopped (optional)
Chopped cilantro (optional)

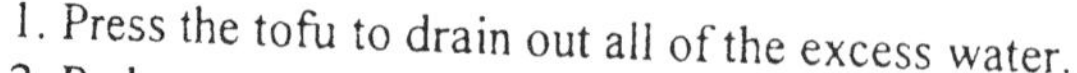

1. Press the tofu to drain out all of the excess water.
2. Preheat oven to 375° F. Lightly oil a 2 ½ to 3 quart casserole dish.
3. In a mixing bowl, combine miso, turmeric, chile powder, oregano, cumin, oil, salt, and pepper. Add broth or water and stir until smooth. Crumble the tofu into the mixture. Add corn and red peppers and mix well. Pour it all into the casserole dish and press it down lightly with the back of a spoon.
4. Mix the tomatoes and corn chips together, spread over the tofu mixture, and bake for 20 to 30 minutes, or until lightly browned.

Liz's Mom's (authentic) Beans and Rice

Music: Shub Niggurath-Les Morts Vont Vite lp (1985)

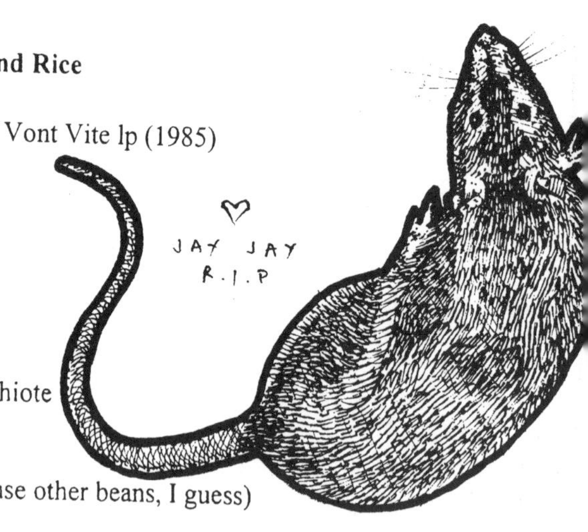

2 cups white rice
2 tsp olive oil
About 3 cups hot water
1 can tomato sauce
1 Tbsp Goya adobo
4 pkg Goya sazon sinachiote
4 pkg Goya sazon conculantro y achiote
1/2 cup Goya sofrito
1/2 cup Goya recaito
2 15oz cans pigeon peas (can also use other beans, I guess)

Brown rice in olive oil. Add hot water, tomato sauce, and all the Goya stuff. Bring to boil, then cover and simmer on low for about 20 minutes. Drain and rinse pigeon peas and add them to the rice when it's cooked. Recipe can be split in half. Mom says, "I usually make this big of a batch because Dad likes it." Freezes well.

Slaytanic Scrambler

Music: Slayer-Show No Mercy lp (1984)

2 ½ cups extra firm tofu
One 14 ½ oz can ready-cut chopped tomatoes with jalapenos
1-1/2 tsp olive oil
1/8 tsp crushed red pepper
2/3 cup chopped onion
4 cloves garlic, minced
1/3 cup chopped green bell pepper
One 6 oz package vegan Canadian bacon, diced
1/2 tsp turmeric
1 rounded Tbsp mellow white miso
1 ½ Tbsp very dry sherry
1 tsp dried cilantro
1 Kerry King solo

Place tofu in large microwave safe bowl and mash with a potato masher. Add Kerry King solo for additional thrashing/mashing power. Press out as much of the water as you can. Set aside. Pour tomatoes into a separate strainer, and set aside to drain. In a 10" frying pan, heat oil and crushed pepper, medium high. Add the next 4 ingredients and saute 5 minutes. Add tofu and stir in turmeric and drained tomatoes. Simmer 5 minutes, stirring frequently. Place miso in a small bowl, blend sherry gradually until smooth and add. Sprinkle with cilantro. Simmer gently 1 minute. Serve with salsa.

As to the human race. There are many pretty and winning things about the human race. It is perhaps the poorest of all the inventions of all the gods but it has never suspected it once. There is nothing prettier than its naive and complacent appreciation of itself. It comes out frankly and proclaims without bashfulness or any sign of a blush that it is the noblest work of God. It has had a billion opportunities to know better, but all signs fail with this ass. I could say harsh things about it but I cannot bring myself to do it--it is like hitting a child.

Samuel Langhorne Clemens

Potatocore

Music: Demigod-Unholy Domain demo (1991)

1 large jar sauerkraut
3 medium potatoes, washed and chopped into 1" chunks
2 packets vegetarian gravy mix

Dump sauerkraut and potatoes into a large pot and cook on medium heat for 10-15 minutes, or until potatoes are tender. Mix gravy according to directions on packet and stir into the sauerkraut. Serve with a soup and warm bread. This was apparently adapted from an old Ukranian recipe.

Joshua Plague's Wild Mock Mallard of the Spanish March

Music: Barón Rojo-Volumen Brutal lp (1982)

Influenced of course by the cuisine of the Iberian Peninsula and with a metal moniker alluding to the outer reaches of Charlemagne's empire, the appropriate listening for this dish's preparation must be both Spanish and hard rockin' Euro-metal. Thus, may I suggest the lp "Volumen Brutal" by Barón Rojo, legends in their own right.

4 to 8 good sized slices mock duck, vegan chicken or tofurkey (or tempeh if you despise fake meat). Marinate these with tamari, ground sage, fresh minced thyme, minced garlic and white wi (or actually Madeira is good) to taste. Set aside.

Preheat oven to 400° F and place in a greased baking dish:

2 cups peeled, diced turnips
2 or 3 cored green apples, cut into thin wedges
1 chopped onion
8 whole cloves
2 bay leaves

Sprinkle with salt, pepper, paprika and lemon juice (orange juice may also be used) and drizzle with some olive oil and bake for 25 minutes. A bit of sugar may be sprinkled on for further effect. While this is occurring, simmer a vegan bouillon cube in1 cup of water for about 10 minutes. Make the liquid into a cup's worth by finishing with a dash of white wine. Set aside.

Remove baking dish from oven, stir the items within and add:

1 chopped or thinly sliced fennel bulb (use 2 bulbs if thou lovest fennel)
several sprigs of thyme
several sage leaves

Spoon some of the wine-bouillon over this and return to the oven for 15 minutes more or until don to your liking. You could also try broiling for the last 5 minutes to throw some good colour on there. Remove, stir, and spoon more bouillon over it. Serve with the following,.which you will have made while all of this was baking.

Take your marinated "duck" slices and sprinkle them with some paprika, black pepper, minced parsley and ground allspice. Next, fry them in some olive oil or melted margarine. You may lightly bread them with fine herbed breadcrumbs first if desired. Cook, turning once, until browne on both sides. You may add onions and garlic to the pan for the frying in order to be more exciting if you wish. Also good to fry along with this: wild mushrooms, particularly wood ear or morel. Serve with the baked concoction in an attractive manner. Finish with minced fresh parsley or chervil and chopped toasted almonds. This is not just a garnish, it completes the dish, mis amigos! A gravy can be made by mixing the rest of the wine-bouillon, pan drippings and leftover marinade in a saucepan and whisking with a teaspoon or two of flour, simmering until thickened a bit.

Good accompaniments to this: Garlic new potatoes; rice pilaf; orzo cooked with wine and saffron; seasoned polenta; wilted spinach or greens with toasted cumin seed, etc.

One variation of this would be to bake figs instead of apples (split them in half, and add 10 minutes later, use a pint), use red wine instead of white and serve with blue potatoes. In this case you would want to listen to Deep Purple.

Sukiyaki 666

Music: Katharsis-666 lp (2000)

1 Tbsp sugar
1/4 cup sake
1 Tbsp mirin (Japanese rice wine)
1/2 cup soy sauce
2 cups watercress sprigs, thick stems removed

8 oz sukiyaki noodles, mung bean threads, or udon noodles
4 oz daikon, peeled and sliced into ½"-thick rounds
1 Tbsp vegetable oil
1 block (about 10 oz) firm tofu, cut into 1" cubes
2 small leeks, trimmed cut on the diagonal into ¼"-thick slices
5 oz shiitake mushrooms, stemmed, wiped and sliced ½" thick

THE HUNGER FOR THE FEAST

If using dried noodles, cook and soak them according to the instructions. Drain and set aside.

Parboil the daikon slices in 3 cups of water until tender but not mushy, about 3 minutes. With a slotted spoon, transfer the daikon to a plate, reserving the cooking water in the pot.

Heat the oil in a large heavy skillet or stovetop casserole until beginning to smoke. Add the tofu cubes and cook over medium-high heat, turning once, until beginning to turn golden on 2 sides. Transfer the tofu to the plate with the daikon. Add the leeks and mushrooms to the skillet and stir over medium-high heat until wilted, about 2 minutes. Add the sugar to the vegetables and stir until mixed. Add the sake, mirin, and soy sauce and bring to a boil. Add 2 cups of the reserved daikon water and bring back to a boil. Stir in the watercress and tofu and add the noodles.

Well, we weren't busted for grave-robbing. We were busted for carrying illegal guns. They *did* confiscate the bones that we had and they tried to run tests on them because we might have killed these people. But they had to drop all the charges.

Interviewer: So how did you get those bones?

That's neither here nor there.

David from Morbid Angel

Extreme Noise Teriyaki Kabobs

Music: Abruptum-Obscuritatem Advoco Amplectere Me lp (1992)

2 cups large TVP chunks
2 cups hot water
2 Tbsp ketchup

Combine and let stand 10 minutes, then simmer until tender. Drain. Now mix the following:

¼ cup shoyu or 6 Tbsp red miso
3 Tbsp white wine
3 Tbsp brown sugar
1 tsp ground fresh gingerroot, or 1½ tsp powdered ginger
2 cloves garlic, crushed
1 Tbsp sesame oil
¼ tsp dry mustard

Add the chunks to the marinade you just mixed. Let soak an hour or longer. If you're going to use wooden skewers, you might want to soak them in water while the TVP marinates…it'll keep the sticks from burning.

Thread the chunks onto skewers, alternating with cherry tomato halves, pineapple chunks, green peppers squares, Vidalia onion squares, and zucchini slices. Put the kabobs on the grill and brush on the extra marinade every few minutes.

As has become an annual event near the end of February, 3,880 hunters in Central Pennsylvania were set loose on a "no-holds barred" hunt in an effort to "help control the coyote population." $15,000 in prize money was set aside for those who brought in the biggest animals from the five-county area. A record 21 coyotes were "netted."

Ray Savel, Mosquito Creek President, had this to say: "They're the smartest animal out there. If they could talk and carry a gun, there'd be none of us left."

Exactly our point, Ray. Fuck off.

Drunken Fist Style Gyros

Music: Dr. Shrinker-Wedding the Grotesque demo (1989)

Whenever my friends in Milwaukee get drunk and it's bar close, first place they head is any of the many East Side gyro shops. I tend to feel left out, as there's not much there for a responsible vegan to eat. Now I can make them on my own. Different, but delicious.

Soak for 10 minutes:
1 cup TVP chunks (NOT granules…check your local natural foods/health food store for this)
1 Tbsp ketchup
1 cup boiling water

Add ½ cup water and vegetable stock and simmer 15-20 minutes on the stovetop, or until tender.

Mix for a dressing:
¼ cup olive oil
1 Tbsp wine vinegar
1 tsp each sea salt, basil, and oregano
¼ tsp black pepper

Mix marinade with cooked and drained TVP chunks

Prepare the vegetables:
1 large tomato, diced
1 cucumber, thinly sliced
½ cup red onion, chopped
¼ Greek Kalamata olives (or black olives), sliced
2 Tbsp fresh mint leaves, chopped
3 cups lettuce, shredded

Have ready, warmed in oven if desired:
6 pita breads, cut in half.

Toss the vegetables in with the TVP. Fill the pita pockets. Eat while reading the new issue of the Onion.

> Thousands of years of human history lay behind us-and all of it a chaos of blood and tears and suffering! Poets have sung, prophets have preached, scientists have studied-and the best they have been able to produce is a world in which millions of abject and degraded people toil without cease in order that a few hundred idle parasites might squander the surplus of their labour.

Upton Sinclair

Viva Zapata Chalupas

Music: Living Death-Back to the Weapons ep (1986)

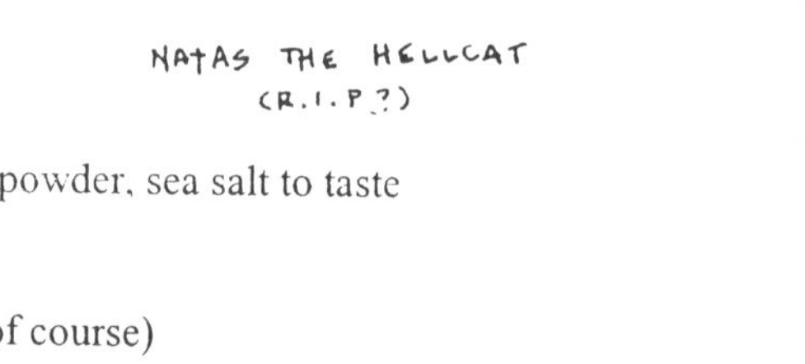

12 corn tortillas
4-6 Tbsp vegetable oil
1/2 package meatless burger crumbles
1-3 tsp cumin
1-3 tsp chili powder
1-3 tsp garlic powder
1/2 tsp lemon pepper
1-3 tsp onion powder
1 can vegetarian refried beans
1 head lettuce, chopped
2 fresh tomatoes, seeded and chopped
1/4 cup finely diced yellow onion
2 avocados, mashed with 2-3 tsp garlic powder, sea salt to taste
Your favorite salsa
Jalapenos
French dressing (make sure it's vegan, of course)

First, in medium-sized skillet sprayed with non-stick cooking spray, crumble ground meatless and add all spices. Cook until all browned. While that's finishing, heat beans either over stove or in microwave.

In large, fairly deep skillet, add vegetable oil and heat until oil forms small bubbles when you dip an edge of the tortilla in it. When oil is fairly hot, fry each corn tortilla on each side until desired crispiness is achieved using tongs. Place on paper towels to drain off excess oil.

Then top each fried tortilla in following order: beans, meatless, lettuce, tomato, onion, avocado, salsa, French dressing and jalapenos. Add sea salt and pepper to taste.

And all the guys who died all the five million or seven million or ten million who went out and died to make the world safe for democracy to make the world safe for words without meaning? How did they feel as they watched their blood pump out into the mud? How did they feel when the gas hit their lungs and began eating them all away? How did they feel as they lay crazed in hospitals and looked death straight in the face and saw him come and take them? If the thing they were fighting for was important enough to die for then it was also important enough for them to be thinking about it in the last minutes of their lives. That stood to reason. Life is awfully important so if you've given it away you'd ought to think with all your mind in the last moments of your life about the thing you traded it for. So did all of those kids die thinking of democracy and freedom and liberty and honor and the safety of the home and the stars and stripes forever? You're goddam right they didn't.

Dalton Trumbo

Warzone Calzone

Music: Ghostrider-Mayhemic Destuction demo (1985)

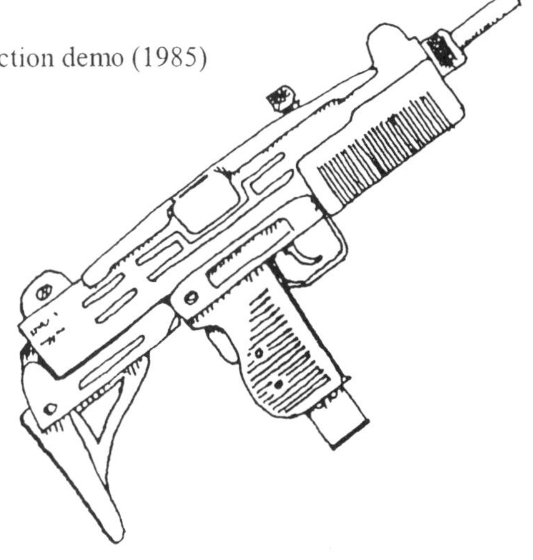

Dough (combine in a mixing bowl):

1 Tbsp yeast
½ cup warm water

Let stand 5 minutes, then add in:

1 cup warm water
2 Tbsp olive oil
½ tsp sea salt
½ tsp oregano
½ tsp basil
4 cups flour

Add a little more four if necessary to make a workable dough. Knead for 10 minutes until smooth and elastic. Oil a clean bowl and turn the dough around in it to coat it. Cover the bowl and set it in a warm place to rise until it's doubled...about 1 hour.

While the dough is rising, work on the filling. Saute the following together until the onions are soft:

2 Tbsp olive oil
1 large onion, chopped
1 green pepper, chopped
8 oz crumbled extra firm tofu (or vegan meat crumbles)

Add:

8 oz can tomato sauce
2 Tbsp soy sauce
1 tsp oregano
1 tsp basil
2 Tbsp nutritional yeast
½ tsp garlic powder
½ tsp red pepper flakes

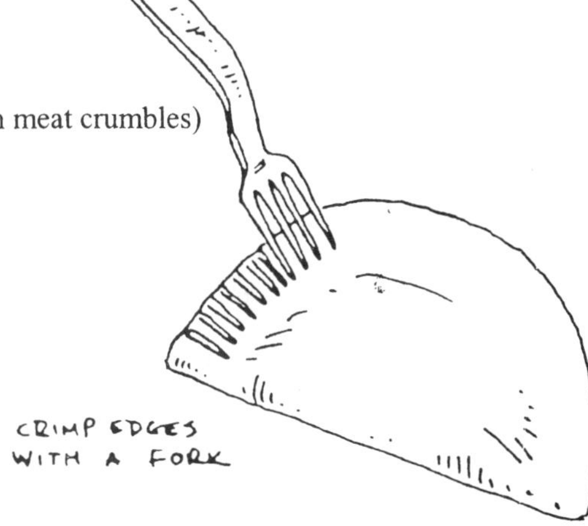

Preheat the oven to 375°F. Punch the dough down and divide into 9 balls. Roll each ball out into a circle ¼" thick. Use flour to keep the dough from sticking to the counter and the rolling pin. Place ¼ cup filling in the center of each. Fold the dough over the filling into a half circle. Moisten the edges with a bit of water to seal well. Crimp the edges with a fork. Now prick holes in the top with the fork. Place the calzones on a lightly-oiled cookie sheet. Bake 20-25 minutes or until lightly browned. Cool on a rack so the bottoms don't get soggy. Enjoy hot or cold.

Don't Tread on Me Tofu Loaf

Music: Militia-Regiments of Death demo (1985)

1 medium onion
1 cup rolled oats 1½ lbs firm tofu, mashed
½ cup chopped parsley
1/3 cup soy sauce
1/3 cup ketchup
2 Tbsp yellow mustard
¼ tsp black pepper
¼ tsp garlic powder

Preheat the oven to 350° F. Mix all the ingredients together and press the mixture into a lightly greased loaf pan. Bake for one hour. Let it cool 15-20 minutes before trying to remove it from the pan. Slice and enjoy with ketchup. It's just short of spectacular as a cold meal the next day.

Hot and Spicy Bean Curd

Music: Malign-Fireborn ep (1998)

2 Tbsp oil
2 green onions, chopped
1 clove garlic, chopped
1 green chili, chopped
1 Tbsp salted black beans (check the Asian market for this)
1 lb bean curd, cubed
1 Tbsp soy sauce
½ cup vegetable stock
1 tsp arrowroot dissolved in 1 Tbsp water

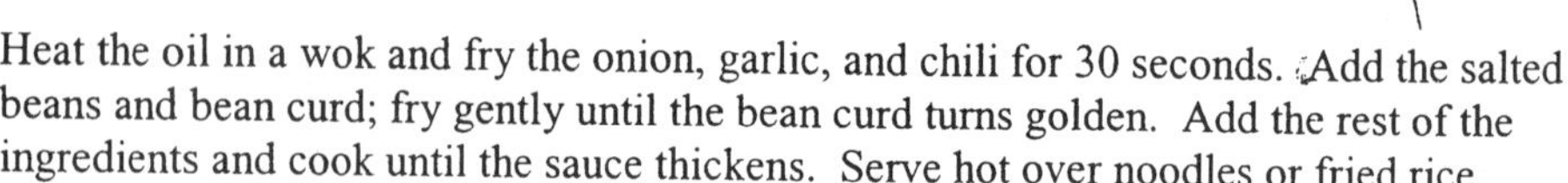

Heat the oil in a wok and fry the onion, garlic, and chili for 30 seconds. Add the salted beans and bean curd; fry gently until the bean curd turns golden. Add the rest of the ingredients and cook until the sauce thickens. Serve hot over noodles or fried rice.

BBQ Onion Sandwich

Music: Fantom-Lucifer Jeleni Meg! demo (1987)

One Vidalia onion
Two Kaiser rolls
½ cup barbecue sauce (homemade stuff is always better, but Sweet Baby Ray's is good)

Slice onion and separate into rings. Saute onion in a few Tbsp of water or vegetable broth. When the onions are soft and limp add about 1/2 cup of BBQ sauce. Scoop this onto your Kaisers and serve them up.

Dehumanization Roast

Music: Necro Schizma-Erupted Evil demo (1989)

This is the closest I've come to what I remember meat loaf tasting like. Good hot, good cold, good with bbq sauce, good on a sandwich. Definitely a favorite.

2 cups vital wheat gluten
2 Tbsp nutritional yeast
1 tsp thyme
1 tsp marjoram
2 cups vegetable broth
1 Tbsp soy sauce
1 small yellow onion, minced
2 cups hot water
2 Tbsp soy sauce
Golden Gravy (see recipe this book)

Combine first 4 ingredients in large bowl; make a well in the center of the mixture. Combine vegetable broth and soy sauce, add to dry ingredients and onion and knead. Transfer mixture to a 9" x 5" x 3" non-stick loafpan. Combine hot water and soy sauce; pour over loafpan. Cover with foil and bake at 350° F for 1-1/2 hours. Let cool before slicing. Serve with golden dawn gravy.

Road Rash Skillet

Music: Turbo-Ostatni Wojownik lp (1987)

1 14 oz package veggie burger crumbles
1 medium sized onion, chopped
1 ¾ cups vegetable broth
1 ½ cups uncooked penne pasta
1 14 oz can diced tomatoes, drained
1 14 oz can cut green beans, drained
2 Tbsp tomato paste
2 tsp oregano
½ tsp garlic powder
½ tsp ground cinnamon

In a large skillet, brown the burger crumbles and the onion over medium-high heat. Add the broth; bring to a boil. Stir in the pasta. Return to a boil and simmer, covered, for 8 minutes.

Stir in the remaining ingredients and return to a boil. Simmer, uncovered, for 7-10 minutes, or until the sauce thickens.

A Blatant Disregard for Tradition: Vegan Red Beans and Rice

Music: Crowley-The Scream of Death ep (1985)

½ cup water 1 onion, chopped
1 green pepper, chopped
1 bunch green onions, chopped
2 cloves garlic, minced
1 8 oz can tomato sauce
1 tsp yellow mustard
½ tsp ground oregano
1 bay leaf
1 tsp cayenne pepper
½ tsp ground thyme
1 tsp ground pepper
1 tsp basil
4 cups cooked small red beans (or 2-3 cans' worth, drained and rinsed)
¼ lb veggie sausage, sliced into ½" rounds
2 Tbsp olive oil
4-6 cups cooked rice

Pour the water into a large saucepot with the onion, green pepper, green onions, and garlic. Cook, stirring occasionally, over low heat for 10 minutes. Add remaining ingredients (minus the sausages, oil, and rice). Cook, covered, over low heat for 20 minutes or until the sauce is simmered down and thickened a bit. While the sauce simmers, fry the sausages and then add it into the mixture. When finished, remove the bay leaf and serve over rice.

Jack Sprat's Jambalaya

Music: Unburied-Veil of Damnation demo (1992)

½ stick margarine
1 cup vegetable stock
1 green pepper, chopped
1 large onion, chopped
1 large tomato, chopped
2 cups cubed tofu, seitan, veggie sausage, or whatever
2 tsp seasoned salt (Zatarain's or see recipe, this book)
½ tsp cayenne
8 cups cooked rice
1 cup tomato paste
½ cup shredded carrot
½ cup chopped scallions

In a medium pot over low heat, melt the margarine. Add the stock, pepper, onion, and tomato. Simmer, stirring occasionally, until the vegetables are tender (about 10 minutes). Add 2 cups meat substitute, seasonings, carrots, and scallions and cook five more minutes. Stir in the rice and tomato paste; continue stirring until the mixture is completely blended. It makes lots so call some friends. Apply hot sauce liberally.

Knowledge is a polite word for / dead but not buried imagination.

e e cummings

Demian's Black Masserole (aka the Potluck Poser Disposer)

Music: Kreator-Coma of Souls lp (1990)

SAUCE:

Margarine
Flour
Soy milk (unsweetened)
Sea salt

REST:

1 24 oz jar sauerkraut
1 1 lb box bow-tie pasta (or whatever)
1 lb extra-firm tofu, cubed
A big bag of tater-tots

Get the pasta cooking. While waiting, you have three things to do: make the sauce, brown the tofu, and toast the taters.

The cream sauce is really a matter of experimentation. Put about a stick of margarine (nobody said this was going to be good for you) into a sauce pan and melt it. Whisk in a cup or a cup and a half of soy milk. Now, start sprinkling in flour. Your goal is a sauce of alfredo-like consistency…if it's too liquidy, add flour…if it's too thick, add soy milk. Sprinkle in sea salt to taste at the end.

Fry the tofu in some olive oil until it's browned and slightly crispy on the outside. Feel free to add some black pepper.

Place the taters on a tray and cook them however the package tells you to.

Now, assume that all the components are ready. Using one large casserole dish or several small ones, put down a layer of noodles. Now dump the tofu cubes over them. Add a layer of sauerkraut over that. Alternate layers if you've got enough materials. Now pour the sauce over the whole thing. Quick glance over at the stereo to make sure Demian isn't trying to put in some whack shit like The Fucking Champs or some sort of 70s prog rock-lite…that nonsense could cause the recipe to go haywire, you know. Finally, place a layer of tater-tots over the top. Put the whole damned thing in the oven and let it cook at 350° F for 10 or 15 minutes or so.

BBQ Wrecking Ball Loaf

Music: Burning Witch-Rift.Canyon.Dreams 12" (1998)

3 cups pinto beans, cooked/mashed
1 cup tomato sauce
1 cup bread crumbs, finely ground
1/4 cup minced onion
1/4 cup quick oatmeal
3 tsp egg replacer mixed with 4 Tbsp water, beaten until frothy
Fresh ground pepper to taste
1/4 cup ketchup or barbecue sauce

Preheat oven to 350° F. Combine all ingredients, except catsup, in a large bowl. Mix well. Turn into a non-stick loaf pan, 9-1/4 x 5-1/4 x 3, and flatten.

Spread ketchup or BBQ sauce over the top.
Bake for 45 minutes.

Eily's Pad Thai

Music: Trouble-self titled lp (1984)

2 quarts water
¾ lb mung bean sprouts
6 oz rice noodles (1/4" wide, if possible)

3 Tbsp fresh lime juice
3 Tbsp catsup
1 Tbsp turbinado sugar
¼ cup soy sauce

3 Tbsp peanut oil (or vegetable oil)
3-4 garlic cloves, minced
1 ½ Tbsp red pepper flakes
2 cups grated carrots
2/3 cup peanuts, chopped
6-8 scallions, chopped

In a covered pot, bring the water to a rolling boil. Put the mung bean sprouts in a strainer and dip them in the boiling water for 30 seconds. This is called "blanching." Set aside to drain well. When the water returns to a boil, stir in the rice noodles and cook 3-5 minutes until tender but firm. Drain the noodles, rinse under cool water, and set aside to drain. Meanwhile, in a small bowl, mix the lime juice, catsup, sugar, and soy sauce.
Prepare the remaining ingredients and have them near-at-hand before you begin to stir fry. Heat the oil in a wok or large skillet. Add the garlic and red pepper, swirl them in the oil a moment, and stir in the carrots. Stir fry for 1 minute. Pour in the sauce mixture and stir everything together. Add the drained rice noodles and mung bean sprouts and toss to distribute evenly. Stir in peanuts and scallions and serve at once.

Tofu Pot Pie in Your Eye

Music: Genocide-Violent Death demo (1985)

Crust:

¾ cup unbleached white flour
½ cup whole wheat flour
½ tsp sea salt
3 Tbsp vegetable oil
¼ cup water

Mix together the four and salt.
Stir in the oil and mix in the water.
Chill the dough while making the filling.

Filling:

2½ cups vegetable broth
3 cups diced potatoes
1 cup finely chopped carrot
½ cup chopped onion
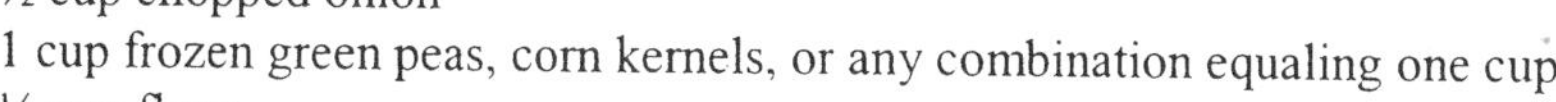
1 cup frozen green peas, corn kernels, or any combination equaling one cup
¼ cup flour
¼ tsp pepper
½ cup plain, unsweetened soy milk
1 lb extra firm tofu, drained, patted dry, and cubed
Sea salt to taste

Preheat the oven to 350°F. In a large saucepan, bring the vegetable broth to a boil over medium-high heat. Add the potatoes, cover, and cook for 5 minutes. Add the carrots and onion. Cover and cook for 3 minutes. Add the peas/corn. Cover and cook for 2 minutes or until tender.

Combine the flour, pepper, and salt. Add the soy milk and beat together well. Gradually add the vegetable mixture, stirring well. Over medium-high heat, stir constantly for about 3 minutes or until the mixture is thickened and bubbly. Remove from heat and stir in the tofu.

Roll out the dough to fit over the top of a 9" square casserole dish. Spoon the tofu-vegetable mixture into the casserole dish and cover it with the remaining crust, cutting off any extra dough and folding over and pinching edges to seal. Cut four or five slits into the top. Bake for about 40 minutes, or until the crust is browned.

> My eyes grew darker from lack of sleep to the point where it looked like I had two black eyes. It had all come full circle. Whereas I had initially felt deadened by the natural imbalances of my serotonin levels, I now felt deadened by the insomnia-inducing medications. I knew I could reduce the dose, but I didn't. There was a latent need to punish myself for my mental weakness.

Killer Kofta Balls in Spicy Sauce

Music: Devotee-Dead and Gone demo (2002)

Balls:

2 cups grated cauliflower
2 cups grated cabbage
1½ cups chickpea flour
1½ tsp sea salt
1 clove garlic, minced
1 tsp garam masala
1 tsp ground cumin
½ tsp ground coriander
½ tsp turmeric
½ tsp cayenne powder
Oil for deep frying

Sauce:

28 oz can crushed tomatoes
1 cup vegetable broth
1 small onion, chopped
1 jalapeno chili, minced
1 tsp paprika
½ tsp black pepper
½ tsp sea salt

Heat the oil in a pot or saucepan. Combine all the kofta ball ingredients in a bowl. Roll into 24 balls, about 1" in diameter. Place as many balls as possible in the oil, allowing them to float "comfortably." Fry over medium heat for 10 minutes, until the kofta is a rich, golden brown. Drain in a colander.

While frying the balls, combine the sauce ingredients in a saucepan, bring it to a boil, and let it simmer 15 minutes, stirring occasionally. Place the kofta in the tomato sauce 5 minutes before serving, as it likes to absorb a bit of the sauce. Serve with the sauce.

One's personal delvings can be considered occult in the true sense of the term only if they remain outside the pale of supernormal faddism. The would-be innovator asks, "If I cannot find food for thought in source material akin to my interests, where then?" The answer is found in the analogy that one does not "find" one's self. One creates one's self. Magical power is accrued by reading unlikely books, employing unlikely situations, and extracting unlikely ingredients, then utilizing these elements for what would be considered "occult" ends. After one has observed the results of such creative unions, what was originally considered "unlikely" will be seen as the most easily understandable methodology.

Anton Szandor LaVey

There comes a time when the moodswings become so violent that their oscillations start to smash indiscriminately against the boundaries and borders which hold our lives together. Our values…our loves and passions…our needs…crumbling like rotted drywall…leaving us nothing but to deeply inhale the anaesthetic-laced asbestos in the hopes of a cheap, disorienting high. Cancerous and numb, we approach the void without want nor regret. Cancerous and numb, we approach the void *without want nor regret.*

The Black Pullet (Chicken Cutlets)

Music: Altar of Perversion-From Dead Temples (Towards the Ast'ral Path) lp (2001)

1 lb extra firm tofu, rinsed and patted dry

Marinade:

¾ cup water
3 Tbsp soy sauce
3 Tbsp nutritional yeast
½ tsp poultry seasoning
½ tsp ground coriander
½ tsp onion granules
½ tsp garlic granules

Coating mix:

½ cup whole wheat pastry flour
¼ cup yellow cornmeal
¼ cup nutritional yeast flakes
½ tsp onion granules
½ tsp sea salt
1/8 tsp ground black pepper

Cut the tofu into ½" thick slices and place them in a wide, shallow mixing bowl.

Place all the ingredients for the marinade in a small mixing bowl and whisk them together. Pout the marinade over the tofu, spooning it over each piece. Turn the slices over so that they are well-coated. Cover the bowl and let refrigerate overnight, or at least a couple hours.

When you are ready to cook the tofu, place the ingredients for the coating mix in a shallow mixing bowl and stir well. Preheat the oven to 400°F. Lightly oil a baking sheet and set it aside.

Remove each slice of tofu from the marinade and dredge it in the coating mix, covering it well all-over. Place each slice on the baking sheet. Bake the tofu until the bottoms are golden brown, or about 15 minutes. Turn them all over and bake until the other sides are golden brown as well.

Arrabiata Antichristos

Music: Bathory-self titled lp (1984)

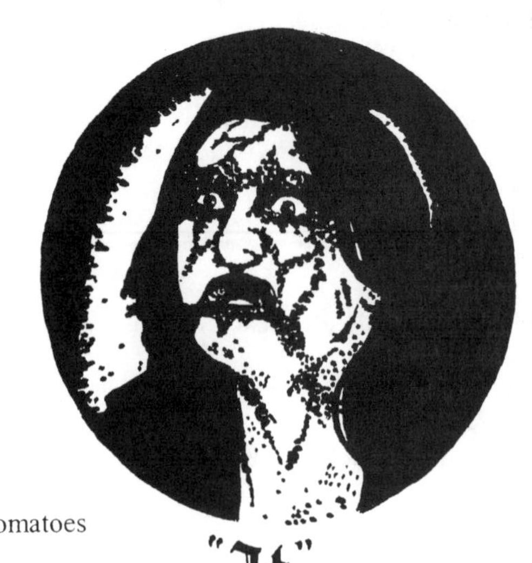

1 tsp olive oil
1 cup chopped onion
4 cloves garlic, minced
3/8 cup red wine
1 Tbsp white sugar
1 Tbsp chopped fresh basil
1 tsp crushed red pepper flakes
2 Tbsp tomato paste
1 Tbsp lemon juice
1/2 tsp dried Italian seasoning
1/4 tsp ground black pepper
2 (14.5 ounce) cans peeled and diced tomatoes
2 Tbsp chopped fresh parsley
As much cooked penne pasta as you'd like

Heat oil in a saucepan or large skillet over medium-high heat. Add onion and garlic; saute 5 minutes. Stir in wine, sugar, basil, red pepper, tomato paste, lemon juice, Italian seasoning, black pepper, and tomatoes; bring to a boil. Reduce heat to medium, and cook, uncovered, about 15 minutes. Stir in parsley. Ladle over hot cooked pasta.

R.I.P Quorthon

Corn Dogs

Music: Last Days of Humanity-Hymns of Indigestible Suppuration lp (2000)

6 tofu hot dogs
6 skewers
1/2 cup yellow corn meal
1/2 cup flour
1 tsp dry mustard
1/2 tsp salt
1 egg's worth of egg replacer
1 Tbsp sugar
1 tsp baking powder
1/2 cup soy milk
1 Tbsp melted shortening

Combine the cornmeal, flour, sugar, mustard, baking powder and salt. Mix well. Add the soy milk, egg replacer, and shortening and mix until very smooth. Pour the mixture into a tall glass.

Put the tofu hot dogs on the sticks and dip them in the cornmeal batter to coat them evenly.

Deep fry in oil heated to 350° F until golden brown, about 2 minutes. Drain on paper towels, then eat with yellow mustard.

Fucking Fool Beans

Music: Hell Militia-Canonisation of the Foul Spirit lp (2005)

One 16-ounce can cooked fava beans
1 large onion, chopped
1 large tomato, diced
1-1/2 Tbsp olive oil
1 tsp cumin powder
1/4 cup parsley, chopped
Juice of 2 lemons
Sea salt, pepper, and red chili pepper to taste
Injeri bread (see recipe this book)

Pour the beans into a pot and bring to a boil. Mix them well and add the remaining ingredients. Bring to a boil again, then reduce to medium heat and cook for about 5 minutes. This dish is usually eaten with injeri and a hangover.

Robyn's Chicken Nuggets

Music: Kat-666 lp (1985)

1/3 nutritional yeast
1/3 corn meal
1/3 flour
Sea salt (to taste)
Paprika (to taste)
Garlic powder (to taste)
Extra firm tofu
Olive oil
Sweet Baby Ray's Barbecue Sauce

Preheat oven to 375° F.
First, use the first six ingredients to make a mixture based on the given proportions…the more you intend to make, the more you should use. For a smaller batch, try a half cup each of yeast, corn meal, and flour.
Cut the tofu into slabs…preferably about 2" X 1" and no less than ½" thick (if they're too thin they'll just get crunchy).
Find a large cooking tray or a cookie sheet that has upturned edges. Coat the pan with about an eighth of an inch of oil…enough to cover the entire surface.

Now, thoroughly coat the tofu, piece by piece, in the yeast/corn meal/flour mixture and set the pieces on the oiled tray. When the tray is full, put it in the oven for 45 minutes or so. About halfway, you'll want to flip all the pieces over. Try and get them golden brown.
Let them cool, then serve with bbq sauce. They're actually best after having been refrigerated.

Steve and Heidi's Authentic Creole Tofu and Rice

Music: Eyehategod-In the Name of Suffering lp (1992)

1 onion, chopped
2 green peppers, chopped
Several cloves garlic, minced
1 couple stalks celery, chopped
Olive oil
2 cups water
Sea salt
Pepper
2 lb extra firm tofu, cubed
Nutritional yeast
Soy sauce
2 Tbsp roux (see below)
Hot sauce
½ little can tomato paste
Basil
Oregano
Thyme
Cayenne pepper
Cajun seasoning (see recipe this book)
As much rice as you'd like

URSUS CAUDA ANNULATA,
FASCIA PER OCULOS TRANSVERSI
AKA "SJUPP"

Roux is a Deep South thickener which can be made as such: Put whatever amount of margarine you want into a saucepan and melt. Add in an equal amount of flour. Stir quickly. The resulting mixture should be doughy in consistency and amber in color. Apparently it becomes a more effective, more flavorful thickener the longer it cooks. Keep refrigerated.

Preheat the oven to 350°F.

Fill the bottom of a small bowl with soy sauce and fill the bottom of another bowl with nutritional yeast. Coat each of the tofu cubes with soy sauce, then with nutritional yeast. Place each cube on a lightly oiled oven tray and cook in the oven for 20 minutes or so.

Next, get the rice going. This will probably take 20 minutes or so as well. In a small pot, boil the 2 cups water. Add the tomato paste, roux, and hot sauce to taste. Reduce to a simmer.

In a large pan or wok, stir fry the onion, peppers, celery, and garlic in a bit of olive oil. Add the salt, pepper, basil, oregano, thyme, and cayenne to taste. Mix the roux/tomato sauce into the stir fried vegetables. Mix in the baked tofu as well. Serve over the rice with Cajun seasoning and extra hot sauce.

Hot Damn Tamale Pie

Music: Infernal Death-Incantation of the Gates demo (1989)

I can barely describe how wonderful this is. Seems like a lot of effort, but I bet it takes less than 45 minutes to make.

Filling:

2 cups cooked pinto or small kidney beans
2 Tbsp oil
½ cup chopped onion
¼ tsp garlic powder
1 tsp chili powder
1 tsp sea salt
1 Tbsp tomato paste
3 Tbsp water
¼ cup sliced ripe black olives
½ cup frozen or fresh corn
½ green pepper, chopped
¼ cup parsley, chopped (cilantro works well, too)

Crust:

2½ cups cold water
1½ cups cornmeal
1 tsp sea salt
½ tsp chili powder

Grind the beans in a blender or mash thoroughly. Mix the tomato paste with the water. In a skillet, saute the onion in oil and add in all of the filling ingredients. Let these cook over medium heat. If the beans were hot to begin with, no more than 5 minutes is needed. Stir frequently and adjust seasonings to taste.

Combine the ingredients for the crust into a heavy pan and cook over medium heat until the cornmeal thickens and comes to a boil. Don't cook it too long or it will get excessively thick. You have to stir this constantly or the cornmeal will stick to the pot. For real.

Grease an 8" X 8" pan or a 10" pie dish and spread 2/3 of the cornmeal mixture over the bottom and sides. Then pour the bean mixture into the cornmeal crust and spread the remaining 1/3 of the cornmeal over the top. Don't panic if it's not perfect. Cook the whole damned thing in the oven at 350° F for 30 minutes. Let it cool a bit before serving.

Here's an idea: If you buy jalepeno peppers in a jar, make sure to save the liquid when they are gone. It never goes bad (or at least I don't think it does) and can be used in chili, refried beans, rice, or whatever for extra flavor and extra heat.

I often ride my bike out to the university-owned deer park to visit with the deer. I find their grace astounding. I like them better than most of the people around here. However, something about the park has never seemed quite right. I found myself suspicious of the signs which clearly state that the deer are "research subjects" which should "only be fed the feed from the machines." I finally cornered one of the employees and got the full, non-visitor story. In addition to simple research (how far does a deer stray in a day?), more complex research on breeding was taking place. The deer were being injected with some sort of chemical which was supposed to interfere with the does' reproductive systems such that they produced only one fawn as opposed to two or more. The ultimate goal was to develop a "humane" means of population control. My first response was one of interest. It seemed like a potentially decent idea. If the deer population could be controlled by nonviolent means, a large strike would be taken against the pro-hunter argument that hunting is a legitimate form of population control. Later, as I reached through the fence to pet a doe, I started to rethink my initial reaction to the research. Our (human's) conceptions of overpopulation are based in a specieist orientation. We encroach upon the territory of these animals, we take their space for our homes and roads and businesses, and then we wonder why the birth rates of these animals cannot be sustained by the amount of "wilderness" we allot them. These animals are not "over" populating. They are populating at a rate which will propagate their species in a world without human-made borders...the rate which their morphology requires. Today a black bear was spotted in the parking lot at the mall. What was the response? "What the hell is that doing here?!...Get it out of here!" Maybe we have to look at it the other way. Why the fuck is there a huge mall complex in the middle of the mountains of Pennsylvania? We (humans) are the true overpopulators. Our population grows exponentially and uncontrollably, year after year. Yet, we seek to control the reproductive systems of other species such that we can maintain the lie that our own reproductive rate is "natural" and "healthy." I swear, those researchers better hope I don't get my hands on that chemical they're developing...I know where I could put it to good use...

Hungarian Potato Paprikash

Music: Intense Agonizing/Necrobiosis-split ep (1994)

4 oz vegetable oil
2 onions, finely chopped
1 clove garlic, crushed
¼ tsp caraway seeds
1 tsp paprika
1-2 cups water
4 lbs potatoes, peeled and sliced thin
2 green peppers, cut into strips
4 tomatoes, peeled, seeded, and chopped
Sea salt

In a heavy-bottomed skillet, heat the oil and fry the onions and garlic. Add the caraway seeds, paprika, and water. Add the potatoes, peppers, and tomatoes. Simmer for 30 minutes.

zechwan Tofu Triangles in Triple-Threat Pepper Sauce

Music: Killing Addiction-Legacies of Terror demo (1990)

lb firm tofu
cup peanut oil or vegetable oil for frying
Tbsp peanut oil or vegetable oil
/3 cup dry sherry or rice wine
Tbsp tamari or soy sauce
½ cups water
cloves garlic, crushed
½ tsp dry mustard
tsp crushed dried red hot pepper
tsp black pepper
Tbsp cornstarch
large green bell pepper, cut into strips
large red bell pepper, cut into strips
large scallions, minced

Cut the tofu into as many triangles as you'd like. Heat the ½ cup oil in a wok or skillet. ry the tofu until the surface gets crispy…about 3-4 minutes for each side. Drain the iangles on paper towels.

Meanwhile, combine sherry, tamari, water, garlic, mustard, and red hot and black epper. Place the cornstarch in a bowl, and whisk the liquid into the cornstarch. Heat ne wok or skillet, add a little oil and saute the bell peppers and scallions for 3-4 ninutes. Pour in the sauce and stir fry 5-8 minutes longer. Add the tofu triangles, stir ently, and serve.

Dave's Super Scallion Pancakes

Music: Negura Bunget-Sala Molksa mlp (2000)

cups flour
tsp sea salt
cup boiling water
tsp peanut (or vegetable) oil
¼ cup sesame oil
scallions, chopped
¼ to ½ cup peanut oil (or, once again, vegetable oil)

Mix flour, salt, and boiling water in a bowl. Cover for about 10 minutes.
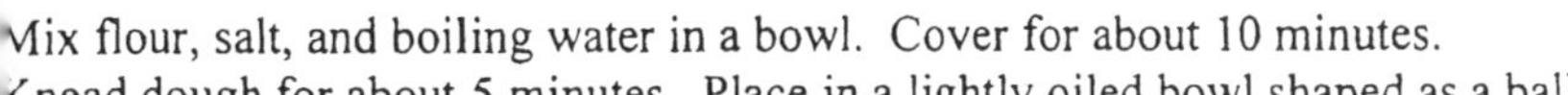
Knead dough for about 5 minutes. Place in a lightly oiled bowl shaped as a ball. the dough in oil, cover the bowl, and let sit about 30 minutes.
Roll out dough into a 10 X 16" rectangle about ¼" thick. Brush dough surface with sesame oil and sprinkle on scallions. Roll the dough into a thick cylinder about 10" long. Cut into 6 equal slices. Roll each slice into a ¼" thick pancake.
Fry as you choose in a pan/skillet/griddle.

Hessian Hash

Music: Holocaust-Heavy Metal Mania 12" (1981)

6 medium potatoes, diced
2 yellow onions, diced
5 cloves garlic, minced or pressed
1 red pepper, diced
1 green pepper, diced
1 tsp chili powder
Several large pinches cumin
Several large pinches oregano
3 tomatoes, diced
2 cups cooked black beans (or a 15-ounce can)
Chopped cilantro

Cook potatoes and onions in a bit of water (a few Tbsp) until onions have softened. Add garlic and peppers, continue cooking until onions are translucent and peppers have softened (more water may be needed). Sprinkle with spices. Add tomatoes and black beans. Bake in 375° F oven until nicely browned and not too saucy. Sprinkle with cilantro and serve with salsa.

I think I discovered Megadeth near the beginning of sixth grade. I was 11 or 12 at the time and was very, very into the likes of Metallica, Anthrax, Iron Maiden, and Dio. There was something about Megadeth though…they seemed more dangerous or something. "Killing is my business…and business is good." Yeah. More skulls, more curses, more anger…it pleased me. I remember feeling like my interest in them set me apart from other people I knew, like my classmates, my teachers, my parents, and so on. It was important to me.

Just last week I found myself sitting in my lawyer's office waiting for a hearing of sorts. There were about ten or twelve of us there…the Bellefonte courts prefer to schedule everyone's hearings at the same time so that they can queue everyone up and have you wait up to five hours for your turn…fuckers. As I sat, I noticed that the background music coming from the secretary's desk had a familiar sound to it. The vocals were vaguely reminiscent of something I'd heard before. Then it hit me…Megadeth. Megadeth was playing on Quik Rock. Washed up, watered down, attorney's office-friendly Megadeth. Nobody was screaming to turn it off. Nobody even noticed it any more than the alterna-rock song before it. First I was confused. Then I cringed under the weight of the irony. All the rebellion, anger, and offensiveness was gone…co-opted, filtered, and sterilized…just like me…hair tied back, beard combed, shirt tucked in, ready to accept a plea bargain…fucking pathetic…

Jennifer's Borrowed Brussels Sprouts Skillet

Music: Acrostichon-Lost Remembrance ep (1991)

I love this dish, especially when the weather starts turning cold and Brussels sprouts are in season. Serves 2-4 and is easily doubled or tripled.

1 lb Brussels sprouts (preferably fresh...it does taste different)
2 tsp olive oil
1 Tbsp peeled, minced ginger
½ tsp minced garlic (the more the better, of course)
6 scallions, thinly sliced *keep white and green parts separate from each other*
1 cup finely diced bell peppers...make it colorful and mix bell pepper types
¼ tsp crushed red pepper
¾ cup water
8 oz uncooked udon noodles
2½ Tbsp dark miso
1-2 Tbsp soy sauce

Trim off the root end of the sprouts, clean off any damaged leaves, and slice lengthwise into halves or thirds, depending on size; set them aside. Next, start heating a large pot of water to a boil. Heat the oil in a large skillet. Add the ginger and garlic to the skillet. Stir constantly while cooking for 30 seconds. Smoke while you're doing it. Add the white part of the scallions, peppers, red pepper flakes to the skillet. Cook, stirring frequently, for about a minute.

Turn off the heat and add the ¾ cup water to the skillet. Put the sprouts in the skillet, cover, and cook over medium high until they are tender yet crisp (they should be bright green), or about 2-4 minutes. If the mixture becomes dry, add water by the tablespoon. Uncover and set aside.

Break the udon noodles in half and cook in the pot of boiling water until just before done. In the meantime, dissolve the miso into some of the noodle cooking water (or hot water) and stir in the soy sauce. Drain the noodles and put them in the skillet with the sprout mixture. Stir in the miso mixture and the scallion greens. Add more soy sauce if needed and stir until hot over medium heat. Serve immediately. Perk up leftovers with soy sauce.

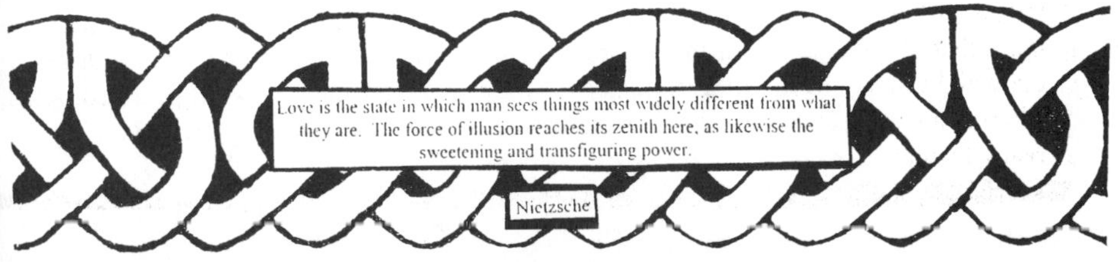

Tofu Almongeddondine

Music: Törr-Armageddon lp (1990)

This dish develops greater complexity and flavor the longer it sits, so if possible make th recipe and let it cool in the refrigerator for 4-12 hours before reheating and serving.

1 lb extra-firm tofu, cut into 1" cubes (herbed tofu works *real* good in this)
2 Tbsp soy sauce
¼ cup soy sauce
¼ cup smooth almond butter
1 1/3 cups water
1 1/3 Tbsp arrowroot or cornstarch
1 tsp sea salt
2 Tbsp olive oil
2 cups thinly sliced yellow onion
1 medium green pepper, thinly sliced
2½ cups thinly sliced carrots
½ cup slivered almonds

Preheat oven to 375° F. Cut the tofu into cubes. Place in a small bowl with 2 Tbsp soy sauce. Toss gently to combine. Place on a lightly-oiled tray and bake for 20 minutes. Remove and cool.

While the tofu is baking, whisk together 1/4 cup soy sauce, almond butter, water, arrowroot, and sea salt over medium heat until thickened. Set aside.

Heat the oil in a large pan and saute the onions, green pepper, and carrots until they are slightly soft to the bite.

In a large bowl, combine the tofu, almond butter mixture, and sauteed vegetables. Toss to combine and season with salt and pepper to taste. Serve over brown rice, garnished with the slivered almonds.

Brent's Septic Pasta

Music: This dish is prepared best with Italian Death Metal. We suggest the Morbid Upheaval/Capra Hircus-split 10" (2005)

¼ cup extra virgin olive oil
1 small onion, chopped
1 green pepper, diced/chopped
½ cup of halved green olives
2 Tbsp minced garlic
¼ tsp garlic salt
¼ tsp white pepper
2 cans artichoke hearts (drained and cut into pieces)
1 can of diced tomatoes
1 small can of tomato sauce
Your favorite pasta (fettuccini works pretty well)

Prepare pasta as directed. Heat ¼ cup of extra virgin olive oil in a skillet. Sauté chopped onion, green pepper, green olives, minced garlic, garlic salt, and pepper until the onions and green pepper are a bit brown and squishy. Now add the cut up artichoke hearts, canned tomatoes, and tomato sauce. Simmer for 10 minutes.

Serve over pasta with your favorite bread.

Beware the Jersey Devil Sorrento-Syle Pasta

Music: Paysage d'Hiver/Lunar Aurora-split lp (2004)

1¼ lbs ripe tomatoes, chopped up
3 oz black olives, pitted
2/3 cup olive oil
1' garlic clove (minced)
1 tsp dried oregano
1 cup chopped fresh basil
1¼ lb spiral pasta (or your choice of pasta)

In a bowl, combine all ingredients but the pasta. Stir well and let sit for about 30 minutes, stirring here and there to mix the flavors. Meanwhile, boil the pasta until done, drain it and throw the rest of the ingredients in and mix again. Serves about 4. Because none of the ingredients (other than the pasta) are actually cooked, it has a very fresh flavor and is best eaten right away!

> If you want a picture of the future, imagine a boot stomping on a human face...forever.
>
> George Orwell

Josh's Old-School Orzo with Asparagus and Roasted Garlic

Music: Derketa-self titled ep (1990)

1 head of garlic (large white one)
1 cup dried orzo (rice shaped pasta)
1 pound fresh asparagus
1 Tbsp margarine
1/4 cup vegetable broth
1 Tbsp finely snipped fresh basil or dried basil
1/2 tsp dried oregano
1/4 tsp ground black pepper

Preheat oven to 400° F, remove most of papery outer skin from garlic, leaving the bulb intact. Trim about ½" off the top of the bulb to expose the cloves. Wrap garlic in foil or use garlic roaster. Bake 25-30 minutes or until soft (make sure you don't overcook the garlic here…I fucked this up once and it's a cooking downer). This step can be done ahead and roasted garlic refrigerated.

Meanwhile, cook orzo according to directions. Drain and keep warm.

While the orzo is cooking, wash and trim the asparagus and cut it into bite-sized pieces. Melt the margarine in skillet; add the asparagus and vegetable broth, and cover and cook until crisp and tender (~3-5 minutes).

Squeeze out roasted garlic pulp and add to broth with the asparagus, basil, oregano, and pepper. Stir. Cook a minute or two more and add the mixture to the orzo. Toss and serve.

Grizzly Bear Gnocchi

Music: Poison-Bestial Death demo (1985)

Boil/bake eight medium sized potatoes, and mash them. Be sure to remove the skin.

Add 1 ½ to 2 cups of flour, and mix gently until everything sticks together but does not stick to your hands. Note: the more you knead, the more flour you'll require, and the more flour you use, the more dense the gnocchi become.

Pull off hunks of dough and roll into 1/2" ropes. Cut into half-inch pieces, and dust with flour. Roll each piece over the back of a fork to make ridges (push the piece against the fork tines, then roll it down and off the fork). Drop gnocchi into boiling salted water. When they float to the surface (2-3 minutes later) they're done. Devour with a spicy tomato sauce.

Hongshao Doufu: Red Cooked Bean Curd Family Style

Music: Transgressor-Twisting Brochus demo (1990)

There are very few people I know who would not sacrifice their lives (or at least pay 6 bucks) for a plate of family-style tofu.

1 lb extra-firm bean curd
9 whole scallions
1/3 cup peanut oil
1½ Tbsp coarsely chopped garlic
2 Tbsp rice wine
2 Tbsp hoisin sauce
2 Tbsp soy sauce
1 tsp turbinado sugar
1 cup vegetable stock
½ Tbsp sesame oil

Pat the bean curd dry with paper towels. Cut the bean curd into 1" by 3" triangles and lay the pieces on a towel to drain. Cut the scallions at a diagonal into 3" long pieces and set aside.

Heat a wok or large skillet on high heat. Heat the peanut oil. Add the bean curd pieces and fry until both sides are golden brown. Make sure it's extra crispy or Robyn will send it back if you try to serve it to her. Remove the bean curd and place on paper towels to drain. Drain the oil and set the wok aside. Wipe and dry the wok and return 2 Tbsp of the oil to the wok. Heat the oil and add the scallions a garlic and stir fry for 30 seconds. Add the rice wine, hoisin sauce, soy sauce, sugar, and stock and bring to a boil. Add the fried bean curd pieces. Cook over high heat for 10 minutes or until the bean curd absorbs most of the sauce. Add in the sesame oil and give a final stir. Serve immediately.

Demise's Broccoli Knishes

Music: Ghoul-Jerusalem ep (1985)

1 cup mashed potatoes
1/3 cup matzo meal
2 Tbsp potato starch
½ onion, finely chopped
¼ cup egg substitute
½ tsp black pepper
¼ tsp sea salt
1 cup fresh or frozen broccoli, steamed and finely chopped

Preheat the oven to 375° F. In a bowl combine the potato, matzo meal, potato starch, onion, egg substitute, pepper, and sea salt. Knead together. Divide the dough into six balls and flatten each. Divide the broccoli evenly into each circle, fold over and press the edges to seal.

Arrange the knishes in a single layer on a lightly greased baking sheet. Place on the bottom rack of the oven and bake for 15 minutes on each side. Serve hot.

Taco Thrash-erole

Music: Artillery-Fear of Tomorrow lp (1987)

2 cups tortilla chips, broken into bite sized pieces
1 large onion, chopped
1 large green pepper, chopped
1 Tbsp canola oil
2 cloves garlic, minced
1 cup frozen hash browns
1 can chopped green chilies
3 cups cooked long grain or brown rice
1 cup salsa
3 Tbsp hot chili powder
2 Tbsp cumin
1 Tbsp leaf oregano
1 can fat free refried black beans

AILUROPODA MELANOLEUCA

Spray 11 x 9 inch baking pan with non-stick cooking spray. Place crushed tortilla chips in the bottom. In large non-stick skillet, add onion, green pepper, oil, garlic and hash browns, cooking until peppers and onions are soft. In a bowl, combine chilies, rice, salsa, chili powder, cumin, oregano and black beans. Add this mixture to onions and peppers and cook until warm.

Transfer mixture to baking dish and bake in 350° F oven for 20 minutes. Top with more crushed chips and serve.

Taco Salad el Grande

Music: Autopsy-Mental Funeral lp (1991)

1 can vegan refried beans
1 can black beans, drained
Several black olives, chopped
1 Tbsp cumin
1 Tbsp chili powder
1 Tbsp "bacon" bits (see recipe this book)
3 dashes liquid smoke
5 dashes hot sauce
Some green leaf lettuce, washed and shredded
A bunch of tortilla chips
Hot salsa

Heat the beans on the stove. Mix in all the spices, the bacon bits, the liquid smoke, the hot sauce, and anything else you see fit. Arrange a layer of tortilla chips on a large plate. Cover the chips with a layer of lettuce. Pour the beans over the top. Sprinkle with olives and add salsa to taste. Consume and feel full for the rest of the afternoon.

Kittee's Chole

Music: Mercyful Fate-Don't Break the Oath lp (1984)

2 medium onions, finely chopped
3-4 Tbsp olive oil
3 cloves garlic, crushed
1 green chile, chopped in thirds
1 Tbsp fresh ginger, grated or minced
5 curry leaves (optional)
1 tsp sea salt, plus more to taste
2 Tbsp ground coriander
1 tsp ground cumin
1 pinch asafetida (optional)
1/4 tsp ground cinnamon
44oz canned chickpeas or about 4-5 cups cooked
1 1/4 cups water
1/2 cup tomato sauce
1 tsp paprika
1/2 tsp garam masala
3 Tbsp chopped cilantro

Heat 3 tablespoons olive oil over medium heat. Add the onions, garlic, green chile, ginger, curry leaves and sea salt. Mix well. Saute over medium to medium-low heat until the onions almost brown, adding more olive oil if necessary. Stir in the coriander, cumin, asafetida and cinnamon. Let cook in the onion and oil mixture for a few minutes until the spices become aromatic.

Add the chickpeas and stir. Quickly pour in the water and then tomato sauce, paprika and garam masala. Stir well. Raise heat until the mixture bubbles. Then, lower heat and cover to simmer slowly for about 30-40 minutes. The chickpeas should break down a little while simmering and mix with the spices and sauce to make a thick brown gravy. Remove the chile and serve topped with fresh cilantro and steamed basmati rice.

Lasagna de Matteo Ruscigno

Music: Animals Killing People-Human Hunting Season ep (2004)

32 oz tofu, mashed
¼ cup extra virgin olive oil
1 tsp sea salt
1 Tbsp oregano
½ tsp garlic powder
1 Tbsp nutritional yeast
Basil and rosemary to taste
2-3 cloves garlic, minced
1 small onion, finely chopped
Red pepper flakes to taste
1 package Gimme Lean Sausage, in small pieces
2 26 oz cans Del Monte traditional sauce
1 package no-boil lasagna noodles

Mix the first seven ingredients well, and marinate them in the refrigerator overnight.

Fry the garlic and onion in some oil over medium heat for two minutes, then add the sausage and fry until brown…about eight minutes. Add 1½ cups sauce and the red pepper; turn down the heat.

Meanwhile, heat up the tofu in a pan until warm. Grease a 15 X 9" pan, then cover the bottom with 1½ cups sauce. Put down three noodles, then most of the sausage mixture. Cover with three more noodles, then most of the tofu and about half of the remaining sauce. Cover with three more noodles and the remaining tofu, sausage and sauce.

Cover with foil and bake for one hour at 350°F or until hot and bubbly. Serve with garlic bread. Hasta la comida siempre!

September 11, 2001

Once the clock struck 9 am I knew it was time. Their offices opened at 9 and it was time to make the call. Shit was fucked. Just the day before, I overheard a friend of mine saying that self-hate was victimless…and therein lay its perfection. He had a point. I'd made that point many times before…so many times that I'd actually believed it. Yet, two days before I had had to explain through abstractions and euphemisms to a crying mother why my life no longer held value to me and why I no longer wanted to live it. My mother. While my father listened silently, unable or unwilling to respond to his failure of a son. This was becoming too common…too fucking routine. The victims of my "victimless" downward spiral were all too clear. They were the people I loved more than anything.

So I called the clinical depression unit. Little did I know that almost at the exact minute I made the call the World Trade Center was blowing up. The phone rang and rang, unanswered. "Busy signal at the suicide hotline." I bet Drowningman thought they were pretty fucking clever. Despair washed up from my center regions, over my eyes, and across my mind. My head dropped to my desk. "Tomorrow," I thought. "Tomorrow."

Carolina Barbecued Tempeh

Music: Cinerary-Rituals of Desecration lp (2001)

1 lb tempeh, cut into four ¼ lb slabs
¼ cup vegetable oil
1 medium onion, chopped
1 chipotle pepper
3 Tbsp cider vinegar
3 Tbsp tomato paste
2 Tbsp molasses
1 Tbsp Dijon-style mustard
1½ cups vegetable stock
2/3 cup coffee

In a large skillet, over medium heat, brown the tempeh slabs in oil and then let drain on a towel. Add the onion to the skillet and saute until browned, about 8 minutes. Add the whole chipotle and cook for 2 minutes more. Add the vinegar and stir. Add the tomato paste, molasses, mustard, vegetable stock, and coffee, stirring each ingredient in gradually. Simmer until the mixture is almost reduced by half. Remove the chipotle, slice it in half, remove the seeds, mince it, and return it to the sauce. Add the tempeh and simmer covered for another 10 minutes. Serve on buns with vegan coleslaw (see recipe this book) on the side.

Snausages

Music: English Dogs-Where Legend Began lp (1987)

1 lb can kidney beans, drained and rinsed
1 cup cooked brown rice
2 Tbsp ketchup
¼ tsp ground sage
1/8 tsp dried thyme
1/8 tsp ground savory
1/8 tsp garlic powder
¼ tsp sea salt
¼ tsp pepper
¼ tsp fennel seeds, crushed lightly

AND THE ANCIENT GODS
LAY AT REST... DREAMING...

Place beans, rice, and ketchup in a large bowl. Sprinkle evenly with spices. Mash well with a fork or potato masher, making sure that the spices are evenly distributed (the rice will be lumpy regardless). Chill the mixture several hours or overnight. Divide the chilled mixture into 12 portions. Roll each portion into a log-link approximately 2½" long. Preheat a large pan over medium heat. Oil it lightly. Cook the snausages until browned on all sides, turning frequently to brown evenly. Oil the pan again if necessary. Serve hot.

But when he came to study those who had thrown off the old myths, he found them even more ugly than those who had not. They did not know that beauty lies in harmony, and that loveliness of life has no standard amidst an aimless cosmos save only its harmony with the dreams and the feelings which have gone before and blindly moulded our little spheres out of the rest of chaos. They did not see that good and evil and beauty and ugliness are only ornamental fruits of perspective, whose sole value lies in their linkage to what chance made our fathers think and feel, and whose finer details are different for every race and culture. Instead, they either denied these things altogether or transferred them to the crude, vague instincts which they shared with the beasts and peasants; so that their lives were dragged malodorously out in pain, ugliness, and disproportion, yet filled with a ludicrous pride at having escaped from something no more unsound than that which still held them. They had traded the false gods of fear and blind piety for those of license and anarchy.

H. P. Lovecraft

Tofu Chorizo

Music: Sarcofago-Satanic Lust demo (1986)

Chorizo is a traditional, spicy pork-based sausage common to Mexico and the Southwest. Try it in tacos, on baked potatoes, or on salads.

3 large, dried ancho chili peppers
4 cloves garlic, coarsely chopped
1 Tbsp dried oregano
2 tsp paprika
1½ tsp cumin seed
1 tsp sea salt
½ tsp fennel seed
¼ tsp ground cloves
¼ tsp ground cinnamon
¼ tsp red pepper flakes
¼ cup peanut butter
3 Tbsp cider vinegar
1¼ cups vegetable stock
1 lb extra firm tofu, thoroughly drained

Cut the chilis in half and remove the seeds and stems. Lay the pieces flat on a skillet and toast them over medium heat for 4 minutes. Press down on them every now and then and turn them once, midway through. Transfer the toasted chili pieces to a blender and add the garlic, oregano, paprika, cumin seed, salt, fennel seed, cloves, cinnamon, and red pepper and puree until the chilis are finely chopped. Add the peanut butter, vinegar, and ¼ cup of stock. Puree, gradually adding the remaining stock until it's fairly smooth. Transfer the mixture into another skillet. Crumble in the tofu and bring to a simmer over medium heat. Reduce heat to medium low and cook until the mixture is considerably dried out. It should be quite crumbly in texture. Be sure not to let it burn on the bottom. Enjoy.

Pat's Orange-Soy Tofu and Vegetables

Music: Wigrid-Hoffnungstod lp (2002)

1 tsp olive oil
4 cloves garlic, minced
½ cup snow peas, sliced
½ cup thinly sliced Napa cabbage
1 carrot, grated
1 8 oz can water chestnuts, sliced
½ red bell pepper, sliced thinly
½ cup orange juice
2 Tbsp soy sauce
2 Tbsp cold water
3 Tbsp arrowroot
Dash of red pepper
½ lb firm tofu, cut into 1" cubes and sauteed
6-8 oz cooked soba or Ramen noodles

In a large skillet, heat oil, add garlic, add the vegetables, and cover. Cook over high he for 4-5 minutes. Lower heat and add orange juice and soy sauce. Cook 3-5 minutes longer. While waiting, mix the water and arrowroot in a small bowl. Stir this mixture into the vegetables to thicken. Cook 3-5 minutes longer and add red pepper, tofu, and noodles. Toss well to coat the noodles with sauce. Serve with mescal.

Cheap-O Chana Masala

Music: Sadistik Exekution-We are Death...Fukk You! lp (1994)

1 can garbanzo beans
1 big onion very finely chopped
1 inch piece of ginger grated
1 clove garlic
1/2 tsp turmeric powder
1/4 tsp cayenne pepper
1/2 tsp amchur powder
1/2 tsp garam masala
2 Tbsp oil
Sea salt to taste

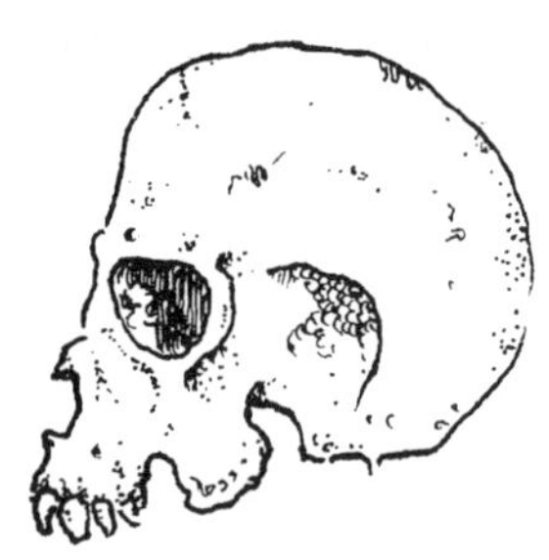

Heat oil in a frying pan. Add chopped onions and fry until golden brown. Add all the spices (except mango powder), crushed garlic and grated ginger to it.

Fry for about two-three minutes. Add garbanzo beans, salt, and mango powder. Add about 1/2 cup of water and cook on low heat for about 15 minutes. This will give some time for garbanzo beans to absorb all the spices. Eat hot with basmati rice and spicy naan.

Indian Tacos of Death

Music: The Ravenous-Three on a Meathook 10" (2002)

Fry bread (recipe below)
Marinade for beans (recipe below)
Pinto beans
Lettuce
Tomatoes
Onions

Fry bread:

1 cup unbleached, white flour
1/2 tsp sea salt
1/4 tsp baking soda
1/2 to 3/4 cup water
A few tablespoons of oil (for frying; olive is the best)

Blend dry ingredients together. Add water. Knead until elastic then tear off some dough and form into small balls. Shape balls until flat and measure about 3" to 4" in diameter. Place dough flats into already heated oil. Fry on both sides until golden brown. Place finished bread on a plate with a paper towel to drain excess oil.

Marinade for beans:

A few tablespoons of vinegar
A few tablespoons soy sauce
Water
Any interesting herbs and spices (varying spiciness to your taste)

Mix these ingredients together and throw in beans. Marinade as long as you like. Then heat them up over the stove and then they're ready to go on top of fry bread along with lettuce, tomatoes, onions, etc.

In what sense is the non-dual reality Void (Emptiness)? The non-dual reality is not constituted of any and all those things (phenomena) which are the products of the activity of superimposition. It is devoid of everything pertaining to the perceptual-conceptual realm. In other words, the non-dual reality is not a thing (an object, a phenomenon); nor is it nothing in the sense of utter absence and blankness; rather, it is no-thing. To be a thing is to be one among many particulars; and to be particular is to have temporal location; and since reality transcends phenomena--particulars--it is non-spatial and non-temporal. Thus reality is not itself a thing; nor is it constituted of things. It is neither one nor many, since it transcends number and plurality. In a word, the non-dual reality is Void--Emptiness. This emptiness is at once Fullness, the fullness of all existence in its inexhaustible variety and multiplicity. Not itself being a phenomenon, the Void, the non-dual reality, is formless and therefore also nameless. Yet it is the fount of all things, all phenomena--all forms and names. If reality is a thing, it will just be one among many things and not all things and therefore reality. Hence it is self-contradictory to think of reality as *something*, no matter how lofty and inspiring.

Ramakrishna Puligandla

Suzi's Mashed Potato Bake

Music: Thorns-Trøndertun demo (1992)

3 cups mashed potatoes
1 cup vegan sour cream (try Tofutti)
¼ cup soy milk
¼ tsp garlic salt
1 cup dried onion
Nutritional yeast

Combine the first four ingredients. Spoon half the mixture into a casserole dish. Top with ½ cup dried onion and sprinkle on some nutritional yeast. Repeat layers. Bake at 350° F for 30 minutes.

Southwestern Tofu Scramble

Music: Disgorge-Chronic Corpora Infest lp (1998)

1 Tbsp olive oil
1 medium onion, finely chopped
1 lb firm tofu, cut into ½ inch cubes
6 corn tortillas, torn into 1 inch pieces
1 16 oz can diced tomatoes
1 4 oz can chopped chilies
1 tsp ground cumin
Sea salt to taste
Flour tortillas, warmed

Heat the oil in a skillet. Saute the onion over medium heat until lightly golden. Add tofu, tortillas, tomatoes, chilies, cumin, and salt. Stir together gently, cover, and cook over medium heat for 10 minutes. Remove from heat, wrap in the flour tortillas, and serve.

Keren's Shakshuka

Music: September-Time of Darkness demo (1992)

Shakshuka is a traditional North African food, traditionally made with eggs. It's a very popular fast food/light meal in Israel and a good way to use vegetables on the verge of rotting.

2 large tomatoes (chopped) or 1 tomato and 1 small can of tomato puree
1 onion
1 garlic clove, crushed
1 red bell pepper, chopped
1 green chile pepper
1 package firm tofu
A pinch of sugar (if using the puree)
Sea salt, pepper, and cumin
Olive oil

In a large frying pan, heat about a tablespoon of oil. Add the onion, garlic, and chile pepper to the pan and fry until the onion starts to brown. Add the tofu and mash it up with a fork. Then add the red pepper and tomatoes and puree and sugar (if used).

Season with salt, pepper, and cumin. Mix throughout the process. Serve hot with pita bread.

Hair of an Angel Knotted by the Persistence of a Mortal

Music: Blasphemy-Fallen Angel of Doom lp (1990)

Because we don't know when we will die, we get to think of life as an inexhaustible well. But everything happens only a certain number of times, and only a very small number, really. How many more times will you remember a certain afternoon of your childhood, some afternoon that is so deeply a part of your being that you can't even conceive of your life without it? Perhaps four or five times more, perhaps not even that. How many more times will you watch the full moon rise? Perhaps twenty. And yet it all seems so limitless... (Jane E. Humble)

Enough angel hair pasta for two
¼ cup pine nuts
2 cloves garlic
¼ tsp sea salt
1 cup firmly packed cilantro leaves
3 Tbsp olive oil

THE WOMAN'S CAUSE IS MAN'S THEY RISE OR SINK
TOGETHER DWARFD OR GODLIKE BOND OR FREE

Toast the pine nuts and the whole garlic in a dry skillet until lightly brown, stirring frequently to avoid burning. Put it all in a blender and grind it into a coarse paste. Cook the pasta (it shouldn't take long), strain it, and mix in the pasta. Share with another.

Barry Immeasurable Difference's Red Hot Beans and Broccoli

Music: Sodom-In the Sign of Evil ep (1984)

1 Tbsp olive oil
1 medium yellow onion, chopped
1 red bell pepper, diced
1 stalk celery, chopped
2 15 oz cans red kidney beans, drained
1 14 oz can stewed tomatoes
1 medium bunch broccoli, cut into small florets.
½ cup water
1 tsp hot pepper sauce
½ tsp black pepper
½ tsp sea salt
½ tsp cayenne
2-3 Tbsp chopped parsley

In a large saucepan, heat the oil over medium-high heat. Add the onion, bell pepper, and celery and cook 5-7 minutes, stirring frequently. Mix in all remaining ingredients except the parsley; cover and cook, stirring occasionally, over medium-low heat until the broccoli is tender...about 12-15 minutes. Stir in the parsley and remove from heat. Set aside for at least 15 minutes and serve.

Misery Wot (Ethiopian Lentil Stew)

Music: Mütiilation-Remains of a Ruined, Dead, Cursed Soul demo (1999)

1 cup dried lentils
2 quarts water
¼ cup minced shallots
1 clove garlic, minced
¼ cup water
2 Tbsp berbere (see recipe this book)
1 Tbsp olive oil
½ tsp onion salt
Additional water as needed

But you stand there so nice in your blizzard of ice

O please let me come into the storm.

Cook the lentils in the 2 quarts boiling water for about 35-40 minutes, or until tender. Meanwhile, cook the shallots in a dry pan until soft and light brown, stirring frequently to prevent burning. Add garlic and continue stirring. Add ¼ cup water, berbere, and olive oil. Drain and mash the lentils and add them to the shallot mixture. Stir in the onion salt. Simmer 30 minutes to 1 hour. You may need to add more water to keep the consistency similar to that of oatmeal. Serve hot or at room temperature with injeri (see recipe this book).

Chicken Fried Steak with Cream Gravy

Music: Watchtower-Energetic Disassembly lp (1985)

Steaks:
1 cup whole wheat pastry flour
3 Tbsp arrowroot
1 tsp sea salt
¼ tsp freshly ground black pepper
¼ tsp cayenne pepper
½ tsp dried thyme
½ tsp onion powder
½ tsp garlic powder
¼ tsp celery seeds
1½ cups water
½ cup vegetable oil
2 lbs seitan (drained, patted dry, and cut into 6-8 cutlets)

Gravy:
3 Tbsp whole wheat pastry flour
2 tsp Cajun Hellspice (see recipe this book)
½ cup water
½ cup plain, unsweetened soymilk
1 Tbsp vegan Worcestershire sauce

Steaks: Place all of the dry ingredients in a large bowl. Add the water and stir to combine. Refrigerate for 10 minutes.

Heat the oil in a large skillet over medium-high heat. Dredge the seitan in the batter and shake off any excess. Working in batches, fry the seitan for 3 to 4 minutes. Turn the seitan over and fry for another 3 to 4 minutes or until golden brown on both sides. Place the cutlets on paper towels to drain.

Gravy: Pour all of the oil from the pan except 3 Tbsp and the pan drippings. Heat the skillet over medium heat. Add the flour and the Hellspice and cook for 3-5 minutes, stirring and scraping the bottom of the pan and lightly browning the flour. Stir in the water, soymilk, and Worcestershire sauce. Increase the heat to high and bring the mixture to a boil to thicken it. Boil for 5 minutes, stirring constantly, until the gravy is thick and smooth. Pour it over the chicken-fried seitan and serve with potatoes and greens.

I was riding my bike to work today. Hadn't slept for anything, barely coherent. And then I catch this little creature out of the corner of my eye. There's this squirrel just standing there in the middle of the sidewalk on the corner of 48th and Cedar. I hardly ever see squirrels by where I live. If they aren't being attacked by feral cats, they're being chased for food by wingnuts. He's up on his rear legs so he's about a foot tall, arms out. He just stares at me with this "what the fuck?" expression. I look back at him and am like "for real man...what the fuck?" I kept riding and he just stood there, bewildered. I'll take my shared empathy wherever I can get it, but dang...it's a sad state of affairs when even the squirrels are walking around in a confused state of malaise.

Sweet Potato Burritos

Music: Ingurgitating Oblivion-Voyage Towards Abhorrence lp (2005)

3 tsp vegetable oil
1 large onion, chopped
4 cloves garlic, minced
6 cups cooked kidney beans, rinsed and drained
2 cups water
3 Tbsp chili powder
2 tsp ground cumin
4 tsp prepared mustard
Pinch cayenne pepper
3 Tbsp soy sauce
4 cups cooked and mashed sweet potatoes
12 (10 inch) flour tortillas, warmed

Preheat oven to 350° F.
Heat oil in a medium skillet. Saute onion and garlic until soft. Add the beans and mash. Gradually stir in the water and heat until warm. Remove from the heat and stir in the chili powder, cumin, mustard, cayenne pepper, and soy sauce. Divide bean mixture and mashed sweet potatoes evenly between the warm flour tortillas. Fold up tortillas burrito style. Bake for about 12 minutes.

Cheeseburger Macaroni

Music: Stiny Plamenu-Ve Spine Je Pravda lp (2001)

3 ½ cups macaroni (uncooked)
½ cup vegan margarine
½ cup flour
3 ½ cups boiling water
1 ½ tsp salt
2 Tbsp soy sauce
1 ½ tsp garlic powder
A pinch of tumeric
¼ cup oil
1 cup nutritional yeast
Paprika
1 package fake hamburger (Morning Star crumbles, etc.)

Cook macaroni and set aside. In a saucepan, melt margarine over low heat. Beat in flour with a whisk, continue to beat over medium flame until mixture is smooth and bubbly. Whip in boiling water, salt, soy sauce, garlic powder, and turmeric. Beat well to dissolve the flour mixture. The sauce should cook until it thickens and bubbles. Whip in oil and nutritional yeast.
Heat fake hamburger in a frying pan. Mix part of the sauce with the noodles, put in a casserole dish. Pour a generous amount of sauce on top and mix together. Mix in fake hamburger. Sprinkle with paprika. Bake 15 minutes in at 350° F oven. Serve.

Crusty Potato Peasant Casserole

Music: Massacra-The Final Holocaust lp (1990)

6 medium (2 lbs) potatoes, very thinly sliced and unpeeled
2 large onions, halved and very thinly sliced
4 large cloves garlic, minced
1 28-oz can tomatoes, drained and chopped
¼ cup tomato paste
1/3 cup olive oil
3 Tbsp water
2 tsp oregano
Sea salt and pepper

Preheat the oven to 400°F. Combine potatoes, onion, garlic, and tomatoes. Beat together the remaining ingredients in a separate bowl. Pour over the vegetables and toss well to coat. Spread in a large, shallow baking dish. Cover with aluminum foil and bake for 30 minutes. Uncover and bake for 45 more minutes, or until the potatoes are crustier than a Gloom show.

Fuel for the Fire: Spicy Szechwan Noodles

Music: Hemlock-Lust for Fire lp (1999)

½ lb udon noodles
¼ cup peanut butter
¼ cup warm water
3 Tbsp soy sauce
1 Tbsp dark sesame oil
1 Tbsp hot pepper sauce
8 ox extra-firm tofu, cubed
5 oz green peas
Toasted sesame seeds
Chopped scallions

Cook the noodles al dente in salted water, then drain. Mix the peanut butter, warm water, soy sauce, sesame oil, and hot pepper sauce. Steam the tofu and peas until the peas are tender. Toss the noodles with the peanut butter sauce, tofu, and peas. Top with sesame seeds and scallions. Serve at room temperature or colder.

> Once in a while, though, he could not help seeing how shallow, fickle, and meaningless all human aspirations are, and how emptily our real impulses contrast with those pompous ideals we profess to hold. Then he would have recourse to the polite laughter they had taught him to use against the extravagance and artificiality of dreams; for he saw that the daily life of our world is every inch as extravagant and artificial, and far less worthy of respect because of its poverty in beauty and its silly reluctance to admit its own lack of reason and purpose. In this way he became a kind of humorist, for he did not see that even humor is empty in a mindless universe devoid of any true standard of consistency or inconsistency.
>
> H. P. Lovecraft

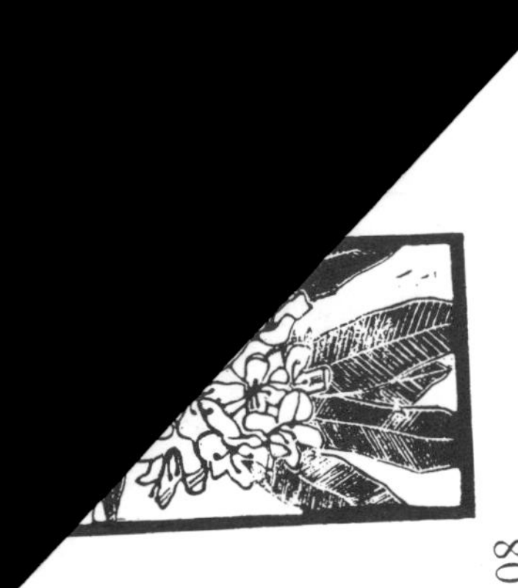

ids 12" (1984)

f vegetable protein derived from wheat gluten
erbs, and spices to tenderize it. It takes 2-3 hours
could just buy it at a natural foods store or
ne-ass who just watches tv all day, too. I decided
ne for homemade tofu as you can find an
Not Oi! Some strict vegans won't eat seitan
ike. By that logic, we shouldn't eat bananas
stency. You decide for yourself. This is one of
...y favorite foods. It's excellent in chili and stir-fry dishes.

The old fashioned way...

Take 4 cups of whole wheat bread flour and dump it into a large mixing bowl. Add enough water to make a nice, firm ball of dough.

Let water run into the bowl (gently) from a tap and knead the dough in the bowl under the running water. Holding the ball together, knead until the water in the bowl stops getting cloudy. Sound easy? Wrong. This is the most labor-intensive step of the process and can take well over a half an hour. I recommend breaking up the big ball and working with it in four pieces, as it is more manageable that way.

Recombine your pieces and roll the very firm dough into a log and cut it into thin steaks or tear off small pieces (about ½ the size of a golf ball). The pieces may look small, but they will swell when they are cooked.

In a large pot bring the following to a boil:

4 quarts water
3 cups soy sauce
1 6" piece of kombu
1 Tbsp peppercorns
2 Tbsp ground ginger
2 Tbsp granulated garlic

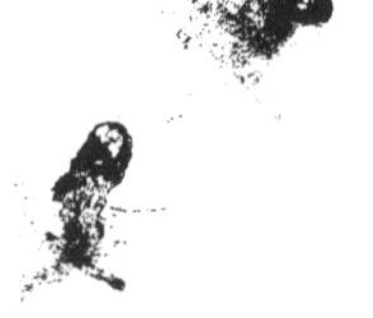

Once boiling, add the steaks or balls, lower the heat, cover, and simmer for 1 to 1½ hours, depending on how tender you want the final product to be (the longer it cooks, the firmer it gets). Poke and stir occasionally to keep the gluten from sticking to the bottom or the sides. If you have any firm tofu sitting around, throw it in as well. It makes a great marinade.

Once done, let the seitan cool and store it either refrigerated or frozen in its broth. Consume with the ferocity of a rabid hyena.

Ghoulash

Music: VON-Satanic Blood demo (1992)

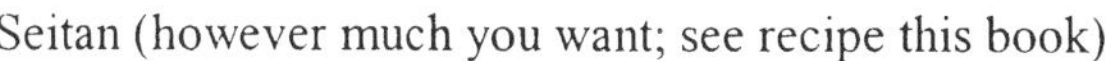

Seitan (however much you want; see recipe this book)
Vegetable oil
1 chopped onion
1 chopped green pepper
Some whole wheat flour
Fresh chopped mushrooms (optional)

Cut the seitan into cubes and fry them in the oil until dark and crusty. Add the chopped onions and the pepper. Season with sea salt and black pepper to taste. Sprinkle flour on it and let it go dark. Add a bit of water to it and let it thicken. Do this again and repeat until the sauce reaches the desired consistency. Add the mushrooms if you must. Serve over noodles or rice.

Seitanic Pepper Steak

Music: Watain-Casus Luciferi lp (2004)

1 lb of seitan in broth (see recipe this book)
1 large onion, sliced into 1/8" wide strips
2 large green peppers, sliced into 1/8" wide strips
¼ tsp black pepper
¼ cup soy sauce
1/8 cup olive oil
1 Tbsp cornstarch mixed with 1 cup water

Slice the seitan into 1/8" wide strips and set the broth aside. Saute the seitan, peppers, and onions in olive oil in a large skillet until the peppers and onions are tender. Add the black pepper, seitan broth, and soy sauce. Quickly stir the ingredients in a skillet until the liquid bubbles. Add in the cornstarch/water mixture and continue to stir until thickened. Remove from heat and serve over rice.

"Speckknoedel" mit Sauerkraut ("Seitanic Bacon Dumplings" with Saurkraut)

Music: Samael-Worship Him lp (1993)

Cut the seitan (see recipe this book) into little pieces and fry it. Season it well with a mix of pepper, sea salt, piquant herbs, and so on. In a separate bowl, peel a few cooked potatoes from the day before and mash them. Add ½ tsp sea salt and 1-3 heaped Tbsp soy flour to the potatoes. The dough shouldn't be too dry or it'll fall apart. If it's too wet, the dumplings will be too mushy. Once the desired consistency is reached, form dumplings out of the dough and insert some pieces of seitan into the center of each. Now cook the dumplings in mildly boiling salt water for about 20-25 minutes. Don't cook them at a rolling boil or the coating will fall off of the seitan. Bring some sauerkraut to a boil in a separate pot and add a bit of sea salt to taste (and maybe some diced and fried smoked tofu if you have it). Serve the dumplings with the kraut and a hearty German beer.

"Caught in a Mosh" Peanutbutter Pasta Spirals

Music: Bolt Thrower-...For Victory lp (1994)

12 oz spiral pasta
2/3 cup smooth peanut butter
3/4 cup water or vegetable stock
3-4 Tbsp soy sauce
2 Tbsp rice vinegar
2 scallions (green onions), sliced
1 Tbsp rice syrup
1/2 tsp ground ginger
1/2 tsp chili powder
1 1/2 cups frozen green peas
Tabasco sauce

Begin cooking pasta. Combine remaining ingredients, except for peas and Tabasco sauce, in food processor and process until smooth. When pasta is nearly done, add peas to the cooking water to thaw them. Drain and transfer to serving bowl. Add peanut sauce and mix well. Serve with Tabasco on the side. This is good warm or cold. The sauce thickens while standing, so you may need to add a bit more water or stock before serving if you don't serve it right away.

Chupacabra Blood Loaf

Music: Necrovore-Divus de Mortuus demo (1987)

3 cups TVP granules
2/12 cups boiling water
¼ cup ketchup
1 tsp basil
½ cup yellow onion, finely chopped
2 Tbsp olive oil
¾ cup whole wheat flour
1 tsp sea salt
¼ tsp pepper
½ tsp each garlic powder, oregano, and marjoram
½ cup parsley, finely minced

Mix the TVP, water, ketchup, and basil in a large bowl and let stand 10 minutes. While waiting, saute the onion in the olive oil. Add the onions to the rehydrated TVP and stir in the rest of the ingredients. Lightly oil a loaf or bread pan and pack the mixture in tightly. Bake at about 350° F for about 45 minutes. If loaf begins to get too brown on top, cover with foil. After removing from oven, let stand in pan for 10 minutes, then ru a knife around the edges to loosen it from the pan. Enjoy with ketchup. If you let it coo off, you can slice it and fry it up (like SPAM!) for sandwiches or whatever.

Jim's Halushki

Music: Sacrilege-Behind the Realms of Madness lp (1985)

1 head of green cabbage, chopped
1 onion, chopped
1 potato, shredded
Whole wheat flour
Oil for frying
Sea salt, pepper, and paprika to taste
Pot of boiling water

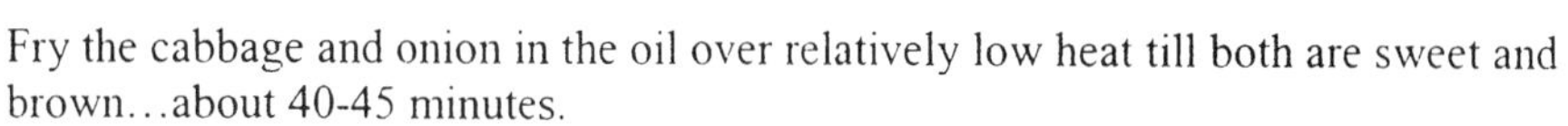

Fry the cabbage and onion in the oil over relatively low heat till both are sweet and brown…about 40-45 minutes.

Squeeze the excess water out of the potato shreds. Mix a bit of the onion into the potato shreds and season with salt, pepper, and paprika. Add enough flour to the potato/onion mixture to make a thick paste. Drop spoonfuls of the mixture into the boiling water and wait for them to rise to the surface. At this point, take the dumplings out of the water and add them to the cabbage and onion. Season with salt, pepper, and paprika to taste.

> If you develop an ear for sounds that are musical it is like developing an ego. You begin to refuse sounds that are not musical and that way cut yourself off from a good deal of experience.
>
> John Cage

Nature's Burgers

Music: Eternal Darkness-Twilight in the Wilderness mlp (1993)

1 15 oz can garbanzo beans
¾ cup rolled quick oats
1 clove garlic, minced
1 tsp sea salt
1 tsp black pepper
1 tsp turmeric
1 tsp liquid smoke
1 Tbsp soy sauce
Vegetable oil

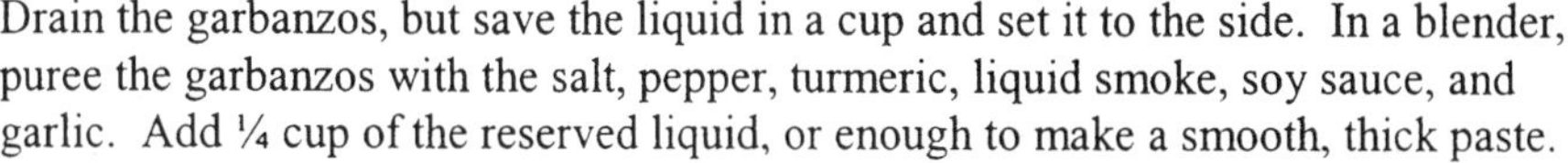

Drain the garbanzos, but save the liquid in a cup and set it to the side. In a blender, puree the garbanzos with the salt, pepper, turmeric, liquid smoke, soy sauce, and garlic. Add ¼ cup of the reserved liquid, or enough to make a smooth, thick paste.

Place the puree in a mixing bowl and add in the oats. Mix in as much of the reserved liquid as is necessary to make a mixture which holds together well and keeps its shape.

Shape the mixture into patties and fry in a little oil until each side is golden brown. Serve on some nice, whole wheat buns.

Lentil Tacos

Music: Hobbs Angel of Death-self titled lp (1988)

1½ cups dried lentils
3½ to 5 cups water
1 bay leaf
1 stalk celery
1 clove garlic, crushed
½ tsp sea salt
1/8 tsp dried thyme
1½ cups tomato sauce
1 Tbsp taco seasoning mix
8 taco shells
1½ cups shredded lettuce
1 medium onion, diced
1 large tomato, diced

Sort and wash the lentils. Combine with the water and the next five ingredients in a pot. Bring it to a boil, reduce heat, and let it simmer 1½ hours. Stir occasionally and add more water, if necessary. When done, remove and discard the bay leaf and celery. Combine the tomato sauce and taco seasoning in a small bowl; stir well. Heat the taco shells and spoon in the lentils, tomato mixture, and other toppings.

Brazilian Vegetable Feijoada

Music: Mystifier-Tormenting the Holy Trinity demo (1989)

2 whole red dried hot peppers
1 tsp ground cumin
1 tsp ground thyme
2 medium sweet potatoes; peeled, sliced lengthwise into quarters, and then into ¼' thick slices
1 large leek (white part only), sliced lengthwise into ½' thick slices
1 red bell pepper, seeded and sliced lengthwise into ½" wide slices
1 medium yellow onion, peeled and sliced lengthwise into ½" wide slices
2 Tbsp lime juice
1 large tomato, sliced into ¼" thick slices
2 16-oz cans black beans
Cooked rice

If all goes well, this should only take 30 minutes or less. Heat a little vegetable broth or water and add the dried red peppers, cumin, and thyme; lower heat and cook 1 minute. Add the sweet potatoes; cook 5 minutes. Add leeks; cook 5 minutes more. Stir in bell peppers and onion; cook 5 minutes. Add lime juice, combine well, and cook 5 minutes more. Add the tomato slices. In a separate saucepan, add the beans and cook for a few minutes until hot; drain. Mix it all together and serve over rice.

Marduk the Destroyer wrought havoc on my apartment for many months. Bread...saltine crackers...tortilla chips...cocoa comets...ramen noodles...all slaughtered indiscriminately. His skills were so sharp that no point of the room was safe from his exploits...save the inside of the refrigerator. "Dude, why do you keep your ramen in the refrigerator?," Matt once asked. I quickly looked about the room. "If only you knew," I whispered. "If only you knew."

McMike's Mexilasagna

Music: Axegrinder-Rise of the Serpent Men lp (1989)

2 cans refried beans
2 cans black beans
12-pack of flour tortillas
Approximately ½-to-1 head of garlic, minced
1 block extra-firm tofu, cut into small cubes
Appropriate spices (soy sauce, cayenne, cumin, chili powder, liquid smoke)
Salsa
Vegan sour cream
Vegan cheese dip (see recipe earlier in book)
Optional layers: shredded iceberg lettuce, diced tomatoes, sliced jalapeno peppers, sliced black olives, etc

This is pretty simple. The plan is to make a lasagna-form dish using bean burrito ingredients. The only real preparation is this:

Make the cheese dip.

Mix all the beans together and heat them on the stove. Add in appropriate spices and garlic to your taste.

Fry the tofu in some vegetable or olive oil. Add in some garlic or spices if you like.

Now, find a large lasagna dish. Put down a single layer of tortilla shells on the bottom. Add a layer of the bean mixture. Add a layer of tortilla shells. Add a layer of tofu. Add a layer of tortilla shells. Add a layer of the bean mixture. Add a layer of tortilla shells. Add a layer of vegan sour cream and shredded lettuce (or whatever). Add a layer of tortilla shells. You can see how this works. Keep alternating layers until you're out of ingredients. Try to save the cheese dip and the salsa for the top layer. Now put it in a 350° stove for about a half hour to heat everything through.

Marduk was deposed during the great purge of October 23, 2001 when I inadvertently took him out with the trash. As I carried the garbage bag out into the hallway, he made a valiant leap from the bag, climbed through the banister, ran off the edge, and took a 10 foot fall down to the first floor. Unfazed, he turned and looked up at me with a sneer before scampering into the open basement door. He knew as well as I did...Marduk the Breadslayer would ride again.

Poncit

Music: Impiety-Ceremonial Necrochrist Redesecration demo (1992)

Filipino cabbage in garlic and soy sauce.

¼ cup vegetable oil
2 cloves garlic, minced
1 onion, minced
1 large carrot, cut into thin strips
1 small cabbage, shredded
3 Tbsp soy sauce
3 Tbsp vegetable broth
3 stalks celery, chopped
8 oz rice stick noodles
1 tsp sea salt
1 tsp MSG
1 green onion, chopped

Saute the garlic in the oil Add the onions, carrots, and cabbage. Season with soy sauce and fry for 2 more minutes. Add the broth and simmer, then add the celery. When the vegetables are cooked, add the rice sticks and season with salt and MSG. Garnish with green onions. Serve with lemon.

It came down to the point where we either had to be terrorists or musicians. Not that we really call ourselves musicians. *Not that we really call ourselves musicians.*

Oblivion of SPK

Superstuffed Pepperbombs

Music: Razor-Armed and Dangerous mlp (1984)

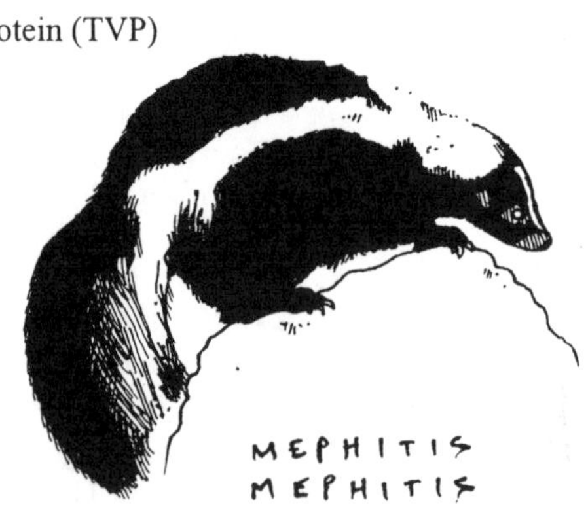

1 cup reconstituted textured vegetable protein (TVP)
1 medium onion, chopped
2 cloves garlic, minced
1 Tbsp olive oil
1 cup cooked rice
1 cup tomato sauce
¼ cup walnuts (optional)
4 bell peppers
2 cups vegetable broth
Seas salt and pepper to taste

Preheat the oven to 350°F.

Saute the onion and garlic until tender. Mix in all ingredients (other than the peppers, of course). Cut off the top of each pepper and remove the stem and seeds. Stuff each pepper with the mixture. Place the peppers in a baking pan and pour the vegetable broth around the base of the peppers. Cover and bake for 30 minutes.

Firestorm Falaf-Hell

Music: Tormentor-Seventh Day of Doom demo (1988)

I realized I hadn't yet put in a falafel recipe, so here it is. This one is special and authentic, as it was sent to me from Israel. Serve with rosewater lemonade.

½ medium potato, peeled
1 tsp vegetable oil
1 small onion, minced
1 15 ½ oz can garbanzo beans, drained
3 Tbsp lemon juice
2 cloves garlic, minced
2 Tbsp tahini
½ tsp paprika
1 Tbsp parsley, minced
Sea salt and pepper

Cut the potato into 1-inch chunks, place it in a pot with enough water to cover it, and boil 10 minutes or until tender. Drain. While the potato is cooking, saute the onion in the oil in a pan until soft.

In a medium bowl, mash the garbanzo beans, potato, and lemon juice with a masher or a fork. Add the onion, garlic, tahini, paprika, parsley, sea salt, and pepper to taste. Mix well to form a consistency similar to cookie dough.

Lightly oil a baking sheet with vegetable oil. Spoon the mixture onto the sheet to form 3-inch patties. Place in the oven and bake for 15 minutes at 350° F. Serve in a warmed pita with lettuce, tomato, and cucumber.

HUMAN LIFE IS A WASTE PRODUCT
CONTAMINATING THE EARTH
MULTIPLYING LIKE CANCER CELLS
DARKNESS GIVING BIRTH
THE WORLD IS INFESTED
WITH HUMANS SUCKING
OUT ITS LIFE DEVOURING
LIKE INSECTS BREEDING
LIKE RATS THE MOST
DESTRUCTIVE POLLUTION THAT
HUMANKIND CREATES IS
MORE HUMAN KIND MORE
HUMAN WASTE... CANNIPTION

I eyed the jump from about 30 feet away. It was big alright. There was one large mound that was about two feet tall. About eight feet after the first mound there was a second, smaller mound. If all went well, I would be using that second mound as a re-entry ramp. If all didn't go well, I would most likely end up a piece of wreckage in the ditch between the two mounds. I looked at the other jumps. I had been able to clear most of them, but then again...they weren't as big as this one. I looked down at my shoes. My dusty old Vans stared back at me...just like they did as a kid. The bike was different, though. My classic, chrome Mongoose Californian had been replaced by a cheap-ass bottom-of-the-line Trek mountain bike. Definitely not an ideal jumper. I eyed the jump again. I hadn't bailed yet today. Then again, I had to bail at some point. I always did...especially as a kid. My elbows and knees told those stories only too well. I slowly pushed off, still uncertain of my intentions. Would I actually do it? Would I swerve at the last moment? I charged at the jump, pedaling as hard as I could.

At full speed, ten feet from the jump, I made the decision. It was time to fly. I remember hitting the jump and looking down...always a big no-no. The ditch passed under me. At least now I knew that that wasn't where I was going to end up. Then came the second mound. I re-entered the stratosphere and onto the second mound and just as I thought I was safe my front tire hit soft dirt, slipped out, and I knew I was going down. I was going fast enough that I was thrown in such a way that it looked like I was sliding in a baseball game...head first. I slid for about 10 or 15 feet on my side with my arms out in front of me. I knew on impact that nothing was broken...not from the way I crashed. I finally came to a stop in a cloud of dust. Lying in a bloody heap in the dirt, I could do nothing more than laugh out loud. I laughed and laughed and rolled in the dirt. So fucking pathetic...the twentysomething boy trying to reclaim his childhood, only to hurt himself just as he always had in the past. The glorious irony of the dirt...soft enough to cause my wheel to slip out, hard enough to shred my shirt and skin to pieces. The had-painted sign staring mockingly at my side... "Jump at your own risk."

HEAVY METAL IS THE LAW

Iere is your challenge, Metal Warrior. For while the lasagna is baking. Or while the pickles are pickling. Or hile the dough is rising. These questions range from the simple to the ultra-obscure. Posers leave the hall, or the kitchen as the case may be.

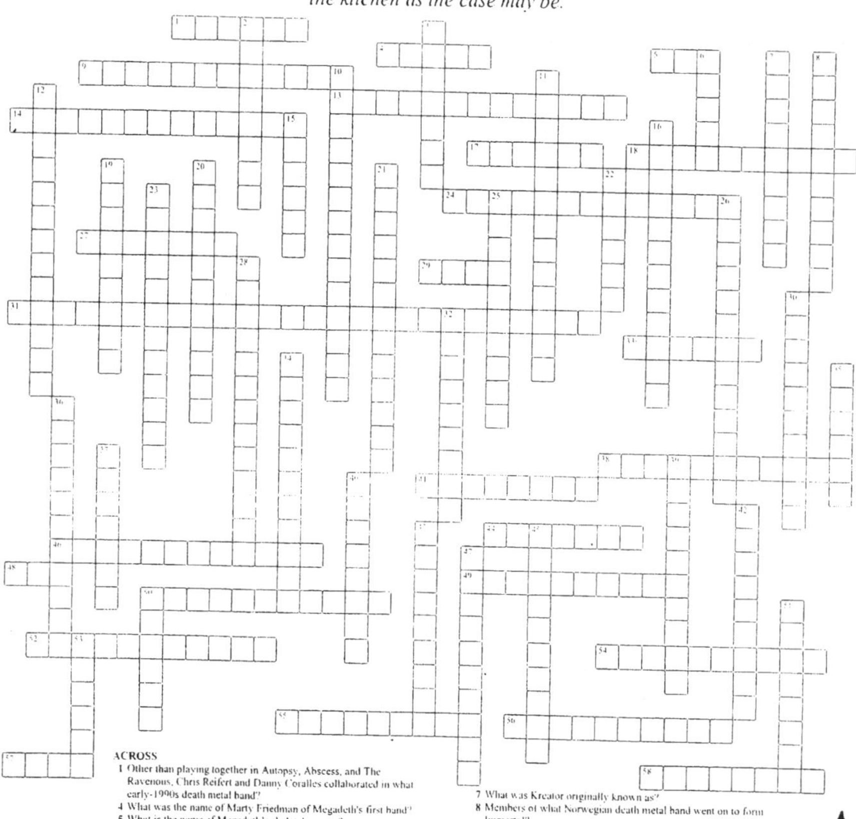

ACROSS

1 Other than playing together in Autopsy, Abscess, and The Ravenous, Chris Reifert and Danny Coralles collaborated in what early-1990s death metal band?

4 What was the name of Marty Friedman of Megadeth's first band?

5 What is the name of Megadeth's skeletal mascot?

9 What record label put out the compilation that Napalm Death's first official track was released on (two words)?

13 The chorus to "Ride the Sky" from Helloween is essentially the same as the chorus from what song from Razor which was released one year before (three words)?

14 What is the name of Nuclear Holocausto's post-Beherit ambient project (two words)?

17 What is the repeated, backwards message at the beginning of Slayer's "Hell Awaits" (two words)?

18 Formed in 1977, who were one of the first (if not the first) entirely African-American heavy metal bands (two words)?

24 Who replaced Ace Frehley in KISS after the "Creatures of the Night" lp (two words)?

27 What is the name of Dawn Crosby's pre-Fear of God thrash band?

29 Complete the following Bulldozer lyric: "Another ________, it's what I need."

31 What does NWOBHM stand for (six words)?

33 What was Death originally known as?

38 Who produced Possessed's "Eyes of Horror" ep (two words)?

41 D.D. Crazy from Sarcofago went on to form what band?

44 The drummer on Death's "Scream Bloody Gore" lp later went on to form what band?

46 What was the full, longer band name that Slayer initially considered using?

48 Justin Broderick of Godflesh played guitar on which side of Napalm Death's "Scum" lp?

49 From what band's lp layout did Necro Schizma photocopy the baphomet image they used on their Erupted Evil demo (two words)?

50 According to the official police report, how many times did Varg Vikernes stab Euronymous (two words)?

52 Two of the members of Sacrilege were once part of what classic UK punk band (two words)?

54 Members of what Italian speed metal band went on to form Necrodeath?

55 What band is responsible for the title of this crossword puzzle (Heavy Metal is the Law)?

56 Who was Metal Forces magazine referring to in the following 1983 quote? "They make Venom sound like the Bee Gees."

57 In 1975, what band checked out Pentagram at their rehearsal space to see if they had "the potential to be a national act"?

58 Sepultura's first vinyl release was a split lp with whom?

DOWN

2 What was the demo version of Metallica's "Four Horsemen" called?

3 What were the headbangers at the front of English heavy metal shows known as?

6 Dana Cosley of the all-female death metal band Demonomacy later went on to play with what classic death-prog band?

7 What was Kreator originally known as?

8 Members of what Norwegian death metal band went on to form Immortal?

10 What does the SS in Death SS stand for (two words)?

11 What was the original, not-used title of Exciter's "Violence and Force" lp (two words)?

12 What did Quorthon falsely claim his real name was in the first edition of Lords of Chaos (two words)?

15 Debbie Gunn of Sentinel Beast briefly sang for what all-female Swedish speed metal band (two words)?

16 What band did Rob Halford of Judas Priest perform live, lead vocals for on November 14th and 15th of 1992 (two words)?

19 Who authored the quote on Eddy's tombstone on the "Live After Death" lp cover (last name only)?

20 The lead singer of what band created Hirax's logo (two words)?

21 What is the name of Glenn Tipton's pre-Judas Priest hard rock band (three words)?

22 Brett Ericksen of Dark Angel previously played guitar for what thrash band?

23 Which mid-1980s thrash band had identical twin brothers in it (two words)?

25 "Piseň Pro Satana" from Root has essentially the same guitar line as the guitar line from what Bathory song?

26 George Emanuelle III is the much-less-cool real name of what guitarist (two words)?

28 What was the name of Quorthon's pre-Bathory oi band?

30 Voivod's "Fuck Off and Die" track was written in response to a contractual dispute with what record label (two words)?

32 From what Canadian town was Blasphemy banned from playing due to show violence?

34 Who played the guitar leads on Septic Death's "Kichigai" ep (two words)?

35 Terri Heggen of the all-female death metal band Derketa went on to play with which other all-female death metal band?

36 Who headlined the 1991 Grindcrusher Tour (two words)?

37 The vocalist/bassist of what band did the inner gatefold artwork for Axegrinder's "Rise of the Serpent Men" lp?

39 Iron Maiden's 1979 demos were also known as the ________ tapes?

40 What band's early line-up included Kerry King of Slayer and Greg Handevidt of Kublai Khan?

42 The U.S. band Genocide later changed its name to what?

43 King Diamond's pre-Mercyful Fate band was called what (two words)?

45 Who is the first Earache Records release by (two words)?

47 In November of 1984, two bands named Slayer had a battle of the bands in Texas to determine who would keep the name. The losing band changed their name to S.A. Slayer. What does the S.A. stand for (two words)?

50 What was Saint Vitus originally known as?

51 What was the name of Hank Shermann's pre-Mercyful Fate punk band (two words)?

53 What was Kirk Hammet's pre-Metallica thrash band?

Side Dishes

BBQ Greens

Music: Tyrant-1978 rehearsals (1978)

2 lbs fresh greens (chard, spinach, or collards)
1 medium onion, chopped
3 cloves garlic, minced
1 can tomatoes, drained and chopped
2 Tbsp maple syrup or mo-lasses
2 Tbsp cider vinegar
2 Tbsp soy sauce
1 tsp paprika
1 tsp ground cumin
2 Tbsp olive oil

Saute the onion and garlic in a large saucepan for 5 minutes. Add the remaining ingredients (except the greens) and simmer partially covered for 15-20 minutes, or until the sauce thickens. Add the greens and cook 5-10 more minutes, or until the greens are cooked through. Serve over brown rice.

Brian's Carolina Curried Sweet Potatoes and Peas

Music: Fatal-A Somber Evocation of Nihilism ep (1990)

2 large sweet potatoes
1 large onion, chopped
4 cups thawed frozen green peas
1 can of diced tomatoes with liquid
1 tsp cinnamon
2 tsp curry powder
Fresh grated ginger
Sea salt to taste

Preheat the oven to 375° F. Cook the potatoes in the oven until tender but still firm (about 40-45 minutes). When they cool enough, peel and dice. Saute the onion in a large skillet. Stir in the remaining ingredients and simmer over low heat for about 15 minutes.

Everything is going to become unimaginably worse, and never get better again.

Kurt Vonnegut

Cold Chinese Noodles in Peanut-Sesame Sauce (aka "Wait, Does Anyone Remember if the Cold Noodles are Vegan or Not?" Noodles)

Music: Loss-Life Without Hope...Death Without Reason demo (2004)

These are the noodles. The ones that every time you go out to eat at a Chinese restaurant someone asks "are the cold noodles vegan?" Everyone looks at each other, but no one really knows. Someone asks the waitstaff. They don't know. "Maybe, maybe not," he or she says. Frustrated, everyone skips the appetizers and goes ahead and orders or one person orders them and everyone watches him or her eat them uncomfortably. Why don't you avoid the hassle and just make them at home?

The recipe makes 1 quart. Dressing will keep well indefinitely in the refrigerator. Use about 2-4 heaping Tbsp of dressing per pound of noodles.

1 lb Chinese-style noodles (or any thin spaghetti/fettucini-type pasta)
2 Tbsp dark sesame oil

DRESSING:

6 Tbsp peanut butter
1/4 cup water
3 Tbsp light soy sauce
6 Tbsp dark soy sauce
6 Tbsp tahini
1/2 cup dark sesame oil
2 Tbsp sherry
4 tsp rice wine vinegar
1/4 cup maple syrup
4 medium cloves garlic, minced
2 tsp minced fresh ginger
1-2 Tbsp hot pepper oil
1/2 cup hot water

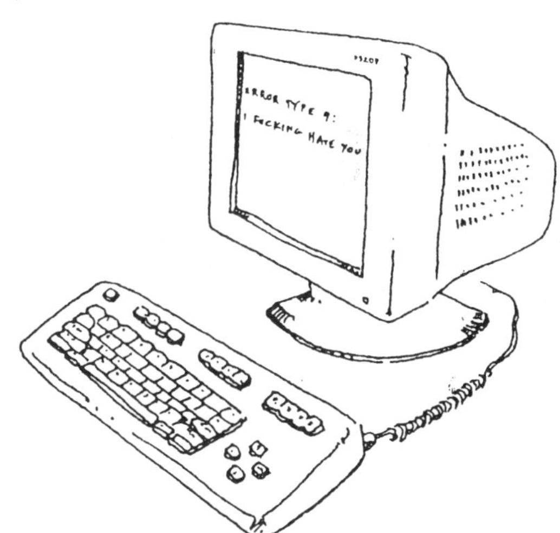

Cook noodles in large pot of boiling unsalted water over medium heat until barely tender and still firm. Drain immediately and rinse with cold water until cold. Drain well and toss noodles with (2 Tbsp) dark sesame oil so they don't stick together.

For the dressing, combine all ingredients except hot water in a blender or food processor and blend until smooth. Thin with hot water to consistency of whipping cream.

Just before serving, toss noodles with sauce. Garnish with cucumber, peanuts, green onion, and carrot curls. Serve at room temperature.

Grandmere Patty's Johnny Cake

Music: Azhubham Haani-On a Snowy Winter Night demo (1992)

The best cornbread I ever ate. Thanks Grandmere!

1½ cups corn meal
½ cup flour
1 tsp sea salt
1 tsp baking soda
1 tsp baking powder
1/3 cup sugar

Mix together. Pre-heat the oven to 425° F. Then mix the following ingredients separately and add to the above mixture:

2 Tbsp melted margarine
1 cup sour soy milk (1 cup soy milk + 2 tsp lemon juice)
1 egg's worth of egg replacer

You have the two mixtures mixed together? Now, put 1 Tbsp of margarine into an 8" X 8" dish and put the dish in the oven until the margarine is melted and bubbling. Take the dish out, pour the cornbread mixture in, put it back in the oven, and bake for 20-25 minutes. Let it cool off and consume with chili.

Cuban Black Market Beans

Music: Merciless-Beyond the Black Door demo (1988)

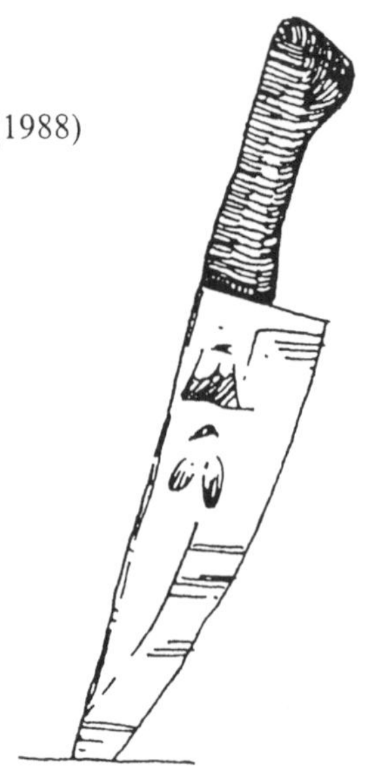

½ lb dried black beans
1 medium onion, finely chopped
½ small green pepper, finely chopped
4-5 cloves garlic, minced
A little oregano
1-2 bay leaves
½ tsp ground cumin
A medium spoonful Dijon mustard
1 Tbsp dark, strong-flavored vinegar
Red wine to taste
¼ cup pimentos, finely chopped
½ tsp cayenne
Sea salt to taste
1 vegetable bouillon cube
1 1" piece of kombu (sea vegetable)

Wash and soak the beans overnight in enough water to cover them. The next day, saute the onion and green pepper until soft. Add the black beans, along with the soaking water. Add the remaining ingredients, stir well, cover, and cook until the beans are soft. Serve over rice with chopped onions on top and a good smoke.

Ellie the Judas Priestess' Drunken Beans

Music: Candlemass-Epicus Doomicus Metallicus lp (1986)

Saute until onions are translucent, approximately 10 minutes:

1 Tbsp vegetable oil
1 cup chopped onions
2 cloves garlic, minced
1/4 tsp salt

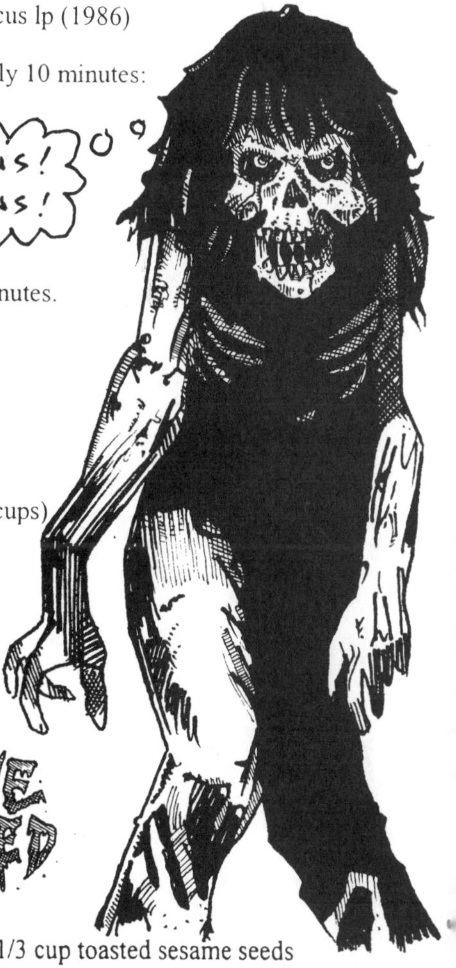

Add 1 tsp ground cumin and cook 1-2 more minutes.

Now add:

12 oz amber beer (i.e., Dos Equis)
2 tsp packed brown sugar
15 oz can rinsed and drained pintos (1½ cups)
14.5 oz can tomatoes with juice, chopped (1¾ cups)
2-3 tsp chipotle adobo sauce
2 tsp soy sauce

Simmer gently about 20 minutes, uncovered.

Eggless Egg Salad

Music: SWANS-Filth lp (1983)

First, the salad:

¾ lb firm tofu
3 minced scallions (white and greens)
1 medium carrot, grated
1 stalk celery, finely minced
1 small bell pepper, finely minced
1/3 cup toasted sesame seeds
Sea salt, to taste
Black pepper, to taste
Soy sauce, to taste

Cut the tofu into dice-sized bits. Add all of the other ingredients except the "to taste" ones. Mix gently. Add the nayonaise (see recipe below). Now, season to taste and mix once again. Chill and serve.

Second, the nayonaise

¼ lb tofu
2 tsp sesame oil
2 Tbsp cider vinegar
½ tsp dry mustard
½ tsp sea salt
½ cup peanut or vegetable oil

Whip together the first 5 ingredients in a blender or food processor. Keep the machine going and gradually drizzle in the oil. When all the oil is in there, turn off the machine. You should have a creamy, eggless nayonaise ready to add to the salad.

Frankenbeans

Music: Impetigo-Horror of the Zombies lp (1992)

1 16 oz can pinto beans, drained
1/3 cup ketchup
2 vegan hot dogs, sliced into ¼" rounds
1 Tbsp soy sauce
1 Tbsp light mo-lasses
1 tsp brown rice vinegar or balsamic vinegar
½ tsp onion powder
¼ tsp dry mustard
Several drops liquid smoke

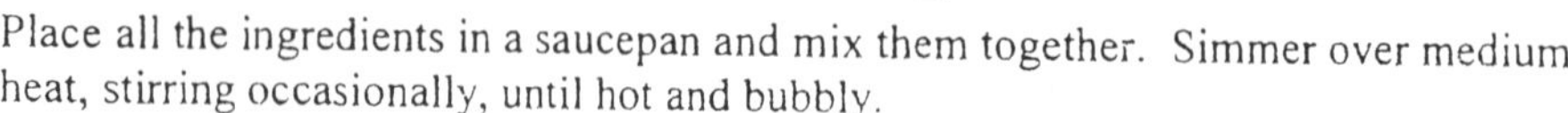

Place all the ingredients in a saucepan and mix them together. Simmer over medium heat, stirring occasionally, until hot and bubbly.

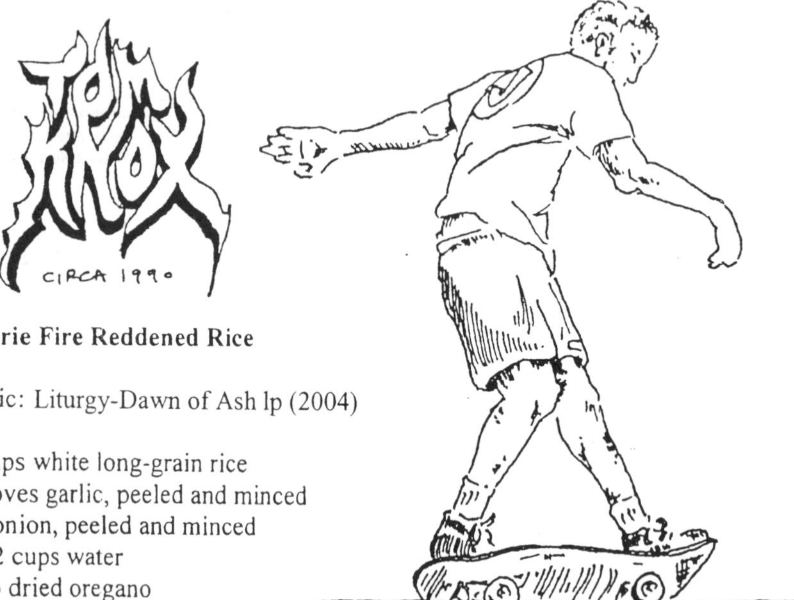

Prairie Fire Reddened Rice

Music: Liturgy-Dawn of Ash lp (2004)

2 Cups white long-grain rice
2 cloves garlic, peeled and minced
1/2 onion, peeled and minced
4 1/2 cups water
1 tsp dried oregano
1 tsp cumin
1 Tbsp minced fresh marjoram leaves
1/3 cup chile powder
1 tsp sea salt

The theory that it degenerates just doesn't hold a truth.
Can't you see the theorists malcontented?
All they need is just to skate and be left alone.
The future's fine, it'll not be circumvented.

In a large pan or skillet over low heat, saute 2 cloves garlic and onion in a tablespoon or so of water, until soft and beginning to dry. Add rice and increase heat to medium-high; dry-toast until golden brown, stirring frequently. Add water and all remaining ingredients, bring to a boil, and cook for two minutes.
Reduce the heat to low, cover, and simmer for 20 to 25 minutes until the water has just evaporated. Remove from heat and let stand five minutes. Fluff up with a wooden spoon.

Rosemary's Potatoes

Music: Witches Hammer-Fuckin' Rights demo (1987)

A whole bunch of small, red new potatoes
Fresh rosemary
Green onions
Garlic cloves
Olive oil

Preheat the oven to 450°F.

Wash the potatoes and cut them into large chunks (leave the skins on, eh?). Put them on a baking sheet (a sheet with sides, that is...you don't want to use a perfectly flat cookie sheet). Slice the green onions and sprinkle them on the potatoes. Cut the rosemary off the branch with scissors directly onto the potatoes. Peel and add your desired number of whole garlic cloves (I say lots). Sprinkle it all with olive oil and stir it all around to coat. Roast it all in the oven for 15 minutes. Remove it, toss it all around, and put it back in the oven for another 20 minutes or until done (tossing more if need be). Phenominal.

There are times when one would like to hang the whole human race, and finish the farce.
Samuel Longhorne Clemens

Zack's Black Bean Artichokehold Spread

Music: Brodequin-Methods of Execution lp (2004)

1 can black beans
1 can artichoke hearts or two of the little jars (preferably not in brine...it's too salty)
Oregano
sea salt
3 cloves garlic, crushed
Black pepper
Basil
Olive oil

Heat up the garlic in a bit of olive oil. Drain the can of black beans and add them in. Mash up the beans and cook for about 6-7 minutes on low heat. Cut up the artichoke hearts and mix them in. Continue mashing while adding about a tsp of oregano. Cook for another 10-12 minutes on low heat and add in the salt and pepper to taste. When it smells good and is cooked into a thick paste, it's done.

Now what to do with it? In another pan, cook a few cut up plum tomatoes in a dash of balsamic vinegar and add in some sea salt, pepper, and a pinch of turbinado sugar. Cook for a few minutes or until warm. Spread the bean mixture onto a bagel or toast and put the tomatoes on top. Consume.

Joe's Ultimate Mashed Potatoes

Music: Minutemen-Bean Spill ep (1982; I'm letting Joe slide here with the metal recommendation)

Massive thanks to Mr. Joe Biel for making this cookbook possible. For seeking me out, for encouraging me to put the book together, for taking the time, effort, and money to press and distribute the book, and for offering technical and emotional support all along the way. I can't tell you how much it all means to me. Thanks, man.

One pile of potatoes
Garlic
Vegenaise (the all-important secret ingredient)
Margarine
Soy milk
Braggs liquid aminos
Nutritional yeast
Sea salt
Pepper
Cumin

Vegenaise is an integral part of making many things (like garlic bread).

Scrub your potatoes but leave the skins. Cut them into 1" pieces and put them all in a large pot of water and get it up to a boil. Cut up the garlic real tiny while the potatoes are cooking and toss it in there too. Play ping pong or watch a good documentary to pass the time while the potatoes get soft. Check your potatoes by sticking a fork in them and seeing if it's difficult to stab them. Once they are soft, strain the potatoes and garlic and get rid of all of the water. Mix in a healthy amount of vegenaise. Add soy milk and mix until you've reached the desired amount of creaminess. Add all other ingredients and continue mixing until they are nicely whipped. If it's not delicious, you didn't add enough vegenaise. Vegans needn't be afraid to put on a few pounds, anyway.

White Bean and Sun-Dried Tomato Pate

Music: Asphyx-Mutilating Process ep (1989)

1 Tbsp olive oil
1 large onion, chopped
2 cloves garlic, minced
1½ cups well-cooked navy beans
¼ cup oil-cured sun-dried tomatoes
Juice of ½ lemon
1 sprig parsley
¼ tsp each: dried thyme, summer savory, sea salt
Freshly ground black pepper to taste

Heat the oil in a skillet. Add the onion and saute over medium heat until translucent. Add the garlic and continue to saute until the onion is just beginning to brown. Combine the onion mixture with all the remaining ingredients except the salt and pepper in a blender and puree until completely smooth. Drizzle with 2 Tbsp water or so, to loosen the consistency if need be. Stop and scrape down the sides as necessary. Season to taste with salt and pepper and serve on crackers or French bread.

Scalped Potatoes

Music: Necrobutcher-Schizophrenic Christianity demo (1989)

1 tsp olive oil
1 white onion, finely chopped
4 cloves garlic, minced
¼ cup tahini
2 Tbsp whole wheat flour
1 tsp sea salt
1 cup water
5 medium white potatoes

Preheat the oven to 400°F. Heat the oil in a skillet and saute the onion and garlic on medium-high heat until the onion is soft and translucent. In a blender or bowl, mix together the tahini, flour, salt, and water. The mixture will be watery. Don't worry about it like I did...it'll thicken upon cooking.

Thinly slice the potatoes. I didn't peel them, but I guess that's up to you and the amount of effort you want to put into it. Arrange the potatoes in a lightly oiled baking dish, overlapping them to cover the bottom of the dish. Spoon the onion and garlic mixture on top of the potato slices. Pout tahini sauce over the top. Cover and bake for 1 hour. Uncover and bake for another 5-10 minutes, or until golden brown.

Vegan Deep-Friedness

Music: Pestilence-Consuming Impulse lp (1989)

1/2 cup TVP
1 Tbsp vegetarian "chicken" bouillon powder
1/2 cup vegan pancake mix, dry (approximately)
2/3 cup crushed cornflakes (approximately)
Sea salt, pepper, other seasonings
Oil for frying

Put 1/2 cup hot water in a bowl. Stir in bouillon powder. Soak TVP in this liquid for 10 minutes. Mix in just enough pancake mix to make a cohesive mixture that can be formed into patties. Mix in salt, pepper, and other seasonings to taste. Put crushed cornflakes in a plate. Dip patties into cornflakes, covering them completely. Heat some oil on medium heat in a heavy frying pan. Fry patties in oil until crispy, turning occasionally.

You gotta eat them hot. Serve with a creamy sauce (perhaps the Golden Dawn Gravy or Super Savory Sauce, see recipes this book), and mashed or oven-fried potatoes.

Spider's Edamame Humus

Music: Alice Coltraine-Universal Consciousness lp (1971)

1 16 oz bag frozen, shelled edamame
1/2 cup canola or other vegetable oil
1/2 cup rice vinegar
2´scallions
Ginger
Sea salt and pepper

Cook the edamame for 5 minutes in boiling water, then drain. While the edamame are cooking, coarsely chop the scallions, then peel and chop the ginger. Put the ginger and scallions in a blender and pulverize. Add the edamame, oil, and vinegar and blend for a minute or two.

Add salt and pepper to taste, and more rice vinegar if it needs some extra zip.

"Now I'm Fucking Pissed" Refried Beans

Music: Bulldozer-The Day of Wrath lp (1984)

So I was making the cheese dip recipe on a Friday afternoon. I was hungry. I had just used up most of my nutritional yeast ($$$) for the recipe. I hit mix on the blender. Then it happened...I didn't screw the bottom of the blender on correctly the last time I had used it...cheese dip mix sprayed everywhere...the carpet, the counter I had just spent a half hour cleaning, the clean dishes. Needless to say, I was pissed. After screaming self-depreciating comments and curses for a good 15 minutes, I cleaned the mess up and made up this recipe instead, salvaging the ingredients I could from the botched cheese dip recipe. Delicious.

1 can vegetarian refried beans
2-3 bottled jalapenos, minced
3-4 Tbsp red bell pepper, minced
2 Tbsp tahini
1 Tbsp soy sauce
1 Tbsp nutritional yeast
½ Tbsp onion powder
½ Tbsp cumin
½ Tbsp chili powder
Two frustrated shakes hot sauce
Several drops super hot sauce (Dave's Insanity Sauce, etc.)
Two angry shakes liquid smoke

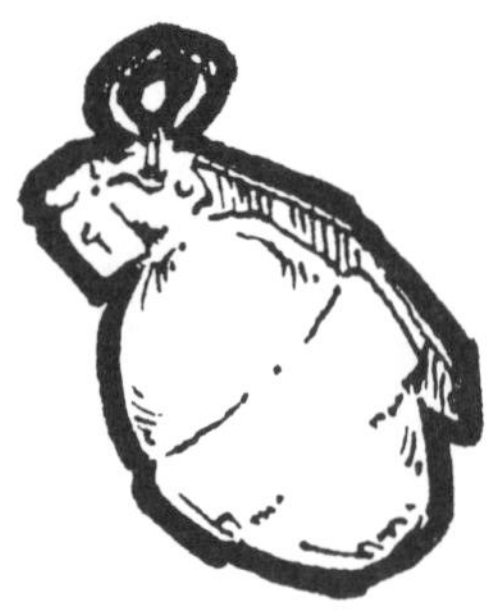

Mix all ingredients together in some sort of pot. Heat it all up. Serve as a dip for chips, burrito filler, taco salad topping, or just throw it at the fucking wall.

Hummous, Reinvented and Rejuvenated by Dave

Music: Athiest-Hell Hath No Fury demo (1987)

2 15 oz cans of garbanzo beans
About six large, fresh spinach leaves
6 cloves garlic, peeled
1 tsp seas salt
1 Tbsp red pepper flakes
1 Tbsp oregano
½ tsp garlic powder
½ tsp cayenne
½ tsp paprika
½ tsp black pepper
The juice of 1 lemon
2-3 Tbsp tahini
1 cup water (or reserved bean liquid)
4/5 Tbsp olive oil for frying

Alright, this require a lot more ingredients than usual but it's just as quick. Put the oil in a large frying pan and turn up the heat near high. Strain the garbanzo beans in a colander (save the liquid if you want to use it instead of water later on...it makes for a richer flavor). Peel the garlic if you haven't done so already. The oil should be pretty hot by now, so dump in the garlic and let it fry for a couple minutes. Now add the garbanzo beans. Sprinkle the salt, red pepper, cayenne, garlic powder, paprika, and black pepper over the beans and mix it all up. Continue stirring occasionally until the beans are soft (5, maybe 10 minutes). Add in the spinach for the last minute or two of cooking. Pour about half of the mixture into a blender. Add the lemon juice, tahini, and about half a cup of water or bean liquid. Blend it until it is smooth and creamy. Put in the rest of the beans and continue to blend, adding a small amount of water or bean liquid when necessary until the dip is smooth, creamy, and the consistency you want it to be. Keep it refrigerated if you don't eat it right away. Serve warm or cold with bagels, raw vegetables, pita, falafels, and whatever else you can think of.

Breaking the Slaw

Music: Judas Priest-Rocka Rolla (1974)

1/3 vegan sour cream
2 Tbsp vegan mayonnaise
2 tsp maple syrup
1 tsp ground mustard
1 tsp celery seed
¼ tsp sea salt
Black pepper
3 cups green cabbage, shredded
1/3 cup carrot, shredded

Mix the first seven ingredients in a large bowl until smooth. Add the cabbage and carrots and toss until the vegetables are fully coated. Let chill in the refrigerator until ready to serve.

Leeks With a Drinking Problem

Music: Tankard-The Morning After lp (1988)

6-8 small leeks, trimmed and washed
1 clove garlic, crushed
1/2 cup red wine
1 tsp red wine vinegar
2 Tbsp parsley, chopped
2 Tbsp margarine
Dash sea salt
Black pepper

War metal drinkers
Pure satanic fukkers
War metal drinkers
Alcohol will crush posers

Barbatos

Melt the margarine and cook the leeks and garlic for 3 minutes over medium heat. Add the red wine and some salt and mix well. Cover and cook for 15 more minutes or until leeks are tender.

Place the leeks on a serving dish and reduce the liquid left in the pan for 2 minutes. Add the vinegar and pepper to taste. Pour over the leeks and garnish with parsley.

Rising from the darkness where Hell hath no mercy and the screams of vengeance echo on forever, only those who keep the faith shall escape the wrath of the Metallian...

Wino Weinkraut

Music: Saint Vitus-Thirsty and Miserable 12" (1987)

1 small onion, grated
¼ cup margarine
2 Tbsp brown sugar
1/2 tsp sea salt
1 tsp cider vinegar
1½ cups dry white wine (not red)
1 cup vegetable broth
1 small potato, grated
1 quart sauerkraut, drained
2 green apples (Granny Smith), peeled, cored, and diced

Saute the onion in the margarine in the bottom of a large pot. Once the onion is tender, add in the brown sugar and let it melt. Dump in the salt, vinegar, wine, broth, potato, and kraut and let it cook uncovered over medium heat for about 30 minutes. Add in the green apples and let it cook at least another 30 minutes…it's really best to let it stew a couple hours. Eat on vegan bratwurst with one liter of your favorite Oktoberfest brew.

Andalusian Wild Asparagus

Music: Wormed-Planisphaerium lp (2003)

This recipe is from the south of Spain (Seville) and it is typically Mediterranean. Yes, saffron is very expensive. Omit it if you don't have any "lying around."

2 bunches wild asparagus
1 Tbsp white flour
1 slice of bread
2 garlic cloves
White wine
Saffron
White pepper
Cumin
Olive oil
Sea salt

Cook the asparagus in bunches.

While they are cooking, fry the garlic cloves and the bread in a frying pan with olive oil until they brown. Then, drain them and place them into a mortar to crush them with the saffron, the cumin, a tablespoon of the oil used for frying and a little of water to thin it down.

Brown the flour in the frying pan and slowly add water, wine and the mix from the mortar to make a sauce. Season it with salt and pepper and let it boil for a few minutes. When the asparagus is cooked, place it on a dish and cover with the sauce.

Method Air Matt's Arnabit (Burned Cauliflower and Tahini Sauce)

Music: Eudoxis-Attack from Above demo (1985)

Cut cauliflower into medium sized flowerettes. Heat a pan on medium high and add olive oil and cauliflower. Add sea salt and pepper to taste. Heat for 7 minutes, only stirring once. Reduce heat to low-medium, and cover for about 8 minutes. Turn it up to medium-high, stir once, add more salt and pepper and cook until mostly burned.

Sauce:

Tahini
Water
Lemon juice
Garlic powder

Start with Tahini, add lemon juice and garlic powder and mix well. Slowly add water until it becomes a sauce like consistency. Everyone likes this sauce different so you have to play with the amounts. Pour an "extreme" amount of it over the cauliflower pieces. Eat until sick.

Springtime Rolls

Music: Mythic-Mourning in the Winter Solstice ep (1993)

2 cups Chinese cabbage, shredded
1 cup bamboo shoots
1 cup sliced water chestnuts
¾ lb bean sprouts
1 cup chopped tofu
1 package eggless pastry wrappers
5 Tbsp sesame oil
1 Tbsp minced fresh ginger
1 clove garlic, minced
¼ tsp black pepper
1½ Tbsp soy sauce
1½ tsp sea salt
1½ Tbsp ground coriander
4 cups oil for frying

In a wok or big pan heat the sesame oil, then add the garlic, ginger, and black pepper. Cover and cook on medium heat for 10 minutes. Add the cabbage and fry for three more minutes. Add the bamboo shoots, water chestnuts, and tofu. Fry three more minutes. Add the bean sprouts, salt, coriander, and soy sauce. Fry two more minutes. Put it all in a colander to drain excess juices.

Heat the 4 cups oil in a pot or wok.

Unwrap the pastry. Have a small bowl of water handy to seal the pastries. In the center of each pastry put 4 tbsp stuffing. Fold the sides over towards the center, roll, and seal. Repeat with all 12 rolls.

Oil should be very hot by now. Fry each roll on each side for 30 seconds or until reddish brown. Drain on paper towels.

Herbed Corn, Roasted and Blackened on the Cob

Music: Expulser-The Unholy One lp (1992)

4 ears of corn, with the husk still on
¼ cup margarine, softened to room temperature
¼ tsp basil
½ tsp oregano
¼ tsp sea salt
¼ tsp pepper

MARMOTA FLAVIVENTRIS

Soak the corn (with the husk still on) in ice water for an hour. Get the grill going in the meantime.

Peel back but do not remove the husks from the corn. Remove the corn silk. In a small bowl, blend together the margarine, basil, oregano, salt, and pepper. Spread ¼ of the herbed margarine on each ear of corn, then close the husk back up over the corn.

Throw the corn directly on the grill and cook until the husk is blackened on the outside and the corn is tender on the inside.

Bumblebee Salad

Music: Sigh-Desolation demo (1990)

2 cans of black beans (16 oz) drained and rinsed
1 10 oz package frozen corn
1 red bell pepper, chopped
1 green bell pepper, chopped
1 Vidalia onion, chopped
2 cloves garlic, minced
¼ cup balsamic vinegar
1 Tbsp to ¼ cup olive oil
1 Tbsp each: fresh thyme, fresh tarragon, and/or fresh dill or sweet basil

Combine all ingredients and chill. Will keep up to two weeks in the refrigerator.

Cannonball Cabbage Salad with Hellfire Peanuts

Music: Omen-Battle Cry lp (1984)

1/3 cup sesame oil
1/3 cup rice wine vinegar
½ cup soy sauce
¼ cup sugar
2 Tbsp fresh ginger, minced
1 tsp fresh chili pepper, minced
Sea salt and freshly cracked white pepper
2-3 Tbsp Tabasco sauce
1 cup unsalted peanuts, shelled and hulled
1 Tbsp vegetable oil
½ head Napa cabbage, outer leaves removed, inner leaves washed and sliced into thin strips
1 cup loosely packed cilantro leaves
3 scallions, white part and bottom 2" of green portion, thinly sliced
1 medium-size carrot, peeled and cut into very thin strips

In a small bowl, combine sesame oil, vinegar, soy sauce, sugar, ginger, chili pepper, and sea salt and pepper to taste. Whisk together and set aside.

In another small bowl, combine peanuts, Tabasco sauce, and vegetable oil, and mix well. Spread peanuts on a small, ungreased baking sheet and roast in a 350° F oven until nicely browned…probably 12-15 minutes. When done, chop roughly.

In a large bowl, combine cabbage, cilantro, scallions, and carrots. Stir the dressing well, then pour on just enough to moisten the ingredients. Toss and coat. There will probably be sauce left over, so you'll have to be creative and find something to put it on. Dump the peanuts over the top and serve.

After a while he pointed to the building and asked...

"What does it look like to you? Like a senseless mess? Like a chance collection of driftwood? Like an imbecile chaos? But is it, Mr. Roark? Do you see no method? You who know the language of structure and the meaning of form. Do you see no purpose here?"

"I see none in discussing it."

"Mr. Roark, we're all alone here. Why don't you tell me what you think of me? In any words you wish. No one will hear us."

"But I don't think of you."

Ayn Rand

Aloo Paratha (Potato-Filled Flat Bread)

Music: Angel Reaper-Végzet Utolér demo (1989)

2 cups chapati four (Indian wheat flour), or 1 cup whole wheat flour and 1 cup unbleached flour, plus extra flour for rolling
½ tsp sea salt
1 Tbsp olive oil
½ to ¾ cup water
3 medium potatoes, peeled, boiled, and mashed
1 small onion, minced
3 to 4 Tbsp cilantro, chopped
1 Tbsp ground cumin
½ tsp sea salt
1 tsp garam masala (see notes)

Combine flour and ½ tsp sea salt in a medium mixing bowl. Stir together 1 Tbsp olive oil and ½ cup water, and add water to the flour. Stir, and add just enough additional water to form a soft dough. Knead for about 5 minutes (the dough should be very soft and spongy). Cover the dough and allow it to rest for about 20 minutes.

To make the filling, combine cooked, mashed potatoes, onion, cilantro, cumin, ½ tsp sea salt, and garam masala in a medium mixing bowl. Mix well. Set aside.

Divide dough into 12 equal balls. Using enough flour to prevent sticking, roll each ball into a flat circle about ¼" thick. Spoon about 2 to 3 Tbsp of potato filling in the middle. Bring up the sides over the top of the filling and pinch together. Very carefully roll out the dough again to be about ¼" thick (be careful not to let the filling burst out of the dough).

Heat a dry, large, non-stick skillet or cast iron griddle on low-medium heat. Place the paratha on the hot skillet and cook until bubbles form on top. This happens fast, so watch the bread closely. Brush the top of the bread with olive oil, turn, and cook the other side until lightly browned. Remove to a warm place (cover with a clean towel to keep the breads from drying out) and repeat with the remaining paratha.

I was walking down a dirt road at night...the moon was out. It was quiet, I think, which was unusual for the woods at night with all the nocturnal creatures typically scurrying about. For some reason, I sensed that something was coming down the road from around the bend. I quickly crawled into the bushes alongside the road and watched to see what it was that was traveling this late at night. I waited for a few moments. Suddenly, without any warning, I felt something heavy slam over my head, as if someone has jumped on top of me from behind. The weight was hot and stifling...too massive to be human. I was completely immobilized by the weight and could not struggle free. Suddenly, I felt the head of the beast swing down to my midsection and rip me open with its teeth. I felt its muzzle pushing into my stomach, violently twitching as it ravaged through my entrails. The initial shock of the ambush intensified into a muted feeling of terror as I realized that my assailant was a bear. I remember feeling my blood spilling out and soaking my clothes. It was hot, very hot...and sticky. Though I still couldn't see what was going on, I remember confusedly trying to push my innards back in. My consciousness was waning, yet somehow I knew that if I tried hard enough I could struggle out. I knew I could fight the bear. The bear kept gouging away, its hot breath pounding on my screaming nerves. Slowly, from the back of my mind, I was consumed by the realization that I was approaching the moment of death. For a split second, I knew I could hold onto my life or let it go. As quickly as the feeling of hope appeared, it was gone, and I consciously decided to let my life go. Darkness washed over me and my mind faded to black, just like it did once when I was anesthetized for surgery as a kid. I felt my soul leave the carnage. The bear was gone, the pain was gone, but the darkness remained. For a moment I felt a strong wave of disappointment. I thought about my family, my relatives, my friends, all that I had done in life, and all that I had hoped to do. It was all gone now. Disappointment faded into a terrified state of excitement. I pictured opening my eyes and seeing warm light....comfort...and happiness...finally, happiness. Things were finally going to be okay. I slowly opened my eyes and found myself staring at the cold, grey corner of my ceiling. My heart dropped into the depths of my body. I tried to move but my arms were paralyzed above my head, still immobile from R.E.M sleep. I completely fucking panicked. My chest was heaving, yet I couldn't breathe. My heart nearly exploded as it strained to maintain equilibrium in a state of self-induced chaos. The joints in my left shoulder loosened and my arm swung down and hit me in the face...my finger still stiff and deathly. I really, truly thought I had died. I thought I fucking let my life go...only to be cast back into reality. I cannot describe the terror...*I cannot describe the terror...*the thought that I had given up my life...everything...and that the afterlife was nothing more than a mockery of my previous existence. Now, thinking back, I wish I had died. Then I wouldn't have to get up every morning afterwards knowing that all the people in my life, all the things I've done, and all the things I hope to do don't mean enough to keep me from giving up my life in a desperate situation.

Sometimes I truly hate myself.

And I still have trouble falling asleep.

Your own aggression generates the dreams you dread. Benediction

Jen's "Best Goddamned Chocolate Pie You Will Ever Eat"

Music: Sacrifice-Forward to Termination lp (1987)

CRUST:

(1) 1¼ cup whole wheat flour
¼ cup Dutch cocoa
¼ tsp baking soda
(2) ½ cup brown sugar or Sucanat
¼ cup vegan margarine
2 Tbsp peanut butter
(3) ½ Tbsp vanilla
1 Tbsp water

Mix together (1) in a small bowl. Mix (2) together really well in a big bowl, then add (1). Now add in (3). It's easiest to mix this all up with your (clean) hands. Just get in there and mash it all up until it's of a gooey ball consistency.

Then press into a big, oiled pie plate (not one of them dinky ones) until up to the edges of the pie plate is filled. Flute the edges (make them wavy) for a fancy effect, then pop it in the oven at 375° F for 8-10 minutes. Let it cool completely before filling it full of:

FILLING:

3 cups pressed medium tofu (I just wrap it up in a towel and put a heavy frying pan on top of it for a while)
1 cup + 1 Tbsp melted vegan margarine
1½ cups sugar
¾ cup Dutch cocoa
2 tsp vanilla
¼ tsp sea salt
1-2 Tbsp soy milk

You'll need a good blender for this. Or if, like me, you have a shitty one, you'll have to keep stopping it, mixing the ingredients around with a chopstick, then starting it again. Either way, blend the ingredients using the liquid to help blend the tofu. Try to blend it as thick as possible while getting it as creamy as possible. When it's as smooth as you can get it (no granular bits left), pour it into the completely cooled pie shell. If you're feeling really fancy, melt some vegan chocolate chips mixed with a bit of soymilk and vanilla, in a metal bowl set over a pan full of boiling water. Dip in strawberries until the berries are coated with chocolate. Then, put the strawberries (pointing inward) around the pie. Then shave some dark chocolate onto the middle of the pie. Make sure to do this stuff *after* the pie has set in the refrigerator for a couple of hours. Then, refrigerate for a couple more hours (4-6 hours total). Finally, eat the best goddamned chocolate pie you will ever eat.

Eric's Pie Crust

Music: Mythra-Death and Destiny ep (1979)

Straight out of Soy Not Oi!

1 cup vegetable shortening
¼ cup boiling water
2 cups unbleached flour
A pinch of sea salt
A splash of soy milk

In a medium sized bowl add the shortening and slowly mix in the boiling water until it has a mayonnaise-like consistency. You likely won't need to use all of the water. Add the soy milk and salt. Add flour by the cup and stir with a fork.

Take a sponge and wet the counter down. Lay one sheet of wax paper on the damp surface...this anchors the wax paper. Throw some four on the wax paper and put the dough in the middle. Squash the dough down with your hands and then four the top of the dough. Put another sheet of wax paper on top of the dough and roll with a rolling pin until the dough is about 1/8" thick.

Carefully take the top sheet of wax paper off and put the pie pan upside-down on the dough. With one hand on the pie pan, use the other to scoop underneath and turn it over quickly. Peel off the wax paper and use a knife to cut around the perimeter of the pan. Flute (make it wavy) the edges to make it easier to serve. You can use the excess dough to make a lattice arrangement on top of whatever you put in the shell.

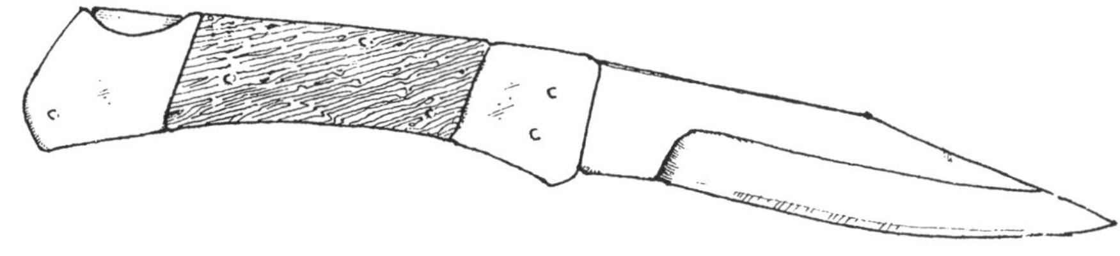

Fat-Free Piecrust

Music: Blitzkrieg-A Time of Changes lp (1985)

1 cup Grape Nuts cereal
1/4 cup apple juice concentrate (undiluted)

Preheat the oven to 350° F.

Mix together the Grape Nuts and apple juice concentrate. Pat into a thin layer on the bottom and sides of a 9" pie pan. Don't worry if there are some gaps. Bake for 8 minutes. Cool before filling.

Strawberry Rhubarb Pie

Music: Fafner-Stycken Hata Kristers Blo demo (1994)

Pie crust, uncooked (see recipe this book)
2 cups washed, hulled, and halved strawberries
4·cups young rhubarb stalks, chopped into ½" pieces
1 1/3 cups sugar
6 Tbsp flour
¼ tsp ground ginger
1½ Tbsp margarine

Preheat the oven to 425° F. In a large bowl, combine strawberries, rhubarb, sugar, four, and ginger; let stand 15 minutes. Dust bottom of pie crust with flour (a tablespoon or so) and pout the filling into the shell. Dot with margarine. Moisten the rim of the bottom crust and cover with a top crust or some sort of lattice arrangement. Seal the edges by crimping all the way around.

Place the pie on a rimmed baking sheet and bake for 20 minutes. Reduce the oven temperature to 400° F and continue baking until the crust is golden brown. Cover the edge of the crust with strips of foil (if necessary) to prevent excessive browning. Serve with vanilla soy ice cream.

Godyammit Pie

Music: Hypnosia-Violent Intensity mlp (1999)

2 medium yams
1/3 cup sugar
3 Tbsp arrowroot powder
1/2 tsp cinnamon
1/4 tsp ginger
1/8 tsp cloves
1/8 tsp sea salt
1-1/2 cups vanilla soymilk
1 fat-free piecrust (see recipe this book, or use a prepared graham cracker crust)

Peel the yams and cut them into 1-inch chunks. Steam in a covered pot over boiling water until tender when pierced with a fork, about 40 minutes. Mash thoroughly. You should have about 2 cups.

Preheat the oven to 350° F.

In a mixing bowl, whisk together the sugar, arrowroot, spices, and sea salt, then stir in the soymilk and mashed yams. Pour into the pre-baked fat-free crust or an unbaked 9" or 10" standard piecrust and bake for 35 minutes. Cool before cutting.

Crunchy Sugar Choco-tomic Bomb Pie

Music: Nuclear Death-Carrion for Worm lp (1991)

3 cups vegan cocoa puffs (I use Finast Cocoa Comets), crushed to make 1½ cups
¼ cup margarine, melted
2 pints chocolate Tofutti, softened
½ cup vegan chocolate fudge ice cream topping (see recipe this book)

Heat oven to 375° F. In a medium bowl, combine 1 cup crushed cereal and margarine. Press into a 9" pie plate. Bake 8 minutes; cool. Spread half of the ice cream over the crust. Drizzle with 1/3 cup fudge topping. Spread on the remaining ice cream. Drizzle with the remaining fudge, then sprinkle with the remaining ½ cup crushed cereal. Freeze at least 3 hours…overnight if possible. Before serving, refrigerate for about 10 minutes to soften slightly.

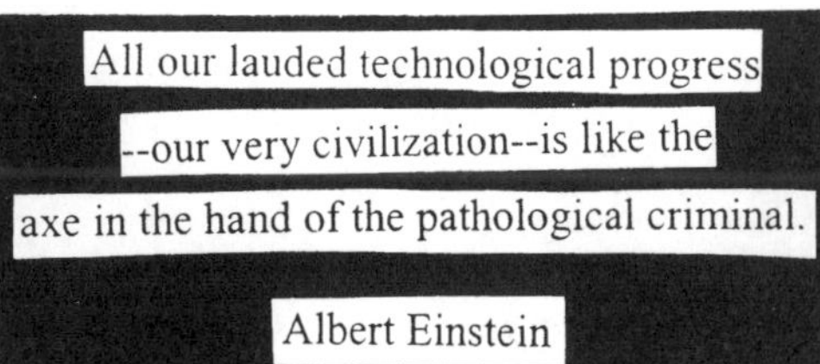

Chai Pie

Music: Jaguar- Power Games lp (1983)

1 ½ cups apple cider
½ cup brewed Assam breakfast tea
3 Tbsp arrowroot
2 Tbsp freshly squeezed lemon juice
2 tsp pure vanilla extract
½ tsp ground cinnamon
½ tsp ground ginger
½ tsp ground cardamom
3 lbs apples, peeled, cored, and sliced
1/3 cup packed dark brown sugar
Prepared or freshly made double-crust 8" pie shell

Boil the cider and tea over high heat until reduced to ½ cup. Allow to cool. Preheat the oven to 450° F. Combine the cooled tea/cider with all of the remaining ingredients except the apples, sugar, and pie crust in a large bowl. Stir well. Put the sliced apples in a separate bowl and coat with the sugar, adding more sugar if necessary to coat the apples thoroughly. Stir the sugar/apple mix into the liquid. Pour everything into the prepared pie crust. Cover with the top crust. Cut slits into the pastry top with a sharp knife. Place the pie on a baking sheet and bake for 15 minutes. Reduce the oven temperature to 350° F and continue to bake the pie until golden brown, about 45 minutes. Serve with vegan whipped cream.

Maple Apple Pie

Music: Mayhem-Deathcrush mlp (1987)

¾ cup crushed gingersnaps (make sure they're vegan)
½ cup turbinado sugar (see notes)
½ cup margarine, melted
½ cup chopped pecans
1 Tbsp all-purpose flour
½ tsp ground cinnamon
1/8 tsp sea salt
6-8 cooking apples...cored, peeled, and thinly sliced
1 9" unbaked pie shell (see recipe this book)
1/3 cup maple syrup

Preheat the oven to 350° F. Combine crushed gingersnaps, sugar, pecans, margarine, flour, cinnamon, and sea salt; set aside. Spread half of the apples in the pie shell. Spread half of the gingersnap mixture over the apple layer. Repeat layers. Bake for 50 minutes. Heat the maple syrup to boiling and pour over the pie. Bake for 15 minutes more. Done.

B & B Blueberry Pie

Music: Possessed-1984 demo (1984)

It is recommended that you get all your ingredients together in advance of boiling the water; once the cornstarch gets involved it's a fast business and you don't wanna be fumbling around with ingredients!

3/4 cup water, boiling

1/4 cup water, cold
1/4 cup corn starch

1 cup turbinado sugar
1/8 tsp salt
3 pints (6 cups) blueberries

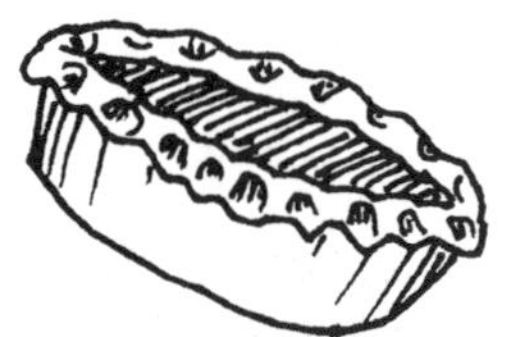

1 Tbsp soy margarine
1/4 lemon, juiced

In a heavy-bottomed saucepan boil 3/4 cup water.

In a separate bowl mix together cold water and cornstarch. Add to boiling water and whisk in as quickly and thoroughly as possible. Add sugar, salt, and 1/2 cup blueberries. Cook on low heat until boiling, stirring constantly and mashing blueberries as you stir. Mixture will be dark blue, bubbly, and syrupy when it is done. Remove mixture from heat and stir in margarine and lemon juice. Pour over remaining (uncooked) blueberries and spoon mixture into prepared pie shells. Chill for at least an hour before serving.

Nancy's Gingerbread Cookies

Music: Iron Maiden-The Soundhouse Tapes demo (1979)

Thanks Ma!

1/3 cup vegetable shortening
1 cup brown sugar
1½ cups dark molasses

Mix these first ingredients thoroughly, then stir in:

2/3 cup cold water

Mix together the following ingredients and then stir them into the above mixture...got it?

7 cups flour
2 tsp baking soda
1 tsp sea salt
1 tsp ground allspice
1 tsp ground cloves
1 tsp ground cinnamon

Divide the final mixture into three patties, wrapping each in wax paper or saran wrap. Chill them for at least one hour. Roll them out on a floured surface to about ¼" and prepare to cut them with a cutter or a knife. It is at this point that you need to decide whether this dough will turn into a house, a bunch of animals, soldiers and tanks, political symbols, or whatever. Keep in mind my Mom would not approve of any violent, offensive, or evil shapes. Choose wisely, then put the shapes on a lightly greased cookie sheet and bake for 10-12 minutes in a pre-heated 375° F oven. Remove immediately and cool on racks.

Chocolate Redemption Cake

Music: Doom Snake Cult-Love, Sorrow, Doom lp (1992)

1 cup turbinado sugar
1½ cups unsifted, unbleached white flour
½ tsp sea salt
¼ cup cocoa
1 tsp baking soda
1 Tbsp lemon juice
1/3 cup vegetable oil
1 tsp vanilla extract
1 cup cold water

Mix ingredients in the order given. Pour into a very lightly greased cake pan.

Bake in a 350° F oven for 30-35 minutes. Wait for it to cool before you eat it...it tastes better that way for some reason. Give a piece to someone you care about.

Leslie's Incredibly Rich Chocolate Cake with the Most Bizarre Ingredients Ever!

Music: Bethlehem-Sardonischer Untergang im Zeichen Irreligiöser Darbietung lp (1998)

Cake:
1½ cups unbleached all purpose flour
¾ cup unsweetened cocoa powder (sometimes I put in a few finely ground cocoa nibs for extra punch)
1 Tbsp baking powder
1 tsp baking soda
2 Tbsp flaxseeds
½ cup pitted dates, soaked in 1 cup hot water for 30 minutes
6 oz extra-firm tofu
1 cup of liquid sweetener (maple syrup or brown rice syrup both taste delicious)
1 Tbsp corn oil
1½ tsp vanilla extract

Frosting:
1 cup semisweet chocolate chips (I sometimes try to melt in as much chocolate in as possible because, hey...why the hell not? It also stiffens up the frosting a bit.)
½ cup raw cashews
6 oz extra-firm tofu
¼ cup maple syrup
1 tsp vanilla extract

Preheat the oven to 350° F. Grease two 9-inch round cake pans and coat a bit with flour, tapping out the extra so there is a nice even but thin layer of flour between the cake and the pan. In a big bowl, mix the dry ingredients, flour, cocoa, baking powder, and baking soda. Get out the Blender! Turn up the music really loud! Grind the flaxseeds to a fine powder. Add ½ cup of water until it is really frothy and thick (30 seconds). Add the dates and the water they were soaking in, along with tofu, maple syrup (or whichever sweetener you used), oil, and vanilla. Blend until smooth, and then put into the big bowl.

Turn down the music, eat some chocolate, and stir the dry ingredients into the wet ingredients, and stir till smooth. Divide the batter evenly between the two pans. Bake until the cakes are slightly springy when pressed, 20 to 25 minutes. Cool in the pans for about 10 minutes then turn them onto wire racks to finish the cooling process.

Oh boy, frosting! Make a double boiler type setup to melt the chocolate but only let the water simmer, SIMMER I say, or the chocolate will get…weird. Stir the chocolate until it's unlumpy, then turn off the stove, and let sit while you…turn up music! In your blender, finely grind the cashews, add 1/3 cup water, and blend until smooth. Add tofu, maple syrup, and vanilla, blend until smooth. Add melted chocolate and again, blend until smooth and evenly mixed. Transfer to a bowl and refrigerate. When everything is nicely cooled and chilled, put the frosting on, with about 2/3 on the bottom and the rest on the top layer.

White Cake

Music: Black Legions Project demo (1995)

1 ½ cups flour
¾ cup sugar
2 tsp baking powder
¼ tsp salt
¾ cup soy milk or other 'milk' (rice milk)
2 tsp vanilla
¼ cup melted shortening or oil (I used melted shortening)
1 egg's worth of substitute, beaten (Ener-G egg replacer)

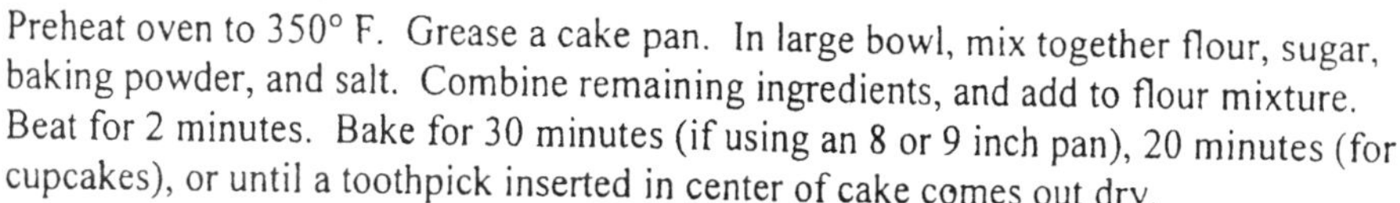

Preheat oven to 350° F. Grease a cake pan. In large bowl, mix together flour, sugar, baking powder, and salt. Combine remaining ingredients, and add to flour mixture. Beat for 2 minutes. Bake for 30 minutes (if using an 8 or 9 inch pan), 20 minutes (for cupcakes), or until a toothpick inserted in center of cake comes out dry.

Sarah's Frozen Key Lime Cheezecake Pie

Music: Immortal-Pure Holocaust lp (1993)

1 box firm silken tofu
8 oz Better Than Cream Cheese (made by Tofutti)
1/3 cup Key lime pulp and juice
1 cup Sucanat or other natural sugar
1 prepared graham cracker or cookie crust (Keebler with 2 extra serving works well)
Vegan whipped topping (see next recipe)

In processor, put tofu and Better Than Cream Cheese. Blend until creamy. Add sugar and lime, and blend again until just blended. Pour into crust. Put pie into freezer, and freeze for 4 hours or until very firm. Just before serving, top pie with whipped topping.

Vegan "Whipped" Topping

Music: Naked Whipper-Moloch: Acid Orgy 12" (1995)

1 package soft silken tofu
2 Tbsp-1/4 cup sweetener, depending on taste
1 tsp vanilla extract

Blend together in food processor until smooth. This isn't very "whipped" but it has a similar taste to whipped toppings.

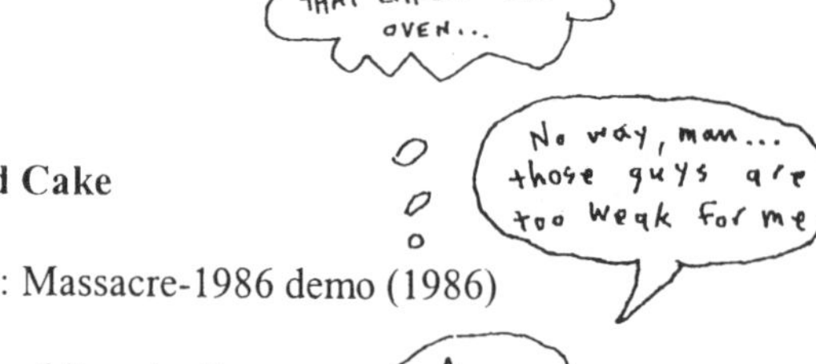

Pound Cake

Music: Massacre-1986 demo (1986)

2 cups white cake flour
4 tsp baking powder
1½ tsp sea salt
¾ cup light maple syrup
15¾ oz soft silken tofu
1 tsp vanilla extract
¾ tsp orange extract

Preheat the over to 350° F. Sift together four, baking powder, and salt. Mix maple syrup, tofu, vanilla extract, and orange extract in a blender until smooth. Add tofu mixture to flour mixture and stir well. Pour into a nonstick or slightly oiled 9" X 5" (or whatever) pan. Bake 30-35 minutes or until golden brown and top is springy to the touch. If needed, cover with aluminum foil for the last 10-15 minutes of baking to prevent burning. Remove the cake from the pan and cool slightly on a rack. While the cake is still warm, wrap it tightly in foil. This will keep it from forming a hard crust.

Curly Jim's Chocolate Chip Cookies

Music: Electric Wizard-Dopethrone lp (2000)

The best vegan cookies I know of.

1 tsp vanilla
¾ cup brown sugar
¾ cup white sugar
2¼ cups flour
1 cup margarine, softened
1 bag semi-sweet chocolate chips (make sure they're vegan)
1 tsp baking soda
½ cup apple sauce
3 Tbsp peanut butter
1 tsp sea salt

Preheat the oven to 325° F. In a large bowl, mix the margarine, brown sugar, white sugar, vanilla, applesauce, and peanut butter until creamy. Then add the flour, salt, and baking soda and mix. Finally, add the chocolate ships.

Place the dough in tablespoon-sized dollops on a baking tray. They will flatten and spread out as they cook. Bake for 9-12 minutes, keeping an eye on them the whole time. The longer they bake, the harder they get. Cool on racks.

Jeff's Safeway Oatmeal Raisin Cookies

Music: Dodheimsgard-Kronet Til Konge lp (1995)

¾ cup margarine
¾ cup turbinado sugar
1 tsp arrowroot mixed with 1 tsp water
1 tsp vanilla
2 cups whole wheat (or unbleached) flour
¾ tsp cinnamon
½ tsp ground cloves
½ tsp nutmeg
½ tsp baking soda
¾ cup soymilk
1 ¾ cups rolled oats
¾ cup raisins

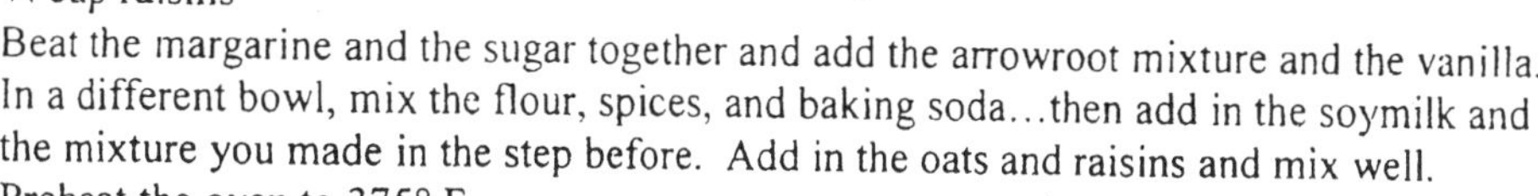

Beat the margarine and the sugar together and add the arrowroot mixture and the vanilla. In a different bowl, mix the flour, spices, and baking soda…then add in the soymilk and the mixture you made in the step before. Add in the oats and raisins and mix well. Preheat the oven to 375° F.

Put spoonfuls on a lightly greased cookie sheet. Flatten the dollops a bit, as they stay in pretty much whatever shape you leave them in. Cook them for about 10 minutes, or until they are a bit browned on the top. You want to undercook cookies, eh? Enjoy.

Pagan Peanut Butter Cookies

Music: Pagan Altar-self titled lp (1982)

¾ cup creamy peanut butter (*not* the natural kind)
1 stick (1/2 cup) margarine
1¼ cups light brown sugar, firmly packed
3 Tbsp soy milk
1 Tbsp vanilla
1 egg-replacer worth of egg (1/2 tsp egg-replacer + 2 Tbsp water)
1¾ cups all-purpose flour
¾ tsp sea salt
¾ tsp baking soda

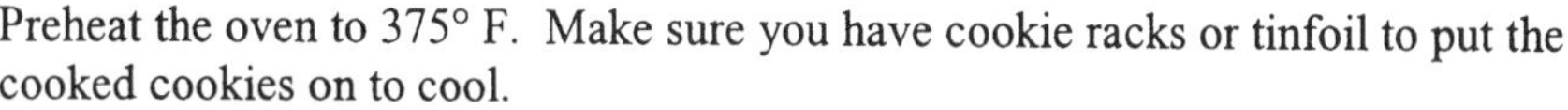

Preheat the oven to 375° F. Make sure you have cookie racks or tinfoil to put the cooked cookies on to cool.

Combine the peanut butter, the margarine, the brown sugar, the soy milk, and the vanilla in a large bowl. Blend it all up using a mixer, a whisk, or a spoon. If the margarine is cold, it may help to heat it up a bit first to soften it. Add the egg replacer and mix it all up a bit more. Add in the sea salt and baking soda. Blend. Add in the flour. Blend.

Drop heaping teaspoonfuls about 2" apart onto an *un*greased baking sheet. Flatten the cookies slightly in a criss-cross pattern using the tines of a fork. Put them in the oven and bake for 7 to 8 minutes, or until set and just beginning to brown. Let them cool on the cookie sheet about 2 minutes before moving them onto the cookie racks or tinfoil to cool completely. Should make up to 3 dozen cookies.

Gotterdamerung Dopple-Chocolate Cookies

Music: Godflesh-Streetcleaner lp (1989)

2 cups all-purpose flour
½ cup oats
1 tsp baking soda
1 ½ tsp baking powder
¼ cup cocoa
2 cups vegan chocolate chips
1 ½ tsp vanilla
½ cup maple syrup
½ cup chocolate soy milk
¼ cup vegetable oil

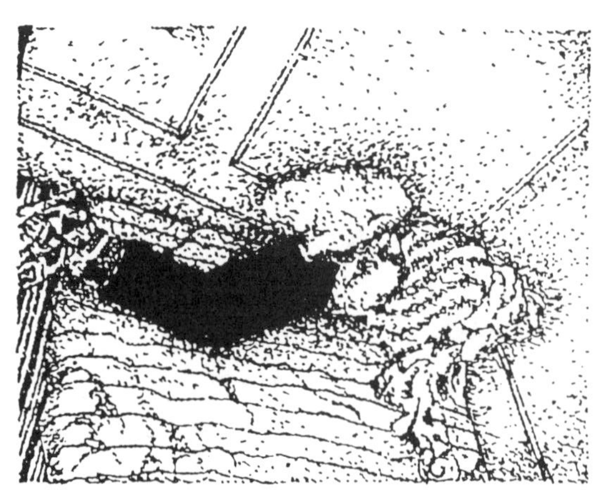

DON'T HOLD ME BACK... THIS IS MY OWN HELL

Preheat oven to 375° F. Mix flour, baking soda, baking powder, cocoa, and chocolate chips in a large bowl. Add vanilla, maple syrup, vegetable oil, and soy milk; mix well. Place spoonfulls on a greased baking pan and cook for 8 to 10 minutes, or until done. Let cool
slightly, then move to a wire rack.

Nilla Wafers

Music: Throne of Ahaz-Nifelheim lp (1993)

½ cup powdered sugar
1/3 cup sugar
1/3 cup vegetable shortening
1 egg's worth of egg replacer
1 tsp vanilla
1/8 tsp sea salt
1 ½ cups cake flour
1 ½ tsp baking powder
1 Tbsp water

1. Preheat oven to 325° F.
2. Cream together sugars, shortening, egg, vanilla, and salt in a large bowl.
3. Add the flour and baking powder. Add 1 tablespoon of water and continue mixing until dough forms a ball.
4. Roll dough into 3/4-inch balls and flatten slightly onto a lightly greased cookie sheet. Bake for 15-18 minutes or until cookies are light brown. Makes 50-56 cookies.

Dainty Tea Cookies

Music: Embalmer-There was Blood Everywhere ep (1995)

2 cups flour
A pinch of sea salt
1 1/2 sticks margarine or Crisco
3/4 cup 10x confectioner's sugar
1 1/2 tsp egg replacer mixed with 2 Tbsp warm water
3 Tbsp almond extract

Combine flour and salt in small bowl; set aside. In a large mixing bowl, cream margarine, sugar, egg substitute, and flavoring in order, mixing well. Add flour mixture and combine thoroughly. Shape into small balls and bake in a preheated 350° F oven for about 6 minutes; cool on rack.

When room temperature, place in a large Ziplock bag into which about a cup of 10x sugar has been placed; gently roll and turn bag to coat cookies with sugar. Makes about 100 dainty fucking cookies.

"Whose Chocolate Cookies? *Our* Chocolate Cookies"

Music: Running Wild-Victim of States Power ep (1984)

2 1/4 cups whole wheat pastry flour
1/3 cup carob or cocoa powder
1 tsp baking soda
1/2 tsp sea salt
1 cup margarine
3/4 cup raw sugar
3/4 cup sucanat, or raw sugar with molasses added
1 tsp vanilla extract
2 eggs' worth of egg replacer
1 package chocolate chips
Some decaffeinated coffee

Preheat oven to 375° F. Stir together the flour, carob or cocoa powder, baking soda and salt in a large bowl. Add in the margarine, sugar, Sucanat, and vanilla. Take your egg replacer and mix it in with coffee instead of water. Add that in too. Stir it up. Throw in splashes of coffee until it looks right if it's a bit dry. It should be velvety and perfect-looking. Put in your chocolate chips. Mix it all around again. Eat some of the dough.

Okay, now you're ready to cook them. Put tablespoon sized dollops onto a cookie sheet, though not too close together as they spread like crazy. Bake for 15 minutes or until they appear done.

Cop-Shop Special (Donuts!)

Music: Blessed Death-Kill or Be Killed lp (1985)

2 cups sifted flour
1/2 cup sugar
3 tsp baking powder
1 tsp nutmeg
Egg replacer, equivalent to 1 egg
3/4 cup soy milk
3 Tbsp oil
Powdered sugar (optional)

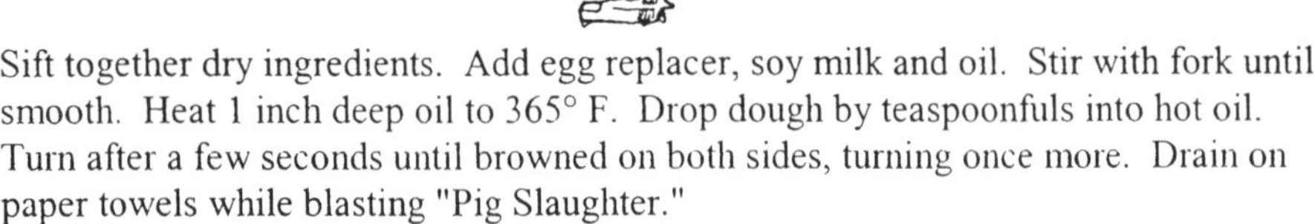

Sift together dry ingredients. Add egg replacer, soy milk and oil. Stir with fork until smooth. Heat 1 inch deep oil to 365° F. Drop dough by teaspoonfuls into hot oil. Turn after a few seconds until browned on both sides, turning once more. Drain on paper towels while blasting "Pig Slaughter."

You can either eat them plain or coat them with powdered sugar. They're really good like that. These get quite hard and dense when cold. Feel free to distribute them at your local Black Bloc meeting to be used as slingshot fodder.

Sopaipillas á la Eva

Music: Mortuary Drape-Tolling 13 Knell lp (2000)

These puffy pastries remind me of the beignets (French donuts) you can buy in the French Quarter in New Orleans. They are best warm, topped with powdered sugar, and as far away as possible from tourists.

1 cup flour
1½ tsp baking powder
1 Tbsp vegetable shortening
A little turbanado sugar
A little sea salt
Oil for frying

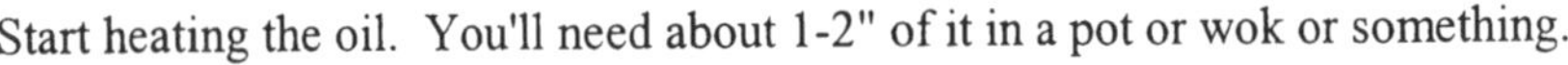

Start heating the oil. You'll need about 1-2" of it in a pot or wok or something.

Combine the flour, baking powder, salt, and sugar. Cut in the shortening. Gradually add 1/3 cup warm water. Stir with a fork. Knead 3-5 minutes on a floured surface. Let the dough sit 10 minutes.

Roll the dough out until it is 1/8 to ¼" thick and cut it into shapes (it really doesn't matter what shapes...just don't make them more than a couple inches in diameter as they will expand immensely when cooked). The oil should be very hot by now, so try frying about 2-3 at a time. When all of the shapes are gone, fry up the scraps to make real twisted and ugly ones. The recipe makes about 20 or so. They can be eaten plain, with jam, or topped with powdered sugar. Be creative.

Broken Jaw Biscotti

Music: Exciter-Violence and Force lp (1983)

1 1/3 cups all-purpose flour
1 cup sugar
½ cup unsweetened cocoa
1 Tbsp instant espresso-coffee powder
¾ tsp baking soda
½ tsp baking powder
¼ tsp sea salt
4 oz egg substitute
1 tsp vanilla extract

About two hours before serving or early in the day:

Into a large bowl measure four, sugar, cocoa, espresso-coffee powder, baking soda, baking powder, and salt. With spoon stir the egg substitute and vanilla extract into the flour mixture until it holds together (mixture may appear dry or crumbly).

Preheat the oven to 325° F. Lightly oil or grease a large cookie sheet. On a lightly floured surface, divide the dough in half. With lightly floured hands, roll each half of dough into an 8" by 2½" loaf. Place loaves about 3" apart on a cookie sheet. Bake 35 to 40 minutes or until a toothpick inserted in the center of each loaf comes out clean.

Remove the cookie sheet from the oven. Turn oven down to 300° F. Cool loaves 10 minutes for easier slicing.

With a serrated knife, cut the loaves crosswise into ¼" think diagonal slices. Arrange the slices cut-side down on the same cookie sheet, making sure they do not tough. Return to the oven and bake 10 to 15 minutes longer. The cookies will seem cake-like in the center but will become characteristically crisp and dry when cooled). Remove the cookies to wire racks to cool. Store the cookies in a tightly covered container. Makes about 3½ dozen cookies.

I thrive on isolation. I need to feel as if I have control over my surroundings...I need to know that I am the only one who decides if the silence around me shall give way to sound or not. Selfish? Maybe...but is it really? In my favorite childhood book, The Phantom Tollbooth (Juster, 1961), there lives a Soundkeeper who maintains sole control over the noises in her kingdom. She even owns a radio which plays silence on all of its channels, any of which can be turned up loud to drown out sound. Silence can be deafening in its intricacies. As the Soundkeeper explains, "...perhaps you know the silence when you haven't the answer to a question you've been asked, or the hush of a country road at night, or the expectant pause in a roomful of people when someone is just about to speak, or, most beautiful of all, the moment after the door closes and you're all alone in the whole house? Each one is different, you know, and all very beautiful, if you listen carefully." I need this quiet. I claim this silence and it is mine.

Sarah's Favorite Blueberry Crunch

Music: Corrupted-Se Hace por los Suenos Asesinos lp (2004)

*I owe many thanks to Sarah for being one of the primary inspirations for the constructic and completion of this cookbook. I greatly appreciate her unconditional support and I very much look forward to seeing *her* cookbook upon its completion.*

1½ cups rolled oats
½ cup whole wheat pastry flour
½ cup chopped almonds
¼ tsp sea salt
1/3 cup safflower oil (cold-pressed, if possible)
½ cup maple syrup
1 pint blueberries
2½ Tbsp arrowroot
¾ cup cold water

Preheat the oven to 400° F. In a large bowl, combine the oats, flour, almonds, and sea salt. In a separate, smaller bowl, whisk the oil and half the maple syrup and add to the oat mixture. In a medium saucepan, bring the blueberries and the remaining ¼ cup maple syrup to a boil. Dissolve the arrowroot into the water and add to the blueberries; cook, stirring constantly, until thickened and transparent (about 2-3 minutes). Remove from heat and set aside.

Oil a 6" X 10" baking pan. With wet hands, press enough of the oat crust (about two thirds) into the bottom of the dish to form a solid layer. Pour the blueberry mixture evenly over the crust. Sprinkle the remaining crust over the blueberries.

Bake for 20-25 minutes, or until the top is nicely browned. Allow to cool slightly, then refrigerate one hour or until the filling is set. Cut into squares and serve.

> What we observe is not Nature itself, but Nature exposed to our method c questioning.
>
> Heisenber

@pple Crisp

Music: Church of Misery (USA)-Sorrows of the Moon demo (1992)

2 medium tart cooking apples, pared and sliced (about 2 cups)
2 Tbsp water
3 Tbsp unbleached all-purpose flour
2 Tbsp turbinado sugar
2 Tbsp margarine
½ tsp ground cinnamon

Preheat the oven to 350° F. Put the apple slices in a small casserole dish (or whatever) Sprinkle the water over the apples. In a separate bowl, mix flour, sugar, margarine, an cinnamon with a fork until crumbly. Sprinkle over the apples. Bake uncovered until t topping is light golden brown and the apples are tender…about 25-30 minutes.

Brice's Flippity-Flapjacks

Music: Ice Age-General Alert demo (1987)

½ stick margarine
½ cup sugar
1 cup syrup
5 ½ cups oats
1 cup raisins
½ cup nuts

Mix all together on low heat. Bake in a lightly greased pan at 300° F for awhile until they're chewy looking. While baking, repeat slowly but surely, "a little nonsense now and then is relished by the wisest men." Cut while hot into bars, cool, and remove. Try adding chocolate chips and other dried fruits if you're feeling crazy.

Cosmic Mars Bars

Music: Assassin-Interstellar Experience lp (1988)

NOUGAT:

2/3 cup of soy milk
3 oz soy margarine
8 oz sugar
2 tsp vanilla extract
2 oz wheatgerm, preferably ground in spice grinder
4 oz dried soy milk

Put the soy milk, margarine, and sugar into a thick saucepan and heat, without stirring, on a low heat until it bubbles all over. Keep at this heat for 2 minutes (if you have a sugar thermometer, it should be 235° F). Cool.

Add the vanilla essence and the wheatgerm. Add the dried soy milk and beat till creamy. Pour into a tray roughly the size of 12 mars bars and freeze for an hour.

TOFFEE:

4 oz sugar
4 oz soy margarine
5 oz soy cream
1 Tbsp golden syrup

Put everything in a thick bottomed saucepan and heat on a low heat till it bubbles all over. Keep at this temperature for 4-5 minutes, stirring constantly. Pour the toffee over the nougat and freeze for another hour. Cut into mars bar size pieces and re-freeze until the toffee is solid (this can take a couple of days.). Melt about 14 oz of vegan chocolate in a microwave if you have one (3 minutes full power for 3.5 oz) or place into a bowl above a saucepan of boiling water till melted. Coat the bars with chocolate and place onto a greased tray. Re-freeze.

Clif-Type Apricot FUBARs

Music: Warhammer-Abattoir of Death demo (1985)

We always take Clif bars on the trails while we're riding. They usually cost at least $1.69 each.

1 cup almond butter, soy butter, or peanut butter
1/2 cup Sucanat or other natural sugar
1/2 cup rice syrup
1/4 cup apricot baby food
1 tsp powdered lecithin (try your natural foods store for this)
2 tsp vanilla extract
3 1/3 cups rolled oats
1/4 cup coconut flakes (optional)
1/4 cup sunflower seeds
1/4 cup chopped almonds
1/2 cup chopped dried apricots

Preheat oven to 350° F. In a large bowl, stir together the nut butter, margarine, Sucanat syrup, and vanilla until smooth. Add all the other ingredients. Mix well. Press the mixture into 13 x 9 inch greased pan. Bake for 20-25 minutes. Do not over-bake. Let cool on wire rack. Cut into bars. Eat while picking the rocks out of your elbows after bailing.

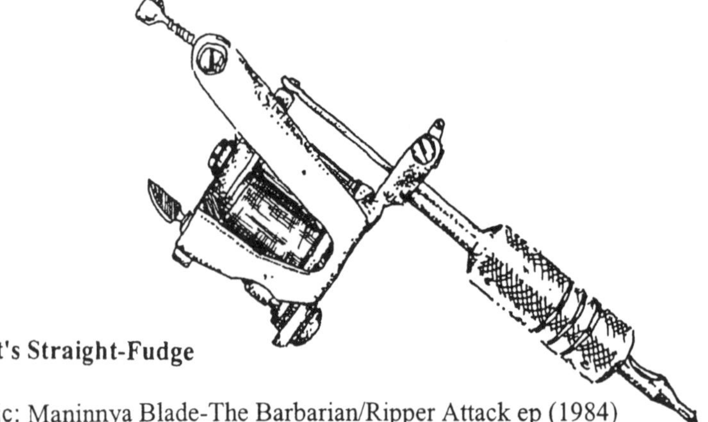

Matt's Straight-Fudge

Music: Maninnya Blade-The Barbarian/Ripper Attack ep (1984)

½ cup sweetener (maple syrup, Sucanat, refined sugar-all work)
¾ cup water
1 cup natural peanut butter
¾ cup carob powder

Stir together sweetener and water over low heat then add peanut butter. Stir until smooth. Stir in carob powder until all mixed well. Pour into a container, keeping fudge evenly distributed, and freeze. I use an 8x8 pan and the fudge is about 1 inch thick. Don't eat until frozen! Once frozen, set on fire, then eat (just kidding). Tastes like peanutbutter cups.

Moshmallows

Music: Vomit Remnants-In the Name of Vomit demo (1997)

3 Tbsp agar-agar
1/2 cup cold water
2 cups sugar
3/4 cup corn syrup
1/2 cup water
1/4 tsp sea salt
2 Tbsp vanilla
Powdered sugar

Mix together the agar-agar and 1/2 cup water and let stand for 1 hour.

After about 1/2 hour, start to prepare syrup. Place in heavy pan over low heat and stir until dissolved the sugar, corn syrup, 1/2 cup water and salt.

When the mixture starts to boil, cover and cook for about 3 minutes. Uncover, and continue to cook without stirring, over high heat, until a candy thermometer reaches 240-244° F.

Remove from heat and pour slowly over the gelled mixture, beating constantly. After all the syrup is added, continue to beat for about 15 minutes. When the mixture is thick but still warm add the vanilla.

Put the mixture into an 8"x12" pan that has been lightly dusted with cornstarch. When it has dried for 12 hours, remove it from the pan, and cut it into squares with cornstarch. Dust each piece generously with powdered sugar. Store the well-powdered pieces in a closed tin.

Fresh Peach Cobbler

Music: Skull Crusher/Second Hell-Metal Deadness split lp (1986)

1/2 cup raw sugar or other sweetener
2 Tbsp arrowroot powder
4 cups fresh peaches, sliced
1 cup water
Ground cinnamon
1 cup whole wheat pastry flour
2 Tbsp sugar
1 1/2 tsp baking powder
1/4 tsp sea salt
3 Tbsp margarine
1/2 cup soymilk or water

Combine sugar and arrowroot in a saucepan, then stir in the peaches and water. Bring to a boil, then boil 1 minute, stirring constantly. Pour into a 9" square baking dish and sprinkle with cinnamon. Preheat the oven to 400° F.

Combine flour, sugar, baking powder, and salt. Cut in margarine until mixture resembles cornmeal. Stir in soymilk until mixed, then drop by spoonfuls onto the hot fruit. Bake until golden brown, about 25 minutes.

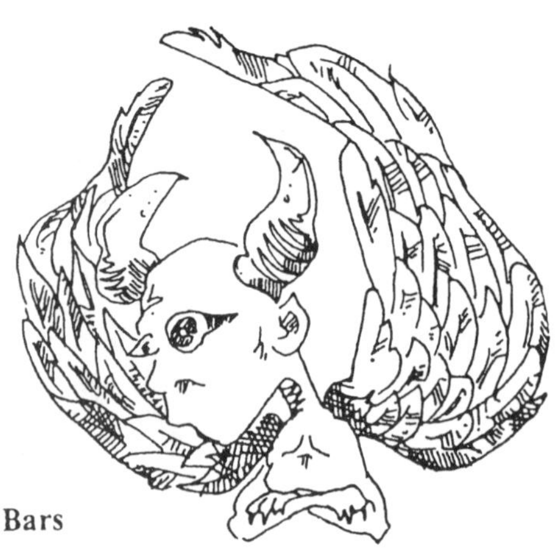

Power(violence) Bars

Music: Nyogthaeblisz-Progenitors of Mankind's Annihilation lp (2004)

1 cup turbanado sugar
1 cup light corn syrup
¾ cup natural peanut butter
4 cups Grape Nuts (or the Finast equivalent) cereal

Line a 9X13" (or whatever) pan with foil and lightly oil or spray with a non-stick cooking spray. Boil the sugar, syrup, and peanut butter in a saucepan for a minute. Apparently, if you boil it for longer than this the bars will be impossible to eat. Add th Grape Nuts and stir. Immediately spread into the prepared pan. Let cool and cut into bars. Wrap the bars in plastic wrap, if you've got it. Sell for $1.59 each (just kidding).

Chris(tine)'s Banana Bread

Music: Filth of Mankind-The Final Chapter lp (2000)

1/3 cup margarine
½ cup maple syrup
2 bananas
3 tsp soymilk
1 tsp vanilla
1 tsp cinnamon
½ tsp ground cloves
½ tsp nutmeg
2 cups flour
1 ½ tsp baking powder
½ tsp baking soda

Preheat oven to 350° F.
Mix together margarine and maple syrup and add bananas, mashing them into the mixture. Add soymilk and vanilla. Add spices. Add baking powder and soda. Mix i flour. Pour dough into oiled bread pan. Bake about 45 minutes, or until you can stick with a fork and have it come out clean.

Karamel Korn

Music: Katodus 609-Ech P1 El 609 Desecratus promo (1993)

Thanks Mom!

2 sticks margarine
2 cups turbinado sugar
½ cup white Karo (corn syrup)
1 tsp vanilla
1 tsp baking soda
Popcorn (about 2 gallons worth)

Boil the margarine, sugar, and Karo for 5 minutes. Take it off the heat and add the vanilla and baking soda. Pour the mixture over the popcorn. Stir it up and bake in one of those tin pans for 1 hour at 250° F, stirring occasionally.

I hate this government and the society that supports it. That means you. You are my enemies and I am justified in killing you.
Toronto resident David Wayne Arisman, sweet-talking a jury considering giving him the death penalty for a murder conviction

Jessica's Blueberry Muffins

Music: General Surgery-Necrology ep (1991)

1/2 cup margarine (soft)
1 cup sugar
2 "eggs" (I use NRG egg replacer)
2 cups flour
2 tsp baking powder
½ tsp sea salt
½ cup soy milk
1 tsp vanilla
2 ½ cups blueberries

Grease muffin pan w/ vegetable shortening. Mix margarine and sugar until fluffy. Add "eggs" one at a time. Mix well after each. Combine flour, baking powder, and salt. Add alternately to creamed mixture with soy milk and vanilla. Crush 1/2 cup of berries and add to batter. Fold rest into batter and spoon into muffin pan. Sprinkle tops with sugar. Bake 30 minutes at 375° F. Let cool. Makes 12.

As a little boy I was tormented by a picture of a scene of a fairytale "Das Gespensterschiff," (the Ghostship) whose captain had been nailed through the head to the topmast by his rebellious crew. I am sure that this was not the "program" of the first movement of the third string quartet. But it might have been, subconsciously, a very gruesome premonition which caused me to write this work, because as often as I thought about this movement, that picture came to my mind. I am afraid a psychologist might use this story as a stepping-stone for premature conclusions. Being only an illustration of the emotional background of this movement, it will not furnish enlightenment of the structure. We must not forget, that a theory for teaching and judgment must be the goal of research, whether it is based on acoustics or on psychology-but it is not as easy as that.

Arnold Schoenberg on the First Movement (Moderato) of his Third String Quartet.

Mud Puddle Pudding

Music: Broken Hope-The Bowels of Repugnance lp (1993)

½ lb firm tofu
¼ cup baking cocoa
¾ cup turbanado sugar
1 tsp vanilla
1/8 tsp sea salt
Soy milk

Blend everything but the soy milk. It should be very thick at this point, so add just enough soy milk to make it smooth and relatively thick. Pour it into a bowl and let it chill overnight. Take it to work in your bag lunch the next day and pretend you're 8 again.

Yet the fact remains--and to have to admit this is rather difficult for a historian--that it is, strictly speaking, impossible to give a reason for Schoenberg's decision of 1907. Those who speak of historical necessity, of the dictates of the historical moment which Schoenberg obeyed, make the event appear more harmless than it actually was. The suspension of the existing order, the proclamation of the musical state of emergency, was an act of violence. And thus the theories with which Schoenberg attempted to justify the emancipation of the dissonance are characterized by a helplessness which prevents us from taking them at their word as being motives for compositional decisions.

Carl Dahlhaus, on Schoenberg's alleged turn to atonality

edrum Truffles

usic: Bunkur-Bludgeon 2Xlp (2004)

oz rich tea cookies
to 2 oz hazelnuts
oz almonds
oz dark jam
to 2 Tbsp dark rum
Tbsp apple juice concentrate
bar dark, vegan chocolate

> Mankind will not be free until the last king
> is strangled with the entrails of the last priest.
> Diderot

lend everything except chocolate in a food processor. Add melted chocolate and mix ell. Pour an extra shot of rum. Down it. Form the mixture into 1 inch balls. efrigerate in an air tight container. Makes around 40 balls.

ockey Pucks

usic: Voor-Evil Metal demo (1985)

cup rolled oats and ½ cup bran
Tbsp sunflower seeds
½ cups whole barley flour
/3 cup turbanado sugar and 1 Tbsp set aside
Tbsp cocoa
tsp baking powder
/3 cup semi-sweet chocolate chips (make sure they're vegan)
Tbsp vegetable oil
tsp pure vanilla extract
Tbsp vinegar
½ cups water

reheat the oven to 400° F. Oil 12 muffin tins to prevent sticking.

n a large bowl, combine all of the dry ingredients (minus the 1 Tbsp sugar) and mix well. Using a spoon, dig three small wells in the flour mixture. Put oil in one, vanilla in another, and vinegar in the third. Pour water over the top of this and mix the whole thing up quickly, making sure the dry ingredients have been moistened.

It's okay for the batter to be kind of lumpy looking. Divide it into the muffin tins. Sprinkle the tops of the muffins with the remaining sugar. Bake 25-30 minutes. Once they've cooled, put them in an airtight container or plastic bag overnight or they may become pucks suitable for playing roller hockey with.

Jessicka's Gobs

Music: Sublime Cadaveric Decomposition-II lp (2003)

1 cup margarine
2 cups sugar
2 "eggs" worth of egg replacer
12 Tbsp boiling water
1/2 cup cocoa
1 cup soymilk
1 tsp vanilla
4 cups flour
2 tsp baking soda
1/2 tsp baking powder
1/2 tsp salt

Mix water and cocoa and let cool. Cream margarine, sugar, "eggs," and vanilla. Sift the dry ingredients. Add the cocoa and sifted dry ingredients to the margarine mixture Mix well. Drop batter by the teaspoon onto an ungreased cookie sheet. Bake at 450° F for 5 minutes.

While the gobs bake, work on the filling:

1½ cups powdered sugar
1 cup vegetable shortening (or half margarine, half shortening)
1/2 cup flour
1/2 cup soymilk
1/2 tsp vanilla
A pinch of sea salt

Mix together and beat. Spread between 2 baked gobs.

Hot Fudge Sludge

Music: Thy Grief Eternal-On Blackened Wings demo (1991)

5 Tbsp warm water
3 Tbsp unsweetened Dutch-process cocoa powder
½ cup Sucanat
1 Tbsp arrowroot mixed with 2 Tbsp water

Pour water, cocoa powder, and Sucanat into a small saucepan; stir over low heat until dissolved. Remove from heat and stir in the arrowroot mixture. Put back on the heat and whisk until thickened. Remove from heat and whisk until smooth. Fucking incredible.

"But i don't want comfort, i'm not looking for shelter. i want conflict, i want freedom, i want real danger. i want love, lust, hatred, despair, poetry, heaven and hell, desire - freedom."
"In fact, you are claiming the right to be unhappy."
"YES, ABOVE ALL, I'M CLAIMING THE RIGHT TO BE UNHAPPY."
"Not to mention the right to grow old and ugly and impotent; the right to have syphilis and cancer; the right to have nothing to eat; the right to be infested with maggots; the right to live in constant apprehension of what will happen tomorrow; the right to be an outcast, a leper, a pariah. You're claiming the right to suffer and die needlessly."
"YES, I CLAIM THEM ALL."

John's Shandygaff

Music: Drunkard-Alcoholic Thrash Attack demo (2000)

The perfect drink for a hot, sunny day...particularly for those of us who don't believe anyone above the Mason Dixon line has any legitimate reason to own air conditioning. Try this with a light beer (the cheap macrobrews work best) and a non-overpowering ginger ale (Canada Dry as opposed to Vernors).

Light beer
Ginger ale
Ice cubes
A hot afternoon
Plenty of time

This is remarkably simple. Put 3-4 ice cubes in a large (frosted if possible) glass. If you're at John's house, you'll pour in 1 part ginger ale followed by 2 parts beer. If you're somewhere else and prefer a slightly sweeter, more traditional 'gaff, you can pour in 1 part ginger ale, 1 part beer. Stir it up. Refresh.

Spicy Bloody Mary Mix

Music: Beherit-The Oath of Black Blood lp (1991)

It's 6:18 AM. You've been out all night drinking. You need one more drink before you crash for the day and you know it ain't gonna be a beer. Here's what you're looking for.

1 46-ounce can tomato juice
4 Tbsp lime juice
3 Tbsp juice from canned jalapenos
3 Tbsp vinegar
2 Tbsp sugar
2 tsp prepared horseradish
¼ teaspoon salt
¼ teaspoon pepper
1/8 teaspoon onion powder
Dash garlic

Combine all ingredients in a 2-quart pitcher. Store covered in the refrigerator. Serve over ice with as much vodka as you need and a celery stalk. Makes 52 ounces.

Merrydeath's Sugarfreakin'free Soy Drink

Music: Acid-self titled lp (1982)

This recipe makes about 1 ½ gallons of soy milk. Change as necessary.

Start with 7 cups raw soybeans, then soak 8-12 hours (make sure you double water to beans when soaking).
Next, drain the water, add fresh water, and cook in a big pot on the stove on medium heat for like 10 minutes. It will be thick looking and the shells will be starting to fall off.
Next, drain off all the water...It's important to keep the water fresh so it doesn't taste entirely like unspiced soybeans...and to keep your booty free of excess gas.
Get a blender. Take 1 cup soybeans and put it in the blender. Add 2 ½ cups fresh water. Blend. Dump it into a large pot. Repeat with that proportion of beans and water until the beans are gone. You'll need two pots that hold two gallons each to hold all the beans and water.
Cook the soybeans on the stove for 30-40 minutes, stirring frequently. Then, turn off the heat and let the milk cool.
Get a colander and line it with cheesecloth (or a clean white t-shirt or any undyed cloth which will allow fluid to pass through it).
Get two containers. Over one container place the colander over it. Add soy milk mixture. Let milk soak through. Then, wrap it up and squeeze the cloth to get all the liquid out. This is your soymilk! Take the pulp and put it into another container. This is called okara and can be used to make burgers (see recipe this issue).
Now, strain it all. You'll have about 1/3 pulp and 2/3 milk. Put all the milk into a pot on the stove. Add ¼ cup vanilla, ¼ cup rice syrup, ¼ cup barley malt, 1 shake of cinnamon, a little ground ginger, and ¼ cup maple syrup. Warm it up for 5-10 minutes and vwala!

Yogi Chai (The Original Sacred Recipe)

Music: Gnome/Nyarlathotep-Legendary Japanese Wolves/Lost Effigy split tape (1999)

3 quarts water
24 whole black peppercorns
24 whole green cardamom pods
12-15 whole cloves
2/3 sticks cinnamon
2" ginger root (peeled and sliced)
1 tsp black tea
Soymilk

Bring the water to a boil. Add the cloves and let them dance for a minute. Add the pepper, cardamom, cinnamon, and ginger. Simmer for 1-2 hours. The longer the better, really. This gives you the base for the tea. You can refrigerate or even freeze it.

When you are ready to drink it, heat up the base to just under a boil and turn off the heat. Add the black tea. Let it sit a minute or two, then strain out the tea. Add soymilk to taste. Delicious hot or iced.

Bubble Tea! That's Right, Fuckin' Bubble Tea!

Music: Satanic Hellslaughter-Advance demo (1990)

Large, dried tapioca pearls (try the Asian market)
Water
Sugar syrup (see below)
1 cup strong, brewed black tea
1 cup soymilk
Ice cubes

You'll need four parts water per one part tapioca. Boil the water. Add the pearls to the boiling water and boil for 30 minutes. Do not, do not, *do not* add the pearls to the water until it is at a rolling boil. If you do so, they'll just disintegrate into a big sludgy mess. It really, really sucks. Stir the pearls occasionally to make sure they aren't sticking to each other or to the pot. Turn off the heat and let the pearls steep for another 30 minutes with the lid on.

While waiting, go ahead and make the sugar syrup. Bring three parts water to a boil. Mix in two parts white sugar and one part brown sugar. Reduce heat and stir until the crystals are all dissolved. Remove it from the heat and let cool.

Once the pearls are done, drain them and rinse in cold water to cool them off. Place them in the sugar syrup, making certain that all are covered. You can store them like this for a day or two.

Now, put it all together. Put about 3 oz tapioca pearls, the tea, the soymilk, the ice cubes, and sugar syrup to taste in a big glass. Hold some sort of lid over the glass and shake it all up. This is traditionally drank with a huge (wide diameter) straw which you can find at Asian markets. The straw is just wide enough for the pearls to fit through. They go "shoomp" every time you suck one up. Now go do something productive or stupid with your buzz.

Immunitea

Music: Evil Blood-Midnight in Sodom demo (1989)

Licorice root
Astragalus root
Ginseng
Green tea
Thyme (optional)
Hyssop (optional)
Crumbled slippery elm bark (optional)

Bring a pot of water to a near boil. Break up a handful of licorice root into it. Now break up four or so pieces of astragalus into it. Let it all simmer for about 15 minutes. Now add some ginseng and couple tablespoons of green tea. If you have a sore throat, add a couple tablespoons of slippery elm and drink it warm. If you have a chest cough or difficulty breathing, add a couple tablespoons each of thyme, hyssop, and slippery elm and drink it cool. If you have a head cold, add the hyssop and drink it hot. Astragalus is incredible for the immune system and the body in general, but *it should not be consumed while you have a fever.* Let whatever combination you decide on simmer for five minutes or so before drinking.

Brewtalitea

Music: Mutilated-Psychodeath Lunatics demo (1988)

Green tea
Red tea
Licorice root
Peppermint leaves

Bring a pot of water to a near boil. Break up a handful of licorice root into it and let it simmer for about 15 minutes. Add a couple tablespoons each of the teas and the peppermint and let simmer for five minutes or so. Great hot or iced.

Insanitea

Music: Insanity-live rehearsal demo (1985)

Licorice root
Ginger root
Cayenne
Orange pekoe tea

Bring a pot of water to a near boil. Break up a handful of licorice root into it. Add about 2 inches' worth of sliced ginger root and let it simmer for about 15 minutes. Sprinkle in some cayenne powder and a couple tablespoons of black tea. Let it simmer for five minutes or so. Great hot or iced.

For us, nothing is sacred any more. A law by which we live, the only sound a broken bell. Entering your shrines, eating your gods, burning your cathedrals.

Lustmørd

Watermintmelon Slushie

Music: Paradise Lost-Frozen Illusion demo (1989)

3 cups cubed watermelon, seeded
½ cup cold mint tea
½ cup soda water
Mint sprigs

Freeze the watermelon overnight. Combine everything but the mint sprigs in a blender and puree until thick and smooth. Pour into glasses and serve with the sprigs of mint. Sip slowly and enjoy the refreshment or gulp quickly and revel in the pain of coolie-head.

How much of your life comes at you through a screen, vicariously? How many times have you rejected the opportunity to play a sport, or watch an animal in its natural habitat, or participate in a drama-filled relationship, or risk danger because you were too busy watching someone else do it on television? When we allow our lives to become less interesting, exciting, and invigorating than the lives we watch on television or in the movies, we cheat not only ourselves but also those with whom we interact. Consequently, our loss is the television programmers' and movie producers' gain. The less we live our own lives, the more dependent we are on them to provide people to live "our" vicarious lives for us...and the more we are willing to pay for it. In the two hours you wasted watching this summer's blockbuster which you found "wasn't as great as it was hyped-up to be after all," you could have cooked an intricate meal for someone you care about or someone you hope will soon care about you. For the $45 you just spent on this month's cable plus premium channels, you could have had enough gas money to drive from the Midwest to New Orleans and still had enough left over to buy a beer or three when you got there. For the most part, we have the power to create our own adventures, our own dramas, and our own entertainment. We simply have to learn to recognize the opportunities. We need to learn how to transform our needs, our desires, and our interests into action. From there, we can reclaim, reinvent, and rejuvenate our lives...no apologies granted. It starts at home. Kill your television. The rest will follow.

"Fade to Carob" Cocoa

Music: Metallica-No Life 'til Leather demo (1982)

1 qt cashew, coconut, or soy milk
3-4 Tbsp carob powder
5 pitted dates
A pinch of sea salt
1/2 tsp vanilla or 1 Tbsp malt syrup
2 Tbsp soy or safflower oil

Liquefy all ingredients except oil until smooth in a blender. Heat, but do not bring to a boil. Add oil slowly and blend again. Reheat and nourish yourself. Healing is a gradual process and must be done on your own terms.

Music: Dripping-Disintegration of Thought Patterns During a Synthetic Mind
Traveling Bliss lp (2002)

Absinthe is an alcoholic drink made with extract of wormwood (Artemisia Absinthium). It is an emerald green drink which is very bitter (due to the presence of absinthin) and is therefore traditionally poured over a perforated spoonful of sugar into a glass of water. The drink then turns an opaque white as the essential oils precipitate out of the alcoholic solution. Absinthe was once popular among artists and writers and was purportedly used by Van Gogh, Baudelaire, and Verlaine, to name a few. It appears to have been believed to stimulate creativity. However, in the 1850s, concern about the results of chronic use developed. Excessive use of absinthe was believed to produce a syndrome (absinthism) which was characterized by addiction, hyperexcitability, and hallucinations. It is widely believed that Van Gogh cut off his ear under the influence of absinthe. This is not the traditional recipe (which is still available in parts of Spain and Portugal) and is consequently not of the same potency or color of earlier times.

1 pint vodka
2 tsp crumbled, dried wormwood
2 tsp anise seed
½ tsp fennel seed
4 cardamom pods
1 tsp marjoram
½ tsp ground coriander
2 tsp chopped angelica root
1 2/3 cups sugar syrup (water that has been saturated with sugar)

Place the vodka in a large jar with a tight-fitting lid. Add the wormwood and shake well. Steep the concoction 48 hours and then strain it. Crush the seeds and pods with a mortar and pestle. Add the seeds and pods and all the remaining spices to the vodka and allow it to steep in a warm place for 1 week. Strain it again. Sweeten it with the sugar syrup. Enjoy your journey.

> What most people don't understand is that you have to gather certain bits of knowledge from varied sources scattered around a large area, and these bits usually aren't what you were looking for, but you must make them yours. It is as simple as turning the day into the night, going down instead of up. Replacing life with Death and seeing Lucifer instead of God.
>
> Glaurung/Warloghe

Thank Christ for the Bodybomb

Music: Bestial Warlust-Vengeance War 'till Death lp (1994)

What if you could make a non-alcoholic drink with medicinal properties that had the power to make you feel instantly really good and as loopy as shotgunning four beers? Well, now you can. Shou Wu Chih is a non-alcoholic Chinese herbal tonic that uses polygonum root and Chinese angelica root as its base. It's in a highly concentrated form and is really meant to be taken two tablespoons at a time. But we all know full-well that taking the recommended dose of anything doesn't get you anywhere in life. Knowing that many people subscribe to this latter perspective, you can often find the drink pre-refrigerated at corner stores. If not there, you can most assuredly find it in a bright orange box on the shelf in any Asian market. It usually runs four to five bucks a bottle. There are many companies that produce the same drink. I prefer the one with the tower in the logo. Rock Star is a non-alcoholic energy drink that you can find just about anywhere. I imagine you could use any energy drink, but my friend contacted Rock Star directly and received confirmation that the drink is indeed vegan. The primary ingredient in question was taurine, and the manufacturer reports that it is taken from a synthetic source.

1 17.5 oz/500 mL bottle Shou Wu Chih
1 16 oz can Rock Star energy drink
Ice (optional)

Very simple. Mix 1/3 of the bottle of Shou Wu Chih with 1/3 of the bottle of Rock Star. Drink it. When the mood strikes you, do it again. Now do it a third time. Enjoy your time on top of the world in the best way you see fit.

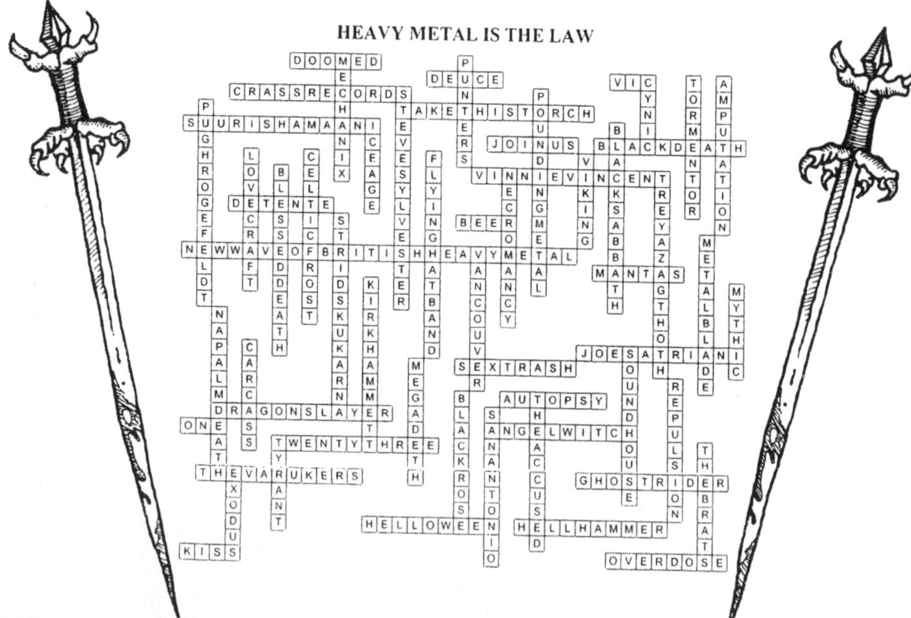

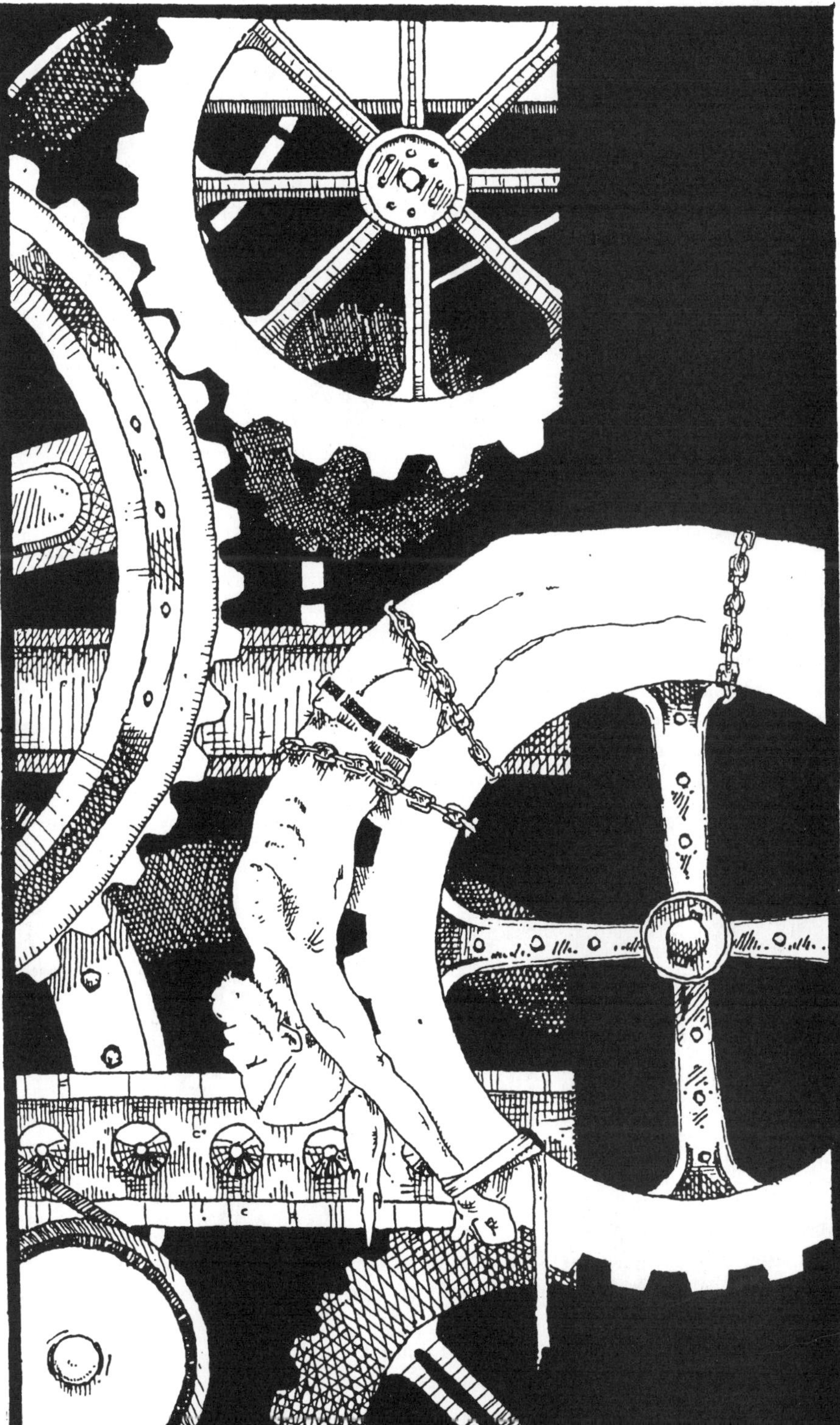

Misc.

LUCIFUGE ROFOCALE

DISMAS ET GESTAS DAMNATUR POTESTAS.
DISMA ET GESTAS DAMNATUR.
AD ASTRA LEVATUR.

Twists of Cain

Music: Ondskapt-Dödens Evangelium 2Xlp (2005)

1 1/3 cups water
2 Tbsp margarine
1½ Tbsp sugar
¾ tsp sea salt
4 cups all-purpose flour
2½ tsp yeast

Also: 4 cups water
1½ baking soda
Kosher salt

Mix the first six ingredients into a firm dough and knead for 10 minutes or so. Cut the dough into short strips, roll into ropes, and form into pretzel shapes. Cover and let rise on a greased baking sheet for 45 minutes. In a non-aluminum pan, bring the 4 cups of water and baking soda to almost a boil. Lower one pretzel at a time into the water for about 1 minute, turning once. Don't let the water come to a full boil, though I'm not sure why. Once removed from the water, place each pretzel on the greased baking sheet. Sprinkle with Kosher salt. Bake in an oven preheated to 475°F for 12 minutes or so. Serve warm with jalapeno yellow mustard.

Cracked Wheat Crackers

Music: Corpse Molestation-Descension of a Darker Deity demo (1992)

1 cup unbleached white flour
1 tsp baking powder
½ tsp sea salt
¼ cup cracked wheat
¼ tsp poppy seeds
2 tsp cold margarine
½ cup ice water

Mix the flour, baking powder, salt, cracked wheat, and poppy seeds in a bowl. Mix in the margarine until it is well blended. Quickly (but lightly) stir in enough ice water to make a dough that holds together. Divide this into two parts and form each into a ball.

Pat each ball into a rectangle on a lightly floured board. Roll it out really, really thin with a rolling pin. Cut it up into 2" squares and bake on a ungreased cookie sheet at 350°F for 10 minutes or until crisp. Cool on racks and store in an airtight container, if possible.

Burned Up, Bled Dry Bacon

Music: Flames of Hell-Fire and Steel lp (1987)

1 lb extra firm tofu, cut into bacon-sized strips
2 Tbsp nutritional yeast
2 Tbsp soy sauce
1 tsp liquid smoke
1 Tbsp vegetable oil

Fry the tofu strips on low or medium heat until they are crispy on the outside. The best way to do this is to lay them in a pan in the heated oil and let them simmer for 10 minutes or so. They should turn easily after that. Turn them, and give them another 10 minutes on the other side.

Mix the soy sauce with the liquid smoke. Now take the pan off the heat. Pour the liquid into the pan and stir the tofu such that all surfaces are coated, then sprinkle the yeast all over the top. Continue to stir over the heat until the liquid is gone and the tofu is covered with sticky yeast.

Kangaroo Bread (Pita)

Music: Portal-Seepia (2003)

1 cup warm water (at about 115°F)
1/8 tsp sugar
1½ packages active dry yeast (1½ Tbsp)
2 Tbsp olive oil
¾ tsp sea salt
3 cups unbleached white flour

Warm a bowl with hot tap water. Empty it and mix in ½ cup of the warm water and the sugar. Sprinkle the yeast on top and stir. When the mixture becomes bubbly after 7 or 10 minutes, add the rest of the warm water. Add the oil, salt, and flour to the mixture and knead thoroughly. Heat the oven to 150°F for 1½ minutes, then turn it off. Put the dough in a bowl, cover it, and place it in the oven (now off) for 15 minutes.

Take the dough out and punch it down. It should be warm and kind of sticky. Knead briefly on a floured board. Divide the dough into four equal parts. Flatten each piece and roll each into a circle that is 6 or 7" in diameter. Dust two cookie sheets with cornmeal and put two pitas on each. Cover and let rest in the still-warm oven for 5 minutes. Turn over carefully, bottom side up and remove from the oven. Preheat the oven to 500°F. Put the cookie sheets in side by side on the lowest rack for 5 minutes. Do not open the oven door during this time. The pitas are puffing up and need to be left alone. Then put the sheet on the middle rack for 3 to 5 minutes. Remove from the oven and cool on cooling racks. After cooling, wrap them in plastic to prevent them from losing their softness.

Flux of Pink Injeri

Music: Antisect-In Darkness There is No Choice lp (1984)

2 cups finely ground teff flour
3 cups lukewarm water
1 tsp dry yeast
1 cup water

You will need a large bowl with a lid or cover, a small bowl, a saucepan, and a 10-12" heavy nonstick skillet with a tight-fitting lid.

Place the flour in a large bowl. Add 2½ cups of warm water, using your fingers to mix and break up any lumps. The batter should be smooth and almost runny.

Dissolve the yeast in the remaining ½ cup warm water, then stir into the batter. Cover and set aside for 2 to 3 days to sour.

When ready to proceed, drain off any water that has separated from the batter and settled on the surface.

Bring 1 cup water to a boil, and stir in ½ cup of the soured batter to blend well. Lower the heat to medium and heat, stirring, until thick and smooth. Remove from the heat and cool until just warm to the touch but not hot. Stir into the soured batter. If necessary to make the batter runny, add a little more warm water and then let rise for 30-60 minutes.

Preheat a large skillet over medium heat. When hot, stir the batter and then scoop ½ cup batter (or slightly less if your pan is less than 12" diameter) into a cup and, beginning near the outer edge of the pan, slowly pour it in a thin stream, moving in a spiral toward the center of the pan. Then tilt the pan so the batter can flow over and cover any gaps. Cover and let cook for 2 minutes, then check to see if it's done: when done, the edges of the bread will begin to curl away from the pan. If not yet done, wipe the lid dry, cover the pan, and cook for about 1 or 2 minutes longer. Use a wooden spatula to begin lifting the bread off of the hot surface, then peel it off, lay it on a towel, and wrap it to keep it moist and warm. Stir the batter well, then cook the remaining bread in the same way.

> Men were designed for short, nasty, brutal lives. Women are designed for long, miserable ones.
>
> Dr. Estelle Ramey

Flour Tortillas

Music: Goat Semen-South American Black Destructive Metal Mayhem demo (2003)

4 cups flour (all-purpose or ½ all-purpose + ½ cup whole wheat)
1½ tsp sea salt
1½ baking powder
4 Tbsp vegetable shortening
1½ cups warm water

Combine the dry ingredients, then cut in the shortening. Make a small well in the center and gradually add water. Knead the dough until it is soft, smooth, and elastic. Set it aside for 10 minutes, then divide it into 12 equally-sized balls. Roll the balls into 1/8" thick circles and cook on a preheated, ungreased grill for about 2 minutes a side, or until the tortilla is lightly speckled. Cover the warm tortillas to keep them soft and pliable.

Sandor's Soy Yogurt

Music: Autumn-The Druid Autumn demo (1995)

Half gallon (60 oz) minus a half cup of soymilk (see recipe in this book)
Half a cup of fresh live culture soy yogurt for starter
Half gallon jar
Insulated cooler

Preheat the half gallon jar and insulated cooler with hot water.

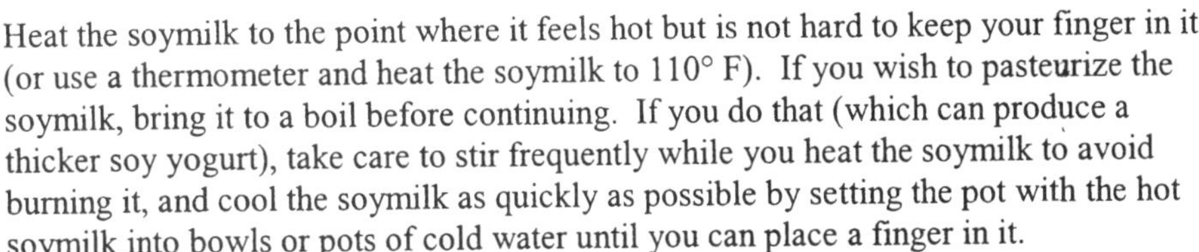

Heat the soymilk to the point where it feels hot but is not hard to keep your finger in it (or use a thermometer and heat the soymilk to 110° F). If you wish to pasteurize the soymilk, bring it to a boil before continuing. If you do that (which can produce a thicker soy yogurt), take care to stir frequently while you heat the soymilk to avoid burning it, and cool the soymilk as quickly as possible by setting the pot with the hot soymilk into bowls or pots of cold water until you can place a finger in it.

Mix the starter soy yogurt into the hot soymilk. Stir well and pour the mixture into the preheated jar, loosely capped.

Place the jar in the preheated insulated cooler. If much space remains in the cooler, fill it with bottles of hot water (not too hot to the touch) and/or towels. Close the cooler. Place the cooler in a warm spot.

Check the soy yogurt after 8-12 hours. It should have a tangy flavor and some thickness. Thickness will vary with the unique cultural and environmental conditions.

Soy yogurt can store in the refrigerator for weeks. Save some of your soy yogurt to use as a starter for the next batch. If after a number of generations your soy yogurt culture seems to be weakening, freshen it by introducing some new starter yogurt.

Self-Inflicted Evisceration Death Sauce (aka Night Terror Sauce)

Music: Insidious Decrepancy-Decadent Orgy of Atrocious Suffering lp (2004)

I've wanted to make my own superhot sauce for a while now...not like Tabasco or any weak-ass stuff like that...more along the lines of Dave's Insanity Sauce. I wasn't able to reach the extremity of Dave's (sorry, no oleoresin capsicum extract), but I was able to make a downright fiery concoction that will tempt you with its fruitiness and then set your fucking head on fire (let alone your arse). Prepare thyself.

12 fresh habanero peppers
1 medium carrot, peeled and diced
1 ½ cups apple cider vinegar
1 ripe mango, peeled, pitted, and diced
½ cup diced red onion
Juice of 1 lime
2 cloves garlic
2 Tbsp turbinado sugar
¼ tsp ground turmeric

In a medium saucepan, combine the habaneros, carrot, vinegar, mango, onion, lime juice, garlic, sugar, and turmeric and bring to simmer over medium heat. Reduce heat to medium-low and cook for 15-20 minutes, stirring occasionally. DO NOT INHALE THE VAPORS or you will pay dearly. Sorry, that's just the way it is *.

Remove the sauce from the heat and let cool slightly. Pour into a blender and blend until it is a smooth, deadly liquid. Bottle and refrigerate.

**Okay, one more real quick story to attest to the powers of habaneros: the other day I made some vegan jello (no, not that kind) from a mix I found in the Indian section of our grocery store. It was a new flavor (orange, my favorite) and I was pretty danged excited to try it. I prepared it, cooled it off for a couple hours, and eagerly devoured the whole bowl at once. About halfway through, I noticed my mouth was burning. From jello? No, it couldn't be. I ate more. My nose was starting to run and my mouth was starting to really get a bit of fire in it. I couldn't for the life of me figure out what was going on. Was it the vegan gelatin ingredient? Why didn't the other flavors burn like this? Then it hit me...I had used the same pot to boil the water and mix the jello that I had used over three weeks before to make the Self-Inflicted Evisceration Death Sauce. The pot had been washed (yes, with soap), and had not been used since. Absolutely amazing.*

Sour Uncream

Music: Yog Sothots-1987 demo (1987)

12 oz lite silken tofu
4 tsp lemon juice
1 Tbsp canola oil
1 Tbsp umeboshi vinegar
Sea salt to taste

Puree the tofu until smooth and creamy in a blender. Add the lemon juice a little at a time. Add the oil while blending. Fine tune the flavor with vinegar and salt. Refrigerate at least 12 hours before using, as the uncream needs time for the flavors to meld.

Dill-icious Pickles

Music: Necrophilia-Death Putrefact demo (1988)

2 cups cider vinegar
1/3 cup sugar
1/3 cup non-iodized salt or canning salt
½ cup (packed) fresh dill
3 white onions, peeled and chopped
3 cloves garlic, peeled and thinly sliced
3½-4 lbs small Kirby cucumbers (enough to fill a 1 gallon jar), well-scrubbed
1 tsp mustard or celery seed

Sterilize a 1 gallon glass jar and lid by immersing them in boiling water for 10 minutes. Set aside to dry. In a large enameled, glass or other non-reactive saucepan, combine six cups water with the vinegar, sugar, and salt. Bring to a boil, then reduce heat to low. Let simmer while proceeding with the recipe.

Place a third of the dill in the bottom of the jar. Top with a third of the onion and a third of the garlic. Starting with the smallest cucumbers, pack one layer horizontally over the garlic. Place another layer crosswise over the first. Continue until the jar is two-thirds full, packing the jar tightly and filling gaps with cucumbers halved lengthwise. Add another third of the dill, followed by a third of the onion and the garlic. Top with cucumbers, packing tightly. Top with remaining dill, onion, and garlic.

Place jar in a large plastic basin and carefully pour the hot vinegar mixture into the jar to fill it completely. Using a long wooden skewer, gently poke the cucumbers deep in the jar to dislodge any air bubbles. Add more vinegar mixture, if necessary. Let it sit for five minutes. Add more vinegar mixture to fill the jar to the brim, and top with mustard or celery seed. If using a metal lid, place a large piece of wax paper over the top of the jar before fastening the lid to prevent corrosion.

Let the mixture cool to room temperature. Remove the jar from the basin and wipe clean. Refrigerate pickles at least 24 hours before eating. The pickles may be refrigerated up to a year.

> The most merciful thing in the world, I think, is the inability of the human mind to correlate all its contents. We live on a placid island of ignorance in the midst of black seas of infinity, and it was not meant that we should voyage far. The sciences, each straining in its own direction, have hitherto harmed us little; but some day the piecing together of dissociated knowledge will open up such terrifying vistas of reality, and of our frightful position therein, that we shall either go mad from the revelation or flee from the deadly light into the peace and safety of a new dark age.
>
> H.P. Lovecraft

Roasted Seed Bread

Music: Root-Poslové Z Temnot (Messengers from Darkness) demo (1989)

1 cup roasted, unsalted sunflower seeds
1 cup sesame seeds
¼ cup millet seeds
¼ cup poppy seeds
1 Tbsp nigella seeds or black caraway seeds
¼ cup dried, minced onion
4-6 cups unbleached white bread flour, divided
2 Tbsp dry yeast
¼ cup sugar
1 Tbsp sea salt
2 cups hot (130-140°F) water
2 Tbsp corn oil

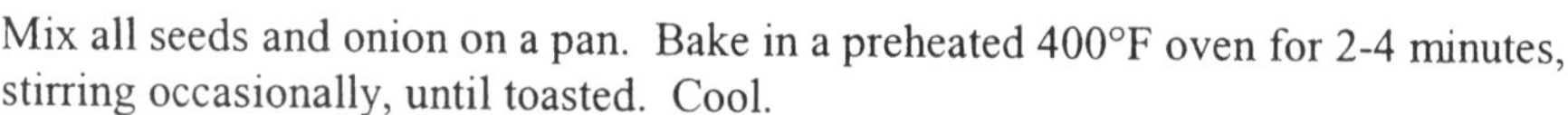

Mix all seeds and onion on a pan. Bake in a preheated 400°F oven for 2-4 minutes, stirring occasionally, until toasted. Cool.

Mix together 4 cups flour, yeast, sugar, and salt. Add the hot water and corn oil and mix 2 minutes by hand. Add cooled, toasted seeds and additional flour ½ cup at a time until a soft dough forms.

Turn the dough out onto a floured surface and knead 8-10 minutes or until the dough is smooth and elastic. Place it in a greased bowl, and turn the dough to coat. Cover the bowl and let rise for 1 hour or until doubled in volume. Punch the dough down, divide into three pieces, and let it all rest for 5 minutes.

Shape the dough into 3 long loaves approximately 3 X 16" and place on a baking sheet that has either been lightly greased or sprinkled with cornmeal. Let it rise for 30-45 minutes.

Bake the loaves in a preheated 370°F oven for 25-25 minutes. Cool on wire racks.

Slice the cooled loaves into ¼" slices and dry in a single layer on baking sheets in a 250°F oven until crisp but not browned. When cool, store in airtight bags or containers.

Brie Cheese

Music: Killers-Mise aux Poings lp (1987)

1 1/2 cups water
2 Tbsp agar-agar (powder or flakes)
1/2 cup raw cashews, finely ground
1/2 cup firm tofu, crumbled
1/4 cup nutritional yeast flakes
1/4 cup lemon juice
2 Tbsp tahini
1 1/2 tsp onion powder
1 tsp sea salt
1/4 tsp garlic powder
1/8 tsp ground dill seed
2 tbsp wheat germ (optional)

Place water and agar-agar in a small saucepan and bring to a boil. Reduce heat and simmer 5 minutes. Place this mixture immediately into a blender or food processor with remaining ingredients (except wheat germ) and blend until completely smooth.

Pour immediately into a 2 1/2 cup round dish or pie plate that has been lightly oiled and dusted with wheat germ, if desired. Cool, cover and chill.

Turn out onto a plate and slice into wedges. Eat with red wine and cracked wheat crackers (see recipe this book).

Vegan Mozzarella Cheese

Music: Necromass-Mysteria Mystica Zothyriana lp (1994)

1 cup water
2 small cloves garlic, roasted
2 Tbsp fresh lemon juice
2 Tbsp tahini
¼ cup nutritional yeast
3 Tbsp quick-cooking rolled oats
1Tbsp arrowroot
1/8 tsp dry mustard
1½ tsp onion powder
½ tsp sea salt
¼ tsp liquid smoke

Place all ingredients in a blender and process until completely smooth. Pour in a saucepan and cook over medium heat, stirring constantly until it thickens. Serve over French onion soup, baked potatoes, broccoli, or whatever.

Big Bear Berbere

Music: Voivod-RRRÖÖÖAAARRR lp (1986)

This is an imitation of and Ethiopian spice which is often difficult to find in the U.S. Definitely use the original, if it is available. It's the best.

1½ Tbsp ground red pepper
2 tbsp paprika
1 Tbsp onion salt
1 tsp garlic powder
1 tsp basil
½ tsp ground ginger
¼ tsp black pepper
1/8 tsp ground cloves
1/8 tsp each: ground cinnamon, ground cardamom, ground nutmeg, ground allspice, ground cumin, ground fenugreek, and ground turmeric

> And behold another beast like a bear stood up on one side: and there were three rows in the mouth thereof, and in the teeth thereof, and thus they said to it: Arise, devour much flesh.
>
> Daniel 7:5

Thoroughly blend the spices.
Place in a well-sealed spice jar.
Makes about ½ cup.

Sage Fugazi (Fougasse)

Music: DAI-The Advent lp (1993)

1 Tbsp active dry yeast
1 cup warm water
3 Tbsp olive oil
2 tsp sea salt
2½ cups unbleached flour
2 Tbsp cornmeal
About 20 whole sage leaves

Dissolve the yeast in the warm water in a large mixing bowl and let it sit 5 minutes. Add 1 Tbsp olive oil, 1 tsp salt, and 1 cup flour. Stir well and add the remaining flour. Dump the dough onto a well-floured counter and knead until smooth and soft (about 10 minutes). Place the dough in a lightly-oiled bowl and turn the dough, so as to coat it. Cover the bowl with a damp towel and let it rise in a warm place for about an hour.

Preheat the oven to 400°F. Lightly oil two baking sheets and sprinkle each with 1 Tbsp cornmeal. Divide the dough in half and roll each ball into a 9" circle and place each on its respective baking sheet. With a sharp knife, cut several 2-3" slits in each loaf. Feel free to be creative. Spread the slits apart with your fingers and brush the tops of the loaves with the remaining olive oil. Press the sage leaves into the dough firmly and sprinkle the loaves with ½ tsp salt each.

Let the dough rise again for about 15 minutes with a clean, damp kitchen towel loosely on top of the loaves. Bake for 20 minutes, or until golden brown.

Dog Biscuits Deluxe

Music: Ulver-Vargnatt demo (1993)

Yep, these are real dog biscuits.

2 cups whole wheat flour
½ cup soy flour
¼ cup cornmeal
½ cup sunflower or pumpkin seeds
1-2 cloves garlic, minced
1 Tbsp nutritional yeast
2 Tbsp margarine, melted
¼ cup unsulfered mo-lasses
1 tsp sea salt
2 eggs worth of egg replacer mixed with ¼ cup soy milk

Mix the flours, cornmeal, and seeds together. Add the garlic and yeast. Combine the margarine, mo-lasses, salt, and egg replacer; set aside 1 Tbsp of this liquid mixture and combine the rest with the dry ingredients. Add more soy milk, if necessary, to make a firm dough. Knead together for a few minutes and let dough rest 30 minutes or more. Roll out into ½ inch thick cylinder and cut into crescents, rounds, or sticks and brush with the remainder of the egg replacer mixture. Bake at 350° F for 30 minutes or until lightly toasted.

Cajun Hellspice

Music: Exumer-Possessed by Fire lp (1986)

4 parts sea salt
3 parts cayenne pepper
3 parts black pepper, ground
3 parts granulated garlic (do *not* use garlic salt or garlic powder)
2 parts MSG
1 part cumin, ground
1 part paprika

Combine all ingredients and blend well. Use whenever you would normally use salt and pepper.

Chili-Roasted Peanuts

Music: Tudor-Spalovda ep (1991)

1½ Tbsp peanut oil
½ Tbsp crushed red pepper flakes
1 Tbsp ground cumin
¼ tsp turmeric
1 Tbsp sugar
4 cups raw peanuts

Preheat the oven to 325°F. Combine all of the ingredients except the nuts in a baking pan and mix well. Add the nuts and toss to mix. Spread the nuts in an even layer and bake for about 20 minutes or until golden, stirring 2 or 3 times.

"I'll be Damned if I'm Gonna Pay $4 for Ny-Quil" Homemade Cough Syrups

Yep, these were lifted directly from Angel Page's amazing D.I.Y Health Guide

Recipe 1, for day-time cough and sore throat:

Music: Morbid Angel-Abominations of Desolation lp (1991)

Ounces (or whatever) can be directly substituted for tablespoons if you'd like to make a larger batch.

2 Tbsp slippery elm bark
2 Tbsp valerian
2 Tbsp comfrey root
1 Tbsp wild cherry bark
2 Tbsp licorice root
1 Tbsp ginger root
1 Tbsp cinnamon bark
4 Tbsp fennel seed
1/8 Tbsp orange peel
Brandy (optional)
Essential oil of peppermint, wintergreen, or spearmint (optional)

Mix all the herbs and such together.
1) Use 2 ounces of the herb mixture for every 1 quart of water. Over low heat, simmer the liquid down to one pint. This will give you a very thick, concentrated tea.
2) Strain the herbs from the liquid. Compost them if possible.
3) To each pint's worth of liquid, add one cup maple syrup (or brown or white sugar).
4) Warm the mixture and stir well. Continue heating for 20-30 minutes. The longer you heat it, the thicker it gets.
5) When finished heating, you may add brandy. Not only will it add flavor and preserve the liquid, brandy also serves to relax the throat muscles and calm spastic coughing. 3-4 Tbsp per cup of liquid should be appropriate. Adding a couple drops of peppermint, wintergreen, or spearmint adds a refreshing flavor and additional medicinal properties.
6) Remove from heat and bottle for use. May last several weeks or months if refrigerated.

Recipe 2, for night-time cough and sore throat:

Music: Internal Suffering-Choronzonic Force Domination lp (2004)
½ pint whiskey
1 lemon
Peppermint candies
Sweetener/thickener (maple syrup, rice syrup, brown or white sugar, or whatever)

Heat the ½ pint of whiskey over medium heat. Add enough sweetener to thicken and sweeten. Add as much peppermint and lemon as desired…these are for flavoring. Continue heating until all ingredients are melted and blended well. Try to drink while hot (obviously not all of it though). It should knock you right the fuck out.

Wonderful Wheat Paste

Music: Mutilator-Grave Desecration demo (1985)

I should hope you know what this is for. If they can plaster their advertisements and political endorsements wherever they please, then why shouldn't you be able to do the same? Just don't get caught using it...once it's on, it's on for real.

To start off, you need to figure out how much you want to make. A six-cup mixture lasts for about 70 fliers, so make lots. The mixture is about 1 cup of wheat flour to every two cups of water, and then add 3 Tbsp cornstarch to that. Put the water in a pot and allow it to heat up slowly on the stove. Slowly add the flour and cornstarch to the water as it is heating (*before* it gets hot...very important). Adding the flour in sprinkles then stirring makes it much easier to manage, and less clumpy.

Once the mixture comes to a simmer, immediately pour the paste into the container that you will be using to transport your mixture. Let cool. Use a paintbrush to apply it. Make sure to paint a layer of paste, administer the propaganda, and then paint another layer of paste over the top of the flier. This way, it will stick and hold up to foul weather better. 1, 2, 3...destroy.

> There is no form of popular music in the industrial world that exists outside the province of mass tonal consciousness. As Richard Norton said so well: "It is the tonality of the church, school, office, parade, convention, cafeteria, workplace, airport, airplane, automobile, truck, tractor, lounge, lobby, bar, gym, brothel, bank, and elevator. Afraid of being without it on foot, humans are presently strapping it to their bodies in order to walk to it, run to it, work to it, and relax to it. It is everywhere. It is music and it writes the songs."
>
> It is also as totally integrated into commercialized mass production as any product of the assembly line. The music never changes from the seemingly eternal formula, despite superficial variations; the 'good' song, the harmonically marketable song, is one that contains fewer different chords than a 14th century ballad. Its expressive potential exists solely within the limited confines of consumer choice, wherein, according to Horkheimer and Adorno, "Something is provided for everyone so that none shall escape." As a one-dimensional code of consumer society, it is a training course in passivity.
>
> John Zerzan, "Tonality and the Totality"

Teeth Whitener

Music: Amputation-Slaughtered in the Arms of God demo (1990)

For those of us who drink strong, dark tea all day, every day.

1 tsp baking soda
Hydrogen peroxide

Mix enough hydrogen peroxide into the baking soda to make a paste.
Brush for a minimum of two minutes.

I feel like you can judge the character of any person simply by asking what his or her favorite Carcass release is. I've found that any post-Tools of the Trade response is reason to be suspicious of serious character and taste flaws. So here it is: my ultimate Carcass interview. To be clear, I did not come up with or ask any of these questions. Rather, I've gone through just about every Carcass interview that exists and have pieced together what I felt were the most interesting and informative questions and responses. The only question that remains for me is this: what the fuck happened in 1992? Was it a conscious decision to turn whack? I mean really, what happened?

Give us an introduction of who Carcass is!

Jeff Walker: Carcass is a psychic reality, making vibrations in the air which, when they are caught up by the human ear, can be interpreted as either: A-Pure Noise. B-Extremely striking, twisted, nauseating music containing varying tempos and a cocktail of bestial growls. Carcass consists of Ken Owen (drums/tenor vocals), Bill Steer (guitar/bass vocals) and myself, Jeff (bass/soprano vocals). (1990)

For those more recent fans and devotees, please elaborate on how Carcass came into being - how did Bill, Ken and yourself meet and when and where did the first rehearsals and songwriting sessions as a band take place?

Jeff: Bill and Ken and a couple of friends when they were really young coined the name "Carcass", I guess was a kinda "bedroom" band, just messing about, you know a sort extreme metal band as they were into early Thrash and Death Metal and so on. I met/was asked to join the band that Bill was in then, they were called "Disattack" and as the name suggests they were a Discharge "clone" band. The then singer asked me to join playing bass, they were changing their name to Carcass as they liked that name and Bill had a logo that a Scottish lad (I believe) had drawn (it looked suspiciously like the Marillion logo to me!) and they were changing "tact" from being a straight ahead hardcore band to doing more "metal" stuff as I guess Bill was starting to speak up and wrestle control/influence away from the rest of the band. One of the first things I did was draw the Carcass logo that the band used! We used to rehearse in Bill's parents house on the top floor- we only had a few rehearsals as a four piece - the drummer kind of lost interest, which was convenient as we kinda lost interest in his pedestrian style (me and Bill wanted a more faster drummer shall we say?)! So anyhow Bill suggested his friend Ken who had just bought a cheap kit and was starting to play, so we started rehearsing with Ken. The vocalist then decided he didn't want to continue so he quit, his final act being to suggest Sanjiv. (2003)

A great many death metal bands, including Obituary, tune their guitars down to D [*D, G, C, F, A, D, low to high*]. In fact, some, like Carcass, even go lower. Is detuning essential to play this style of music?

Mike Hickey: Carcass tunes down to B. By that I mean we take a normally tuned guitar and then drop each string down two-and-a-half steps, so they go: B, E, A, D, F#, B, low to high. To counteract the string slackness created by this tuning, we use pretty heavy gauges--.012 to .056, I can't remember the ones in the middle, but the G string's a plain .022. B isn't the most practical tuning in the world, but it's probably the heaviest, and we're stuck with it whether we like it or not! (1994)

Bill Steer: It's like playing something that's almost halfway between a guitar and bass, actually. We've tuned this low ever since the band started, because it's so crushing--there's nothing else quite like it. Having said that, it has a lot of shortcomings in terms of tone because it's a very unrealistic tuning; we've really had to struggle to make it work. Since we've been doing it so long we can just about pull it off, but to be brutally honest, I think D, or, at a push C# [*C#, F#, B, E, G#, C#, low to high*], are the best tunings. (1994)

Do you know anyone who broke his or her hi-fi equipment while listening to Carcass' first LP?

Bill: I don't know anyone who's blown any speakers while playing the first Carcass LP. Perhaps it might have caused some damage if the pressing hadn't been so quiet, but the guy at the pressing plant told Dig that it had to be that way or else the bass frequencies would take over completely. He said that he had never heard such low frequencies (sometimes touching 25 hz) on an album! (1990)

Who writes your texts and what are they about?

Jeff: I write the most of the texts nowadays. What they are about??!! There is no special theme about them. There are some few cryptic ideas behind them, but they are mainly written just to be scary, firm and extremely repulsive. Anybody with intelligence should find them repulsive but harmless, while anybody who thinks they're disgusting and even dangerous deserves to bathe in their own stupidity. (1990)

What inspired you to sing about gore?

Bill: Well, the idea had been around since 1985, when Ken came up with lyrics to songs like "Feast on Dismembered Carnage" and "Psychopathologist," and I suggested the name Carcass for our band. From then on, we felt that if ever we got a band off the ground together, it would have OTT, medically accurate, grotesque lyrics. There was the odd death metal band with splatter-film influenced songs, but we saw there was obviously plenty of room to take the whole "gore" genre a stage further. With us though, the concepts never came from films - they were drawn from books, real-life concepts and so on. (1991)

Was the idea behind Carcass from the very beginning to incorporate extreme imagery and lyrics?

Jeff: Maybe from Bill and Ken, but to be honest the actual "Reek Of Putrefaction" cover is a result of Dig's (Earache) encouragement. When we were recording the album he turned up with a Forensic Medicine book suggesting we use a picture from it - he basically wanted a more "extreme" album cover then Big Black's "Headache" (the limited edition one)...so I went away and encouraged by the fact that he said Lydia Lunch had a sleeve that was a collage I did the "Reek..." sleeve. The lyrics are a result of Ken's twisted imagination (plus the influence of Death and Repulsion, etc.). I kinda added the "medical dictionary" twist as I basically just hijacked my sister's (who was training as nurse) dictionary! Oh I must point out Bill wrote about a third of the lyrics on "Reek..." as well, it was a real "collaboration." (2003)

It's maybe ironic that a lot of the bands influenced by Carcass emphasized only the sicker aspects of the [band] for less savory reasons, did you perhaps feel they had therefore misinterpreted what Carcass was about?

Jeff: Well if people write "sick" lyrics and there's no irony there, and they're "serious," then yes they've definitely "misinterpreted" Carcass - it was all very tongue in cheek, even if that was a severed one inside the mouth of a dead fetus. (2003)

Another topic of dispute is the association with vegetarianism. As a vegetarian, I like the idea of such an intense, truly hard band with a seemingly morose platform as a harbinger of fleshless nutrition, yet in things I'd read, you [Bill] avoided the issue.

Bill: I haven't tried to distance myself from it, certainly. It's not that at all. This is what we find annoying, really, because it's just impossible to get the matter straight. I mean, no one in the band eats meat, and it's to different degrees. In Mike's case he merely doesn't eat meat, he still has seafood and all that other stuff, the other two guys in the band are merely vegetarian, and then I have vegan eating habits, but the point is these are just personal choices and we don't want to ram it down anyone's throats. I really don't subscribe to that ram it down people's throats kind of thing where people who do eat meat are made to feel guilty. I personally can't understand why anyone would want to eat it, but fine, I'm not going to preach to anyone because I can remember years ago when I did eat meat if there's one thing I didn't appreciate it was someone trying to tell me how to live my life or whatever. (1991)

What are your politics?

Bill: None of us have politics that are possible to define in such brief space. Suffice to say that all of us detest sexism, racism and bigotry in general, and none of us have eaten meat (or dairy produce in me and Jeff's case) in years. (1991)

Who would be your perfect woman?

Bill: Again, an awkward question to answer properly. My girlfriend is (I think) perfect for me as there's no-one else I'd rather be with, but to suggest that she's actually "perfect" wouldn't be fair to her or me. I realize that this will sound pathetic, but surely it's best to love someone despite their faults, as opposed to loving them out of a naive belief that they're "perfect?" The main thing that annoys me about this notion of a "perfect" woman is that the standard, expected answer would be a "sex object" type female. Human beings (and sex) are never perfect - and treating a woman as pieces of meat is sick as far as I'm concerned. (1991)

How do you deal with the racist element that has been creeping into the death metal scene?

Jeff: In the past we've had problems in Portland and Phoenix and...well, we played Portland a few nights ago and didn't have any problems, but when we played there the first time there were like a hundred people causing shit. But again our new album has a peace symbol on the cover, so hopefully some people are getting the message. The last time we played Phoenix I walked off after two songs and people were shouting Axl Rose at me and such. But there were fucking people fucking sieg hieling and shit. It really pisses me off that a few hundred people will just stand there and let them do that, fucking up the whole show and being total arseholes. So I said fuck them and just walked off. I mean rather than me go out into the crowd by myself and get killed trying to fight these fuckers, I'd rather leave it to the rest of the people to handle their own scene. But they seemed pretty content to let them do that and that's definitely a big problem. Part of our rider now is that if we see any right wing or White power t-shirts then we're going to pull the show. (2003)

What do you think of straight/total edge?

Bill: I appreciate the idea behind it all, but the fashion aspects are rather laughable. I haven't drunk alcohol in years (and was never into smoking or drugs) but that has nothing to do with the bands I listen to, nor did I feel the urge to shave my head, scrawl an "X" on my hand or wear "positive message" T-shirts. In other words I can't see why some people have to advertise their personal habits and beliefs so much. (1991)

Where did you get all of these sick pictures?

Jeff: I don't understand why they are sick. The pictures are real suffering and accidents. We are not trying to promote these pictures as anything else than scary art. (1990)

Do you listen to Bathory, if so what do you think?

Bill: It's been ages since I last listened to Bathory. I loved the first and second LPs when they came out, but all round I think they (he?) have been very overrated. (1991)

What do you think of all those bands, like General Surgery, that sound like old Carcass?

Jeff: That's actually Matti from Dismember, a good friend of mine. It sounds better than we ever did. They do a better version of Carcass, but there's just the fact that we did it seven years ago. So it kind of makes it irrelevant, but I was flattered that someone is into it that much. There are loads of bands, from Finland, fucking hundreds in Europe. If people ever complain that Carcass doesn't sound like it used to, then they can go listen to those bands; it's as simple as that. (1994)

That's all, anything you would like to add?

Jeff: No, except use your brain. (1990)

Build Your Own Tattoo Machine

Music: Antaeus-Cut Your Flesh and Worship Satan lp (2000)

The construction of this machine is highly variable and flexible. If you find parts that work better, use them. This is just the basic design. If the words don't seem to clear, refer to the drawings. The elegance of this machine lies in the juxtaposition of its simplicity and its destructive capability.

A plastic knife or a 90°, "L" shaped metal bracket
Toy car motor (leave the wires on so you won't need a soldering iron)
2 AA batteries
A Bic "Round Stic" ballpoint pen
Two small rubber bands
Duct tape
Wire (old speaker wire, whatever)
Sewing needles
Bass string ("G"; optional)
Small hammer
Pliers
Pocket knife
Small nail
Soldering iron (optional)

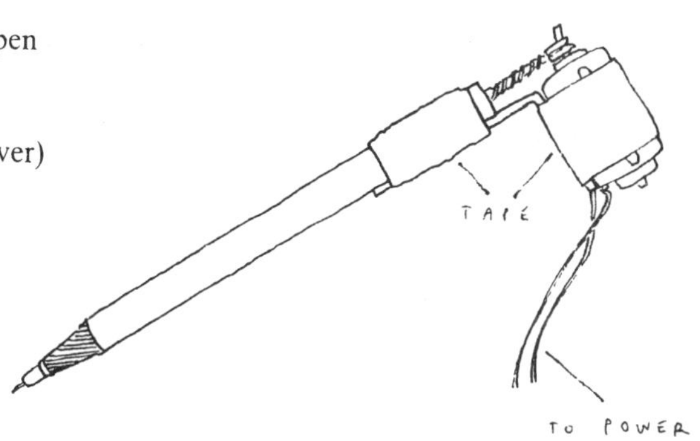

Step 1: Making the Machine Body

Cut off the blade of the knife such that only the handle remains. Bend the handle into an "L" shape, such that the bottom of the "L" is approximately the same length as the motor. You could use a stove, lighter, or some other heat source to heat the handle enough to bend it. Or, you could just use an "L" shaped metal bracket. Again, the bottom of the "L" should be approximately the length of the motor and no more than ½" wide.

Step 2: The Motor

Find a small, cheap "remote" control car. The controller (forward, reverse) should be attached to the vehicle by two wires (typically in the same rubber housing). Dollar stores are a good source for this sort of toy. Small motors can be taken out of old cassette walkmans as well...just make sure that the motor looks approximately like the drawing, that it has two wires coming out of it, and that it can be powered by two AA batteries. Remove the motor from its source. Now, take the pliers and bend the drive shaft of the motor approximately 30-35°. Attach the motor to the machine body in the manner illustrated in the drawing by wrapping wire around it and then wrapping the wire in a couple of layers of duct tape.

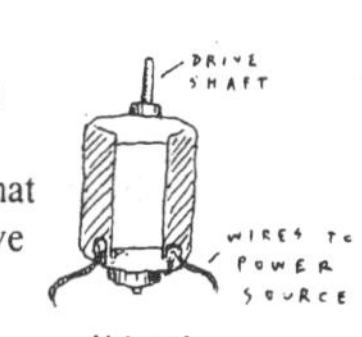

Step 3: The Needle Tube

Using the pliers, pull the pen tip and attached ink reservoir out of the pen. Leave the tapered portion of the pen intact. Using a knife, pop the end cap out of the pen. What you should have left is a hollow tube which tapers at the end. Attach the tube to the machine body in the manner illustrated in the drawing by wrapping wire around it and then wrapping the wire in a couple of layers of duct tape.

It should go without saying that clean needles, safety, and decontamination are very important issues when working with a machine like this. But apparently it doesn't, so it will be henceforth printed here. Clean your needles in an autoclave or always replace them. It's not worth the risk of spreading blood-bourne disease.

Step 4: The Needle

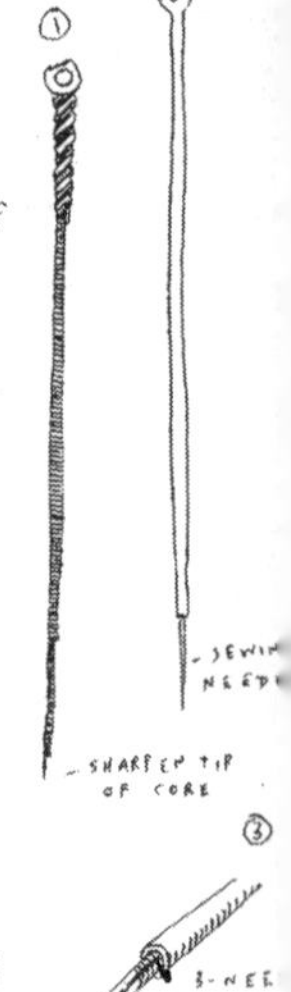

This step has the most flexibility, I've found. Do what works best for you. Here are a few suggestions: 1) Use a bass guitar string. The thinnest string ("G") tends to work well. Leave the loop on the top and cut the other end off at about 6". Unwind about ¾" of the outer wrapping of the string and cut the outer wrapping here. This should leave about ¾" of the string's core exposed. The core will be trimmed and sharpened to better fit the machine in the final assembly stage. 2) Take the pen tip and attached ink reservoir that you pulled from the pen and remove the pen tip which houses the ballpoint. Remove all of the ink from the tube and clean it thoroughly. This can be quite messy. At one end of the tube, smash the last centimeter or so with a hammer such that it is flat, yet not too thin. Now, make a hole in this flat portion which is big enough for the drive shaft of the motor by heating a small nail and pushing it through. Attach a sewing needle with the eye cut off to the other end. You may want to wait until the final assembly stage to do this, such that the needle is attached in a manner which fits the machine. 3) If using the second method, you may want to build a three-needle liner. This will provide a thicker, more solid line when tattooing. To do this, take three sewing needles and cut off the eyes such that they are all the same length. Wrap them tightly in wire such that they hold a tight pyramid arrangement. Use a soldering iron to solder the needles together. Once cooled, remove the wire and attach the needles to the ink reservoir as described in the second method. You may want to wait until the final assembly stage to do this, such that the needles are attached in a manner which fits the machine.

Step 5: The Batteries

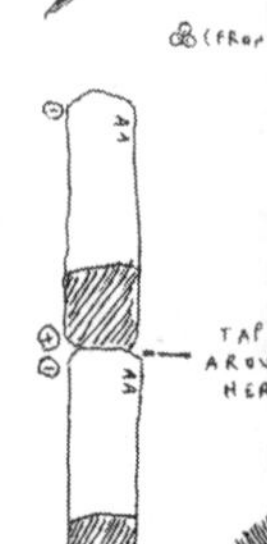

If you found a toy car with an attached remote, this step is very simple: Do nothing other than put batteries in the remote. When you press "forward" on the remote, the machine will run. If you are using a walkman motor or if the motor was necessarily removed from the remote there is an additional step: tape the two AA batteries together endwise, such that the positive end of one is connected to the negative end of the other. To use the machine, you will place one of the wires from the motor on the positive end of the batteries, and the other on the negative end. The wires may be secured with tape for extensive running time.

Step 6: Final Assembly

Push the needle down into the needle tube such that the point sticks out of the tapered end of the needle tube. Place the loop at the end of the needle on the drive shaft of the motor. As the drive shaft turns, it will cause the needle to bob up and down. Now that you can see how much needle is sticking out of the tip of the machine, you can determine where the needle will need to be attached or cut (depending on what needle method you used). You probably will only want about 1/8" to stick out of the tip.

Final considerations:

Obviously, using a machine like this is not sterile. Do your best to sterilize the needles before using them. Infected tattoos could result if you don't. DO NOT use the machine or any of its parts on more than one person. It cost you what, $2 to make? Make 10 if you have to. Just don't use it on multiple people. Doing so could spread Hepatitis C, HIV, and so on. Wear latex gloves when using it. Don't be dumb.

Tinker around with it. If the needle is wobbling around too much, try placing small rubber bands in strategic places (see illustration). If the needle is going too deep, make a new, shorter one or cut the one you have shorter. If you find better parts, use them.

I don't suggest asking tattoo artists for machine design or technique advice (unless you know the person very well). Many artists are very protective of their "art" and will flip out on you (or quickly become indignant) if you ask too many questions.

Practice on oranges and such. Check books for advice on technique. You're never going to produce Guy Aitchison or Paul Booth quality work with this, but that's not the point, is it? Recognize the limits of your creation and act accordingly.

Haggard and scared, he picked up his crutches and hobbled away. Considerably slowed, overwhelmingly restricted, yet comfortable in his methods.

Please Don't Feed the Bears
supports the brave warriors of
the Animal Liberation Front
the Earth Liberation Front
and
the Sea Shepherd Conservation Society

MICROCOSM
PUBLISHING

invisible summer